Cornwall and the Cross

Christianity 500-1560

An England's Past for Everyone paperback

Cornwall and the Cross

Christianity 500-1560

NICHOLAS ORME

Nicholas Orme

+ Will Truro

40th Anniversary of Priesthood

29th September 2007

Michaelmas Day

Phillimore

First published 2007

A Victoria County History publication
Published by Phillimore & Co. Ltd, Madam Green Farm Business Centre, Oving, Chichester, West Sussex, England in association with the Institute of Historical Research at the University of London.
www.phillimore.co.uk

ISBN 978-1-86077-468-3

British Library Cataloguing in Publication Data. A cataloguing record for this book is available from the British Library.

Typeset in Humanist 521 and Minion

We wish particularly to thank the following EPE and VCH staff for their efforts during the production of this volume:

John Beckett – Director of the Victoria County History
Matthew Bristow – Historic Environment Research Manager
Catherine Cavanagh – Project Manager
Coral Pepper – Education Coordinator and Administrator, VCH Cornwall
Nafisa Gaffar – Finance and Contracts Officer
Aretha George – Education and Skills Manager
Mel Hackett – Communications Officer
Stephen Lubell – Production and Editorial Controller
Neil Penlington – Administrator
Andrew Stokes – Web Manager
Alan Thacker – Executive Editor of the Victoria County History
Elizabeth Williamson – Architectural Editor of the Victoria County History

Printed and bound in Great Britain

Cover image: Detail of early 16th-century stained glass window from St Neot church: St Neot and the Pope.

Contents

List of Panels

Foreword by the Bishop of Truro

Nicholas Orme's new book is full of good things about people and places and a deep local and historical knowledge. It ends with a few sentences which, in themselves, sum up why this book is so important for anyone who wants to know something about the history of Christianity in Cornwall.

> The story is partly that of Cornwall itself shaped by its special character. But the story also takes us beyond the Tamar showing us that the Cornish were part of a wider Church: shaped by that Church and helping to shape it in turn. As with all local history we can fully understand the history of the Church in Cornwall only when we consider it as part of a wider history. And we can fully understand that wider history only when we make Cornwall part of it.

So the book carefully separates legend and romance from history, making it clear, for instance, that the lives of many of the Cornish saints were written long after their death and tell us more about the period in which they were written than about the life of the saint.

We are told about the effect of the Norman Conquest and about the place of monasteries in Cornwall, about the development of parishes and we even learn about the difference between rectors and vicars. We hear something about church furnishings, and about the place of the Church in the lives of ordinary people and the significance of the architecture of church buildings. We are helped to see the buildings as organic and telling something about the communities they served as they developed and grew.

We are taken through about a thousand years of Christian history ending with the Reformation and its effects and, of course, the famous Prayer Book rebellion of 1549 which centred on Cornwall and parts of Devon.

So Cornwall and its history is put in the context of a wider picture but the author's skill is shown by the balance he keeps between the relevance of the local and the importance of the national and sometimes international pressures, which helped to shape it.

The illustrations are well chosen and help the reader to remember that this Christian history, about which Professor Orme writes with such love and knowledge, is something living and ongoing.

All the time the names of villages, hamlets, towns, and communities, part of our contemporary life, keep occurring in the text and remind us that we ourselves have a continuing part in this story.

The Christian faith in Cornwall is more than fifteen hundred years young and it could not have a more dedicated learned and attractive writer to help us all to be aware of the heritage which is ours. As T. S. Eliot famously said in 'Little Gidding': 'A people without history is not redeemed from time, for history is a pattern of timeless moments.'

+ Will Truro

The Rt Revd William Ind
Bishop of Truro

Preface

This book is a simple account of the first thousand years of Christianity in Cornwall, from about the year 500 to the beginning of the reign of Queen Elizabeth I in 1560. It is based on the larger and more detailed survey that I have written in *The Victoria County History of Cornwall*, volume II, published in 2007. Readers who wish to know more than is told here are referred to that book, where they will find additional information and references.

Cornwall and the Cross is the second of the new paperbacks from England's Past for Everyone (EPE), the VCH's new venture intended to open up local history to a wider audience and to involve local people in historical research. EPE has been made possible by a generous grant from Heritage Lottery Fund and the support of partners from around the country. The book is complemented by an interactive website which allows the reader to explore relevant images, documents and audio-visual material and which can be searched by people, places and themes. We keep putting up material as we discover it at www.England'sPastForEveryone.org.uk/Cornwall.

The Cornish are a critical people where their history is concerned. Not all will be happy that this volume appears in a series called 'England's Past for Everyone', or that the author is not Cornish! In my defence I plead a long-standing love of the county (I demanded to be taken there for the first time when I was twelve) and years spent studying its history in archives and libraries. I have not tried to write from any particular standpoint – Cornish or non-Cornish – but to cover as much of the subject as possible and as truthfully as I can.

I am grateful to the many organisations and people who have supported and helped with my research. They include those (too many to mention here) whose names are listed in the VCH volume and the volunteers who worked so hard on the project to list religious sites and features, and whose work will appear on the website. My thanks are also due to the staff and consultants of the VCH and EPE listed elsewhere in this volume. I should end by acknowledging the constant and warm support that I have received from the members of the VCH Cornwall Trust over the past few years. This book is dedicated to them all with my very best wishes.

Nicholas Orme
May 2007

Chapter 1 The Early Middle Ages

Figure 1 St Neot and the pope. Later legend made Neot a monk of Glastonbury Abbey who journeyed to Rome and ended his life at St Neot. Episodes from his legend appear in the early Tudor windows of St Neot church.

STARTING AT THE BEGINNING

There is a story that the Devil made a journey through England, looked towards Cornwall, and decided to go no further. 'Over there, everywhere's called St This and St That, and anything strange that moves they put into a pasty.' Cornwall is certainly a holy land in terms of its place-names. Many begin with 'St': St Agnes, St Austell, St Columb, St Germans, St Ives. Others are names of saints without the 'St', like Constantine, Germoe, and Perranzabuloe, and some well-known places whose names do not appear to be religious really are, like Bodmin ('a dwelling by church land'), Launceston ('the church site of St Stephen'), and Penzance ('the holy headland').

Religion also permeates Cornwall in visible forms. You can hardly travel through a town or a piece of the countryside without seeing a church tower or a Victorian chapel, and perhaps an ancient cross or a holy well. Christian worship has been going on in some of these places for a thousand years or even longer, and not only Christian worship. Christianity has inspired people to produce works of architecture, art, literature, and music. Then there are all the other ways in which religion comes into everyday life: people's names (like Andrew, Mary, or Peter), the festivals of Christmas and Easter, and the dating of the year from the birth of Christ. Even the tax year starts on Lady Day, an old feast in honour of the Virgin Mary, delayed by 11 days to 6 April because of the calendar change in 1752. Parishes and parish councils, hospitals and schools, libraries and books, and roads, bridges, and harbours all stem from Christianity or have been affected by it.

This book tells the story of how Christianity came to Cornwall and how it developed there over the thousand or so years from about AD 500 up to the end of the Reformation in 1559. Before the story begins, however, you need to know something about the Cornwall to which Christianity first came. If you think back to the early centuries of Cornish history, the word 'Celtic' will probably come to your mind as a word to describe the people of that time and their civilisation. Historians nowadays dislike the word 'Celtic' because it was not a word that these people used themselves. It is also too broad, like the word 'European', to do justice to the different countries, peoples, and eras that get lumped together under the 'Celtic' heading: ancient Britain, Brittany, Cornwall, ancient Gaul, Ireland, Scotland, and Wales. In this book the Cornish are referred to as 'Britons' up to about the 900s when Cornwall became officially part of the kingdom of England, and their language and culture as 'Brittonic'. This is a narrower term and applies only to Brittany, Cornwall, and Wales, which were a distinctive part of the 'Celtic' world, fairly close together and populated by speakers of a similar language.[1]

Jesus Christ died in about the year 33 of the Christian era. At that time what is now the South West of England (Cornwall and Devon) was inhabited by people speaking a form of the Brittonic language, the ancestor of Cornish. The Romans called them the Dumnonians, in Latin *Dumnonii*. Ten years after Christ's death, in 43, the Romans invaded Britain and united most of it into a province under their rule. The Dumnonii were integrated into this province and their leaders were made to help govern the South West under Roman supervision from a new Roman city at Exeter. Roman rule lasted until about 410, by which time it was weakening and the regions of Britain were turning back into independent kingdoms. Cornwall and Devon became such a kingdom, known as Dumnonia, but little written information survives about it. We hear of a ruler named Constantine who was alive in about the mid-500s, and a king called Gerent who was living around 700. By Gerent's time the South West was coming under pressure from the English

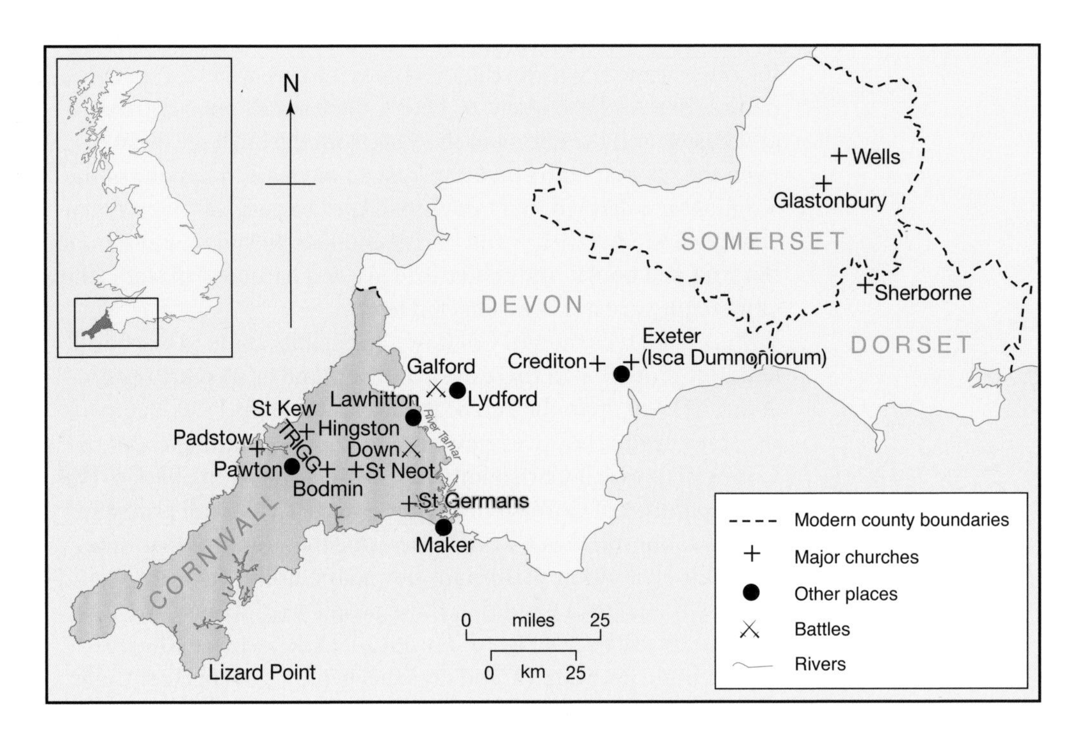

Figure 2 The South West of England from about 600 to 900.

(see Figure 2). East of it lay the English kingdom of Wessex, which stretched from Dorset to Hampshire, and the kings of Wessex were ambitious to extend their power over Devon and Cornwall as well.[2]

The English conquest of the South West was marked by occasional fighting but for the most part probably took place peacefully. English immigrants would have entered from further east or north, and the Britons, especially in Devon, would have gradually adopted English speech and customs. The Brittonic kings of the area, however, remained a powerful force for a long time, and they fought a series of battles with the English for control of Devon and Cornwall from the early 600s to the early 800s. The last of these battles took place in 835 at *Hengestdun*: very likely Hingston Down near Callington. In it Egbert, king of Wessex (802–39), won a victory over a combined force of Britons and Scandinavian Vikings, and put Cornwall – by that time the only area ruled by Brittonic leaders – permanently under his control and that of his successors. A Brittonic king in Cornwall survived for a time, probably as a vassal of Wessex, because a Welsh chronicle called the *Annales Cambriae* records Dungarth, 'king of Cerniu [Cornwall]', as having drowned in the year 876.[3]

Dungarth may have been the last such king. The next ruler recorded as being active in Cornwall was Egbert's grandson, King Alfred of Wessex (871–99). Alfred owned property there and is recorded hunting and visiting a saint's shrine, probably at St Neot.

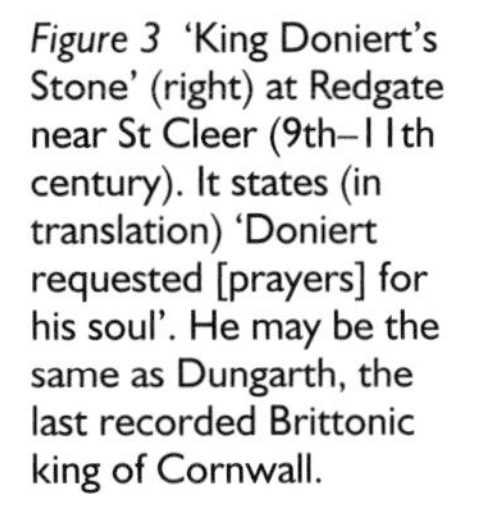

Figure 3 'King Doniert's Stone' (right) at Redgate near St Cleer (9th–11th century). It states (in translation) 'Doniert requested [prayers] for his soul'. He may be the same as Dungarth, the last recorded Brittonic king of Cornwall.

Alfred's grandson King Athelstan (925–39) was the first king to rule most of England, and Cornwall was integrated into England by his time. It became an English county for purposes of government and a unit of the English Church for religious purposes.[4]

THE COMING OF CHRISTIANITY

It is possible that there were individual Christians in Cornwall, either visitors or natives, from the first century onwards, but they have left no traces. The earliest recorded may be two bishops, Instantius and Tiberianus, who were deposed at the Council of Bordeaux in 384 on charges of heresy and exiled to an island beyond Britain called *Sylinancim*, which could have been the Scilly Isles. The Emperor Constantine granted toleration to Christians throughout the Roman Empire in 313, and during the rest of the fourth century Christianity increased its status in the Empire and became an organised and official religion: the Church, as we may now call it. It established bishops, clergy, churches, and congregations, but in Roman Britain this seems to have happened chiefly in towns like Exeter, which may have had a church by about 400. It is doubtful how far Christianity had taken hold of rural areas like Cornwall by the time that Roman authority in Britain disappeared in the early 400s.[5]

Figure 4 An early inscribed stone, undated, from South Hill churchyard. It carries the name (in Latin) of Cumregnus son of Maucus.

The first real evidence for Christianity in Cornwall comes only after the end of Roman rule. One pointer towards it is to be found in a number of pillar-shaped stones with inscriptions, about 80 of which are now known in the South West. The fashion for raising stones of this kind originated in south Wales whence they spread to most of Cornwall, with a few outliers in Devon. They record the names of nobility, chiefly men, and may have served as gravestones, boundary markers, or just commemorative stones alongside roads. Their dates probably range from the 400s to the 1000s, but many seem to belong to the 6th and 7th centuries (500–700). Most of their inscriptions are in Latin (see Figure 4), and some carry the Christian 'chi-rho' symbol: the X and P that are the first two letters of 'Christ' in Greek.[6]

The inscriptions imply that by about the 500s the leading families of Cornwall and Devon regarded themselves as belonging to the Christian Latin culture of western Europe. This conclusion is supported by the only writer of this period to mention the South West: the Welsh cleric Gildas, who wrote his *Ruin of Britain* in the middle of the sixth century. Gildas singled out the ruler of Dumnonia for denunciation as a tyrant, an adulterer, and a murderer. He alleged that this man, Constantine, had killed two royal youths and their guardians in a church near an altar, to which they had presumably gone for refuge. The mention of the church, followed by an exhortation from Gildas that the tyrant should repent and seek forgiveness, indicates that the ruler and his family were Christians, at least in name. If Constantine had been a practising pagan, Gildas would hardly have failed to say so.[7]

Many Cornish people today will probably imagine that the best evidence for the coming of Christianity to Cornwall is to be found in the medieval 'Lives' or biographies of saints such as Cadoc, David, Petroc, Piran, Samson, Winwaloe, and so on. Unfortunately that is not the case. The Lives claim to tell us about Christianity in Britain, Ireland, and Brittany in the period after the Romans, in other words during the 400s and 500s, but they were all written long after the events that they profess to describe. The earliest of them, the so-called 'First Life' of St Samson, is now thought to have been put together about 170 years later than Samson lived. The next Lives, those of Paul of Leon and Winwaloe, were not composed until the late 800s (300 years or more later), and those of Cadoc, David, and Petroc not until the 1000s (over half a millennium later).[8]

None of the Lives, with the possible exception of Samson's, shows any sign of knowing anything reliable about former times. They were essentially new inventions, based on the beliefs and folklore of the times in which they were written, and we shall not consider them here as evidence for the coming of Christianity to Cornwall. They are more useful in shedding light on later periods of history, the periods in which they were written. The First Life of Samson is the only written Life that comes even remotely near the lifetime of its hero. He is also the sole early saint for whom there is a *possible* contemporary reference: he may have attended a Church council at Paris in 562 and, if so, he probably died ten or twenty years afterwards.

The First Life claims to be the work of a cleric from Brittany who visited Cornwall and gained information from an elderly man living there in a monastery founded by Samson. This man's uncle, Henoc, had been Samson's cousin and companion, had been told stories about him by Samson's mother, and had written an account of him. If true, these lifespans would suggest that the Life was written by about 650, but the latest editor of the Life observes that it quotes from the English scholar Bede (active *c.*700–35), and proposes a date of 750 or thereabouts. In this view, the links with Samson claimed by the author cannot be true, so that what he wrote was not an account close to the events of the saint's lifetime but a collection of traditions made after a long stretch of time.[9]

The Life asserts that Samson was the child of noble parents in south-west Wales. He was brought up by a famous saint, Illtud, in

Figure 5 St Samson, as he was imagined long after he lived, in a late-medieval carving from the church of St Samson (Golant).

the monastery of Llantwit Major (Glamorgan), becoming a monk and eventually a bishop. Later he came by ship to Cornwall with his father Amon and a company of followers. After landing (probably in the estuary of the River Camel), Samson went to a monastery called *Docco*, identifiable with St Kew. Its monks refused to receive him, with the excuse that his standards were too high for them, so Samson and his party travelled onwards through the countryside of Trigg, the part of north Cornwall east of the River Camel.

Here local people were holding games at a pillar or image. Samson regarded what they were doing as pagan, but he won them over through a miracle and the nobleman who led them, named Vedian (*Vedianus*), asked him to confirm their baptisms. Vedian then told Samson about a huge serpent which lurked in a cave and troubled its neighbourhood. Samson destroyed the serpent, and went to live in the cave where a spring of water appeared in response to his prayer. He founded a monastery nearby, leaving his father Amon to run it and ordaining his cousin Henoc as deacon. Then he crossed the English Channel to Brittany where he lived for the rest of his life. More than one site has been suggested for Samson's monastery, but the location remains an open question.

This information is interesting, but it is too late and limited to be regarded as a literal and connected account of what happened. We cannot even be sure that Samson's exploits were true or took place in the order described. The episode of the serpent looks like something borrowed from legend rather than fact. The Life's portrayal of Cornish society in the 500s as nominally Christian but still engaged in some pagan practices may not be far from the truth, but may equally be a romantic notion that enabled Samson's achievements to seem more dramatic. This idea appears in a more exaggerated form in some later legends of Cornish saints, in which the saints are shown in a struggle with pagans, notably with a wicked ruler named Teudur. There is no satisfactory evidence that any saint was ever martyred in Cornwall, and even Samson's Life does not imply such happenings.

The greatest value of the Life, like that of all the Brittonic saints' Lives, is to tell us about the time in which (not about which) it was written. And in this case, the 700s, we can link it with some other pieces of evidence. Round about 700 an outstanding English cleric and scholar called Aldhelm (died 709) interested himself in the affairs of Dumnonia (see Figure 6). He wrote a letter to the Brittonic king of the region, Gerent, and to his clergy, urging them to adopt the practices of the Catholic Church in the way in which the clergy cut their hair and calculated the date of Easter. These were two key points on which the English and the Britons disagreed at that time. Aldhelm also visited Dumnonia at least once,

Figure 6 St Aldhelm (died 709) is the earliest Englishman recorded as visiting Cornwall. He was interested in its Church and became the first bishop of Sherborne, with responsibility for the Britons living under the rule of the king of Wessex.

humorously describing his journey as taking him 'to dire Devon through comfortless Cornwall'. This is one of the earliest clear references to Cornwall as a region. During the journey a storm arose and he sheltered for the night in a church, attending worship led by local clergy.[10]

Putting these pieces together we learn that, by the 700s, there was a Christian king of Dumnonia, whom Aldhelm regarded as influential in its Church. There were also clergy. Some of the clergy lived in monasteries, two of which are mentioned in the First Life of Samson: Docco and the unnamed church that Samson was said to have founded. Since the Life seems to deal chiefly with central Cornwall, that would leave room for other monasteries. Although the *Dumnonii* and the English were periodically at war, there were also peaceful relations between them at times, shown by Aldhelm's letter and journey. Indeed, a much later list of gifts to the church of Sherborne (Dorset) states that 'King Gerontius', very likely King Gerent, granted the church an estate at Maker in south-east Cornwall, a grant that indicates a link between the Britons and a church that was, by about 700, a long way inside English territory.[11]

We can also begin to sense Cornwall as being in touch with neighbouring lands in three directions. Samson was believed to have come from south Wales, and *Docco* was also the name of a monastery in Glamorgan which had presumably set up or inspired the foundation at St Kew. Samson's Breton biographer, if we can believe him, came to Cornwall from Brittany, and Aldhelm and Gerent illustrate contacts between the Britons and the English. The king of Wessex too seems to have appreciated Aldhelm's links with the *Dumnonii*, and made him the first bishop of a new diocese based at Sherborne which covered the lands of Wessex in Devon, Dorset, and Somerset. He would thus have looked after the Britons in the east of this region.

THE CORNISH CHURCH AND THE KINGS OF WESSEX

The glimpses of Cornwall that we get from these sources are followed by a period of obscurity, which ends only after Egbert's conquest in the early 800s. Later records claim that he used his power to grant estates in Cornwall to the bishop of Sherborne, especially Pawton in St Breock and Lawhitton near Launceston. Egbert may have intended that the bishop would visit Cornwall or send deputies there to supervise or develop the local Church.

Cornwall remained so different from Wessex, however, that, for a long time to come, it needed Church leaders who were ethnically Britons. Between 833 and 870, we hear of a bishop named Kenstec who was based 'in the monastery of *Dinuurrin*', from where he made a vow of obedience to the archbishop of Canterbury. The location of this monastery has been plausibly identified as Bodmin. King Alfred, whom we have seen was powerful in Cornwall, also recognised the need of the Cornish for a bishop who was a Briton. Bishop Asser, a Welshman who wrote a biography of Alfred, tells us that, in about the 880s, the king gave him the church at Exeter 'with all its territory [*parochia*] in the Saxon lands and Cornwall [in *Saxonia et Cornubia*]'. It looks as if Alfred put him in charge of

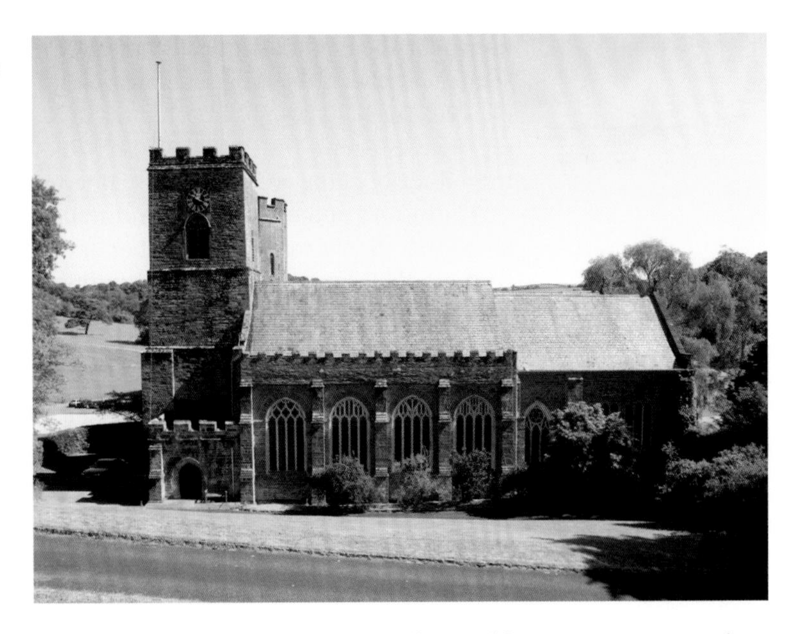

Figure 7 St Germans. The present parish church was formerly a priory church, and stands on the site of the ancient cathedral of the diocese of Cornwall.

the Church in Devon and Cornwall, possibly as an assistant to the bishop of Sherborne.[12]

When a new bishop of Sherborne was needed in the 890s, Alfred gave the post to Asser as well, making him leader of the Church of the whole South West. This had the merit of placing the Cornish under a trusted royal servant, while providing for their special needs with a bishop whose language and religious traditions were similar to their own. By the time that Asser died in 909 the South West was regarded as too large for one bishop to look after, and the diocese of Sherborne was divided. Somerset was given a bishop based at Wells and Devon one located at Crediton, just outside Exeter. The main account of this reorganisation is a letter written at Canterbury in the 980s. It states that the bishop of Crediton received three of the estates in Cornwall which Egbert had given to Sherborne, so that he 'might visit the Cornish people every year and repress their errors, for formerly, in as far as they could, they resisted the truth and did not obey the apostolic decrees'.[13]

It may be that, for a decade or two after 909, Cornwall came under the authority of the bishops of Crediton, but if so this arrangement did not last long because we hear of a bishop of Cornwall named Conan by 931. The Canterbury letter (or a later addition to it) says that King Athelstan gave Conan the bishopric of Cornwall 'as far as the Tamar flows', in other words all the land west of the river, and that King Edred (946–55) awarded Conan's successor Daniel the three estates that had been given to Crediton. Conan was evidently a Briton from Cornwall, Brittany, or Wales, and so, it seems, were Daniel and Daniel's successor Comoere (also known by the English name of Wulfsige). The appointment of such men reflects the fact that Cornwall still differed enough from Devon to need its own bishop, but (as in Kenstec's time) it was regarded as part of the English Church and its bishop was under the authority of the archbishop of Canterbury.[14]

The history of the Church in Cornwall becomes clearer after about 900, thanks to a larger number of written records. In theory the Catholic Church of which Cornwall was part claimed to be an independent self-governing organisation. In practice it depended a good deal on the power of kings and noblemen. King Athelstan established or re-established the bishops of Cornwall, and two royal charters exist granting lands and rights to the churches of St Buryan and St Kew. This does not mean that the Church in Cornwall led a calm and untroubled existence under royal protection. Royal authority was disrupted from time to time, notably by the Viking invasions of the reign of King Ethelred the Unready (978–1016). In 981 the Anglo-Saxon Chronicle recorded that '*Sancte Petroces stow* [either Padstow or Bodmin] was laid waste', presumably by a Viking attack, and at some point St Petroc's relics and clergy moved from Padstow to Bodmin, perhaps as a result of that event.[15]

At least two Cornish churches had property stolen from them by powerful lay people between the ninth and 11th centuries. The ancient monastery of *Docco* at St Kew lost most or all of its lands during this period, and we learn from Domesday Book that Harold earl of Wessex (see Figure 15), who was briefly King Harold II in 1066, seized an estate belonging to the church of Bodmin. The English also exploited Cornwall for the benefit of churches elsewhere in southern England. Tavistock Abbey

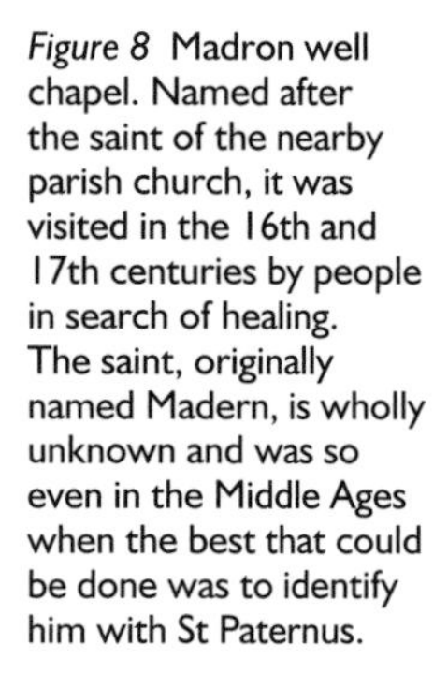

Figure 8 Madron well chapel. Named after the saint of the nearby parish church, it was visited in the 16th and 17th centuries by people in search of healing. The saint, originally named Madern, is wholly unknown and was so even in the Middle Ages when the best that could be done was to identify him with St Paternus.

(Devon), founded in 981 by a Devonshire nobleman, was partly financed with estates in eastern Cornwall, and Cornish lands and churches were transferred to other religious houses after the Norman Conquest. Holy relics were removed as well, notably the bones of St Neot and St Rumon, which were taken from St Neot and Ruan Lanihorne to St Neot's (Hunts.) and Tavistock respectively.[16]

From one point of view this was religious plunder. But it was also a sign of English respect for the Cornish saints. The bodies of the saints were holy, and the English wanted to have the benefit of their holiness and to venerate them. This veneration is most notable in the case of St Petroc, who was buried at Bodmin. He was chosen as the patron saint of more than a dozen parish churches in Devon, Somerset, and Hampshire in about the 900s or 1000s. One of the churches was in Winchester, the chief city of the Anglo-Saxon kings, implying that these kings wished to have Petroc's presence there along with the other saints whom they honoured and trusted to help them.[17]

BISHOPS AND CHURCHES IN CORNWALL, 900–1066

The bishops of Cornwall in the 10th and 11th centuries were chiefly based in the church of St Germans (see Figure 7). This was their cathedral and adjoined a large estate that supported the bishops, their household, and the cathedral clergy. Elsewhere in Cornwall they held the former Sherborne estates at Lawhitton and Pawton, and probably two other major properties: the manors of Treliever consisting of the lands around Penryn, and Tregaire covering much of the Roseland peninsula. Eventually they also acquired the church of St Petroc and its property, a church whose saint and clergy were first located at Padstow but, by at least the 11th century, had moved to Bodmin.

Eight bishops ruled the Cornish diocese from Conan onwards. After the 990s they had English names alone, reflecting the fact that, even if they were Cornish, they were coming under a stronger English influence. At first the diocese of Cornwall fitted in with the Church organisation of southern England. Most of the counties of Wessex had their own bishop, and these bishops were often based at a rural estate like St Germans. During the 1000s, however, opinion in England came to favour larger dioceses with richer more powerful bishops and cathedrals based in towns. The Cornish diocese did not meet these criteria and, as Cornwall grew more closely linked with England, it lost some of the special character that had caused it to be treated separately.[18]

Figure 9 St Germoe's chair in Germoe churchyard, first recorded in 1542. Germoe (originally Germoc) is another unknown saint. The purpose and age of the 'chair' (three canopied seats) is mysterious.

The new shape of things was foreshadowed in 1027 when Lyfing became bishop of Cornwall. He was an Englishman who had been abbot of Tavistock and was already bishop of Crediton, which he continued to hold along with Cornwall. In 1038–9 he added a third diocese, Worcester, to his collection, making it unlikely that he spent much time west of the Tamar. When Lyfing died in 1046 he was succeeded both in Cornwall and at Crediton by Leofric, who may have been Cornish or Welsh since he is once described as a Briton. Leofric was a reformer who sought to build stronger Church institutions. In 1050 he got the agreement of the king to join the two dioceses permanently together, and that of the pope and the king to establish a new cathedral in the city of Exeter. After 1050 Cornwall formed part of the diocese of Exeter, although it had some separate status as an archdeaconry by the

1120s, and it remained part of Exeter until the diocese of Truro was created in 1877.[19]

We know little about the organisation of the diocese of Cornwall during the 10th and 11th centuries. It was not large and its supervision, until Lyfing's reign, would not have been a difficult task for the bishop and his household of clergy. The bishop would have lived at St Germans or on his other estates, travelling around the county from time to time with his household or sending his servants to carry out tasks in his place. No charters or records of the bishops of Cornwall survive before 1050, except for some mentions of Bishop Wulfsige Comoere freeing serfs or slaves at the church of St Petroc (Bodmin or Padstow) in the second half of the 10th century. The bishops must have ordained clergy and provided some means for their education, probably at Bodmin and St Germans in

Figure 10 The religious houses of Cornwall in the 11th century.

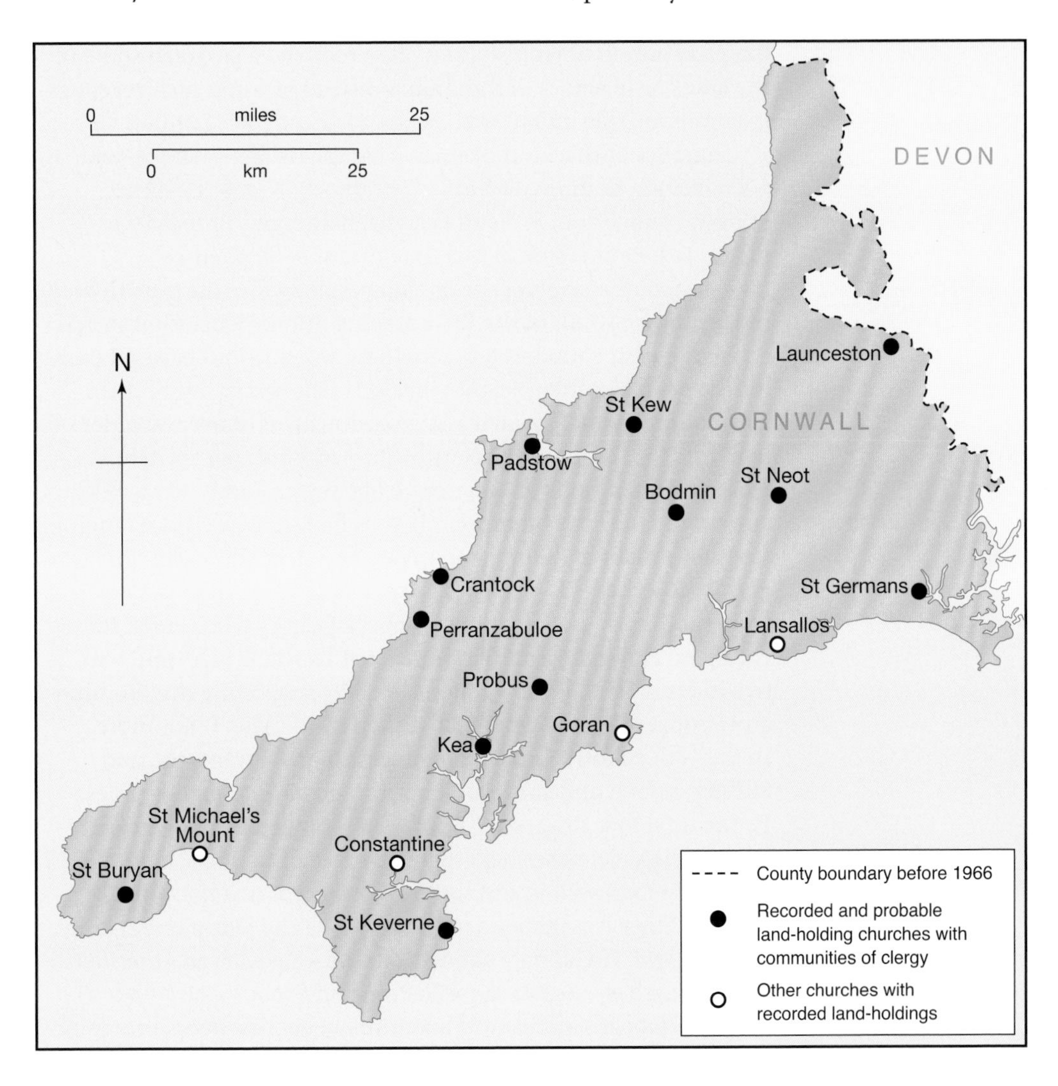

particular. A pupil named Boia is mentioned at St Petroc's church (Bodmin or Padstow) in the 10th century. Some conversational dialogues for teaching students Latin occur in a manuscript that has associations with St Germans, and may have been used in a school attached to that church.[20]

By the 900s we can begin to glimpse other churches in Cornwall for the first time since the First Life of Samson. Some were religious houses staffed by groups of clergy, others were lesser churches likely to have been served at most by a single clergyman. By this period none of the religious houses was a monastery in the usual sense of the word: a church staffed by monks who were unmarried, lived communally, and shared their possessions together. Instead they were churches of the kind that historians call minsters, run by groups of clergy described in contemporary sources as canons, priests, or clerks. Minster clergy lived in separate houses rather than a common dormitory, and often received a personal share of the lands or revenues of the church instead of using such revenues in common. They might even be married and have families.[21]

Churches of this kind likely to have existed between 900 and 1066 include Bodmin, St Buryan, Crantock, Kea, St Keverne, St Kew, Launceston, St Neot, Perranzabuloe, and Probus (see Figure 10). Launceston at this time meant St Stephen-by-Launceston, the original site of Launceston before the growth of the modern town south of the River Kensey. All the Cornish minsters acted as parish churches too, providing worship and pastoral care for the people of their neighbourhoods. The wealthiest of them was Bodmin, which owned a large endowment of over 30 hides of land by 1066, part held directly by its clergy and part by tenants who paid them rents or services. A hide was roughly 100 acres of cultivated land. The other foundations had smaller estates ranging from four hides at Launceston to one or less at St Buryan, Probus, and St Keverne.[22]

In no case do we know the number of clergy who served these churches. However, a similar minster at Hartland (Devon), with two hides of land, had 12 canons in 1086, suggesting that Bodmin and Launceston may have been staffed by as many if not more. In the 13th century Crantock had ten canons, Probus six, and St Buryan four, and such numbers may go back to earlier times. By the time that Domesday Book was compiled in 1086, nearly all the religious houses held their land free of taxation, a privilege distinct to Cornwall in the South West since it was not usual in Devon. Either it originated in the period of the Dumnonian kings or else it was a deliberate concession by a king such as Athelstan. Three churches – St Buryan, Padstow, and Probus – also had special rights of sanctuary in later times, enabling people accused

Figure 11 St Just-in-Roseland church, in a wooded waterside setting. The church site goes back to at least the 10th century, although the church building dates from the 13th and 15th centuries.

of crimes to take refuge on their lands. These rights may have had a similar origin to that of the exemption from taxation.[23]

Far more numerous than the minsters were what we may call lesser church sites, meaning places that came to have a church or chapel without large landed possessions or bodies of clergy. A revealing source about them is a list of saints compiled in Brittany or Cornwall in about 900. The list contains 48 names without an explanation of why it was made. Many of the names, however, are those of saints of Cornish churches, and parts of the list follow a topographical order showing that the compiler was thinking not only of the saints but also of where their church sites were located. Thus Just, Entenin, Gerent, Fili, and Rumon appear together (these are the saints associated with the churches in the Roseland area), and later on we encounter the saints of St Austell and its modern neighbours Creed, Goran, Mevagissey, and St Mewan. In these two regions most of the later parish church sites were evidently in being by about 900, and there is no reason to suppose that this situation was unusual.[24]

By about 1100, if not earlier, there was a church site every three miles or so all over Cornwall with the exception of the moorland areas of the interior. Most of the minster churches lay close to the sea or to estuaries, probably in places where lords had estates or people could gather easily because of travel by water. Bodmin and Launceston differed by being inland, but they too reflected communications since they were on or near the main road from Cornwall to southern England. A few church sites, like the latter two, lay close to settlements or caused settlements to grow up beside them. The typical Cornish church site, however, tended to lie in rural isolation, by a road but adjoined by no more than a farm or a couple of cottages: what was known in later centuries as a 'church town'. Good examples include Paul and Zennor.

Isolated sites of this kind may have been chosen for more than one reason. A couple, St Endellion and Tintagel, appear to have been pre-existing ancient graveyards (Figures 33, 80), and other churches may have had a similar origin. Some sites show signs of having been 'rounds': the small farming settlements common in Cornwall during the Iron Age and Roman periods, enclosed by a bank and ditch. Deserted rounds would have been suitable places for churches and churchyards because they were the right size and were already provided with boundaries. One such round, at Merther Uny in Wendron parish, has been excavated, showing that a chapel was built there in or after the 10th century. The nature of settlement in Cornwall was another major factor, since most people lived apart in farms and hamlets rather than clustered in villages. Church sites had to minister to a scattered population, and most were therefore placed in a fairly central part of the area that they served.[25]

We know little about the appearance of these early church sites. They may have included a graveyard, a cross, a church building, or more than one of these, but the lack of surviving buildings from before the Norman Conquest and the difficulty of investigating church sites archaeologically mean that their nature is still indistinct. More certainly they christianised the landscape as well as the people, aided in this respect by the inscribed memorials and by holy wells.[26]

THE CORNISH SAINTS

Most of the names of Cornwall's early church sites are Brittonic ones. Some of these are place names, such as Egloshayle ('church on an estuary'), but many appear to be names of people like Gwithian, Probus, and Sithney, and by the 10th and 11th centuries the owners of these names were regarded as saints. In due course the word 'St' was often prefixed to the church name, giving us modern names such as St Austell, St Buryan, and St Winnow, although equally often it was omitted, especially in everyday speech, as in the three examples mentioned above. The association of churches with local saints on such a large scale has parallels in Brittany and Wales,

Figure 12 The probable shrine of St Endelient, one of Cornwall's many unique saints, in the church of St Endellion. Built of skilfully carved catacleuse stone from St Merryn in about 1400, it survived the Reformation through being reused as the tomb of a local gentleman.

but differs sharply from most of medieval England. There most churches were dedicated to well-known national or international saints, and relatively few to local ones.

There were at least 185 church sites in medieval Cornwall named after, or associated with, people believed to be Brittonic saints from Cornwall, Wales, and Brittany. The saints themselves numbered 140, since some had more than one site. Just over half of them (78) were venerated only in Cornwall, most of them at a single site so that many were unique to the places associated with them.[27] The rest of the saints (62) were venerated in Brittany, Wales, or both, as well as in Cornwall. Welsh saints, including Cybi and David, were honoured at a handful of churches and chapels, chiefly on the north coast of Cornwall and in the area north-west of Looe. Breton saints, such as Samson and Winwaloe, gave their names to a larger number of sites, especially in Kerrier north of the Lizard peninsula but also scattered over most of the county.

Not all Cornish churches were linked with such saints, however. By 1066 there were also places that honoured the famous saints of the whole Christian Church. The two earliest known are St Michael's Mount and St Stephen-by-Launceston, and several other Cornish churches came to be dedicated to these two saints as well as to Martin, Mary, and similarly well-known figures. The variety of church dedications in Cornwall – local, regional, and international – shows that the history of Cornish Christianity was a complicated process. The influences from outside, which we have noted in the 700s, helped to bring about the presence of saints from Brittany, Wales, England, and continental Europe. There were also unique Cornish saints, implying that there was religious activity purely by Cornish people within Cornwall. Not everything in Cornish Christianity can have been triggered by missionaries from outside.

The original identities of the Brittonic saints honoured in Cornwall are generally unknown. This is true not only of the saints unique to Cornwall, but of most of those who also had church sites in Brittany and Wales. We have seen that all their Lives were written long after the saints were supposed to have lived, and I have argued that the Lives were not based on earlier historical records, which it is clear that the authors did not possess, but on local folklore and contemporary views of what a saint should be like. The Lives placed their heroes and heroines in an imagined 'age of the saints', which the authors seem to have envisaged in about the 400s and 500s. The saints were visualised as holy men and women who came to Cornwall from elsewhere, usually Ireland or Wales, after which they founded a church and a holy well, and sometimes met a violent death for religious or other reasons.[28]

Little or nothing of this can be confirmed. Although the inscribed stones, the monastery of *Docco*, and perhaps the First Life of Samson point to links, there is no evidence for a widespread missionary movement from Wales to Cornwall. Links with Ireland are even more elusive. No saints are known to have been martyred, and even their personal saintliness cannot be proved. Most likely they were important local people – Cornish people, clergy or laity – who founded churches or were buried in graveyards that came to be named after them. Graveyard names may then have been transferred to the churches built inside them, and eventually the names were regarded as those of saints. Their owners could have lived at any period before the 10th or 11th centuries, not excluding pre-Christian times.

The Lives are more valuable for what they reveal about those who wrote them, between about AD 900 and 1500. In general they tell us that people in Cornwall, well after their incorporation into England, saw their past as linked with Ireland and Wales, not with England or Rome. To that extent the Cornish had a different understanding of themselves from most people in England. Individually most of the Lives are rather parochial. They portray the saint as 'our saint': of Bodmin, Breage, Gwinear, and so on. They associate him or her with local landmarks – a hill, a church, a well, or a path – thereby explaining the origin and significance of such places. Even when a church, like St Agnes or St Michael's Mount, did not have a local saint, people could still imagine that the saint had visited their parish. Agnes was believed to have killed a local giant, Michael to have sat in a seat on a rock. Sometimes the

PANEL I

St Piran

St Piran is a typical example of a legendary Cornish saint. His name is first recorded in 960 at Perranzabuloe, a name that means 'Piran in the sand', where the church was later believed to contain his bones. In the 12th or 13th century a Life of him was written in Latin for the church or for Exeter Cathedral, to which the church belonged. The author of the Life believed that Piran was identical with a similarly named Irish saint, St Ciáran, so he took Ciáran's Life and made it the basis of Piran's. He stated that Piran was a saint from Ireland who became a bishop, eventually sailed to Cornwall, made his home there, performed many miracles, and died on 5 March.

The Life was written hundreds of years after Piran was thought to have lived, and there is no reason to suppose that he was Irish. No evidence survives that Irish saints ever came personally to Cornwall, and there is little sign that they were even venerated there in medieval times. It is much more likely that he was an early Cornish cleric or nobleman who founded, served, or was buried at Perranzabuloe church, and that the veneration of him spread from there to the other churches and chapels that are known to have been dedicated to him. They included Perranarworthal and Perranuthnoe in Cornwall, a chapel at Cardiff in south Wales, and Trézildé (and possibly other churches) in Brittany.

A 19th-century depiction of St Piran at Bodmin parish church

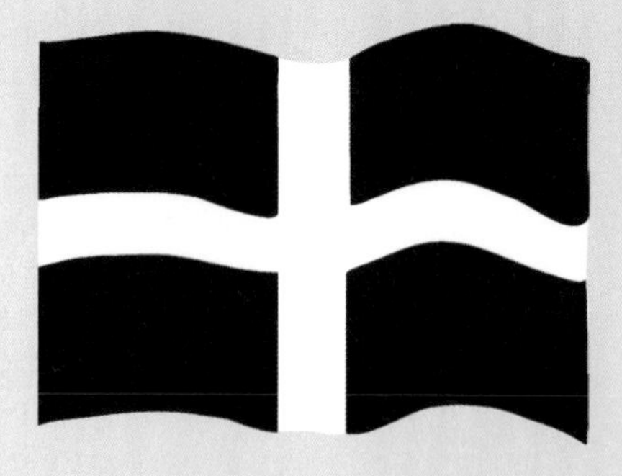

The flag of St Piran is first mentioned in 1838, when it was stated to have once been 'the standard of Cornwall', but the evidence for this statement is unknown. In modern times Piran has come to be widely accepted as the patron saint of Cornwall, and his flag as its flag. Historically, however, Cornwall has never had an official patron saint. Petroc was the most important one before the Norman Conquest, and Mary and Michael the most popular from then until the Reformation.

Lives depict the saint as having been more important than other local saints, reflecting a parish's jealousy about its status.

Most of the saint cults that probably started in Cornwall were also parochial in failing to spread outside their home parishes. Even the most popular saints of Cornish origin acquired only a handful of church sites, even in their home county: Piran three, Euny five and Petroc six. Only Neot, Petroc, Piran, and Rumon became widely known in England through relics, church dedications, and inclusion in church calendars, lists of saints, or collections of saints' Lives. There were too many better-known saints in the outside world – Biblical, European, Brittonic, and English – for the Cornish saints to make much headway there. They made their greatest and most enduring impact in Cornwall itself.

CHURCH LIFE IN CORNWALL, 900–1066

As churches developed they acquired a range of resources including clergy, possessions, and patrons. Clergy needed equipment for their work, such as vestments, holy vessels, crosses, and bells. St Petroc's bell, a portable one, is mentioned being taken from Bodmin to Liskeard on one occasion in the 11th century to validate a grant of freedom to a woman there. No such object exists today from pre-Conquest Cornwall, but some did so in the later Middle Ages. In 1281 Perranzabuloe church owned a silver bowl, two pastoral staffs (one jewelled, one of bone), and a little copper bell, all attributed to St Piran, while Veryan church had a 'small bell of St Symphorian', its patron saint.[29]

Books have been more fortunate survivors. At least three remain that were probably used in Cornwall during the 10th and 11th centuries. All are in Latin. Two would have been used in Church services. These are the 'Bodmin Gospels', now in the British Library, which contain the texts of the four gospels (see Figure 14), and the Lanalet Pontifical, a book containing the rites and sacraments carried out by bishops. The first belonged to the church at Bodmin, and the second to St Germans and now in the municipal library in Rouen. The third book is an anthology of texts known as the *Codex Oxoniensis Posterior*, which includes a commentary on the mass or eucharist, two works by famous Christian authors (St Augustine of Hippo and Caesarius of Arles), and conversational dialogues for teaching students Latin, known as *De Raris Fabulis*. These books (and a few others may also be relevant) show that the Cornish clergy, at least at the bigger minsters, were using the same Church service books and scholarly books as clergy elsewhere in England or western Europe.[30]

Figure 13 A harvester cutting grain, the most valuable form of tithes. Tithes were a tenth of the crops and animals produced on the land, and existed in England from the 10th century until 1936. Originally they were paid in physical form, but gradually this was replaced by money.

The rights of churches came to extend over surrounding territories, known as parishes. It is difficult to date the origins and boundaries of Cornish parishes, but they are likely to have developed into a widespread system during the 900s and 1000s as they were doing at that time all over England. Not until 1291, however, do we possess a complete list of the parish churches of Cornwall, and only then can we begin to analyse the nature of their parishes, which we shall do in the following chapter. Parishes represent the turning of the Church from a missionary organisation into a ruling one, as society became more thoroughly Christian. The clergy of each parish church had spiritual authority over everyone who lived within their parish, and won the right to take resources from the parish for their livelihood. These resources were of two kinds, lands and tithes, of which lands were usually the less important. Only the major churches, those that were also religious houses, had significant landed estates. Most parish churches owned nothing more than a few fields in the parish that the clergyman could farm or let for farming, known as the 'glebe' or 'sanctuary'.[31]

The chief endowment of parish churches by about the 10th century consisted of tithes: a tenth of the crops and animals grown on the land. Tithes were originally voluntary but, at about this time, they turned into a compulsory payment which formed the main income of the Church in England until about the 19th century and was not abolished until 1936. They were used to pay the clergyman of the parish – the rector, as he came to be called – and, because tithes were valuable, it was possible for most parishes to be relatively small and still manage to support their own clergyman. The rector, in return for receiving the tithes, became responsible for maintaining his house, taking care of the chancel of the church where services were said, and providing hospitality to travellers and alms for the poor. The parishioners, as well as paying their tithes, had also to look after the church nave, the public part of the building.[32]

The early medieval Church existed in a society whose ruling classes exerted a considerable influence over every aspect of life, including the Church. Vedian, the Cornish nobleman in the First Life of Samson, is portrayed as a powerful local man who protected Samson and helped him establish a monastery. When lords like Vedian built and endowed a church, it was natural for them to claim rights over it, rights known by the 12th century as an 'advowson', the owner of which was the 'patron'. The principal right of the patron was to nominate the clergyman of the church, or the chief clergyman if the church was a religious house, but in practice he probably had a more general influence over the church and how it worked. This enabled important people – kings, bishops,

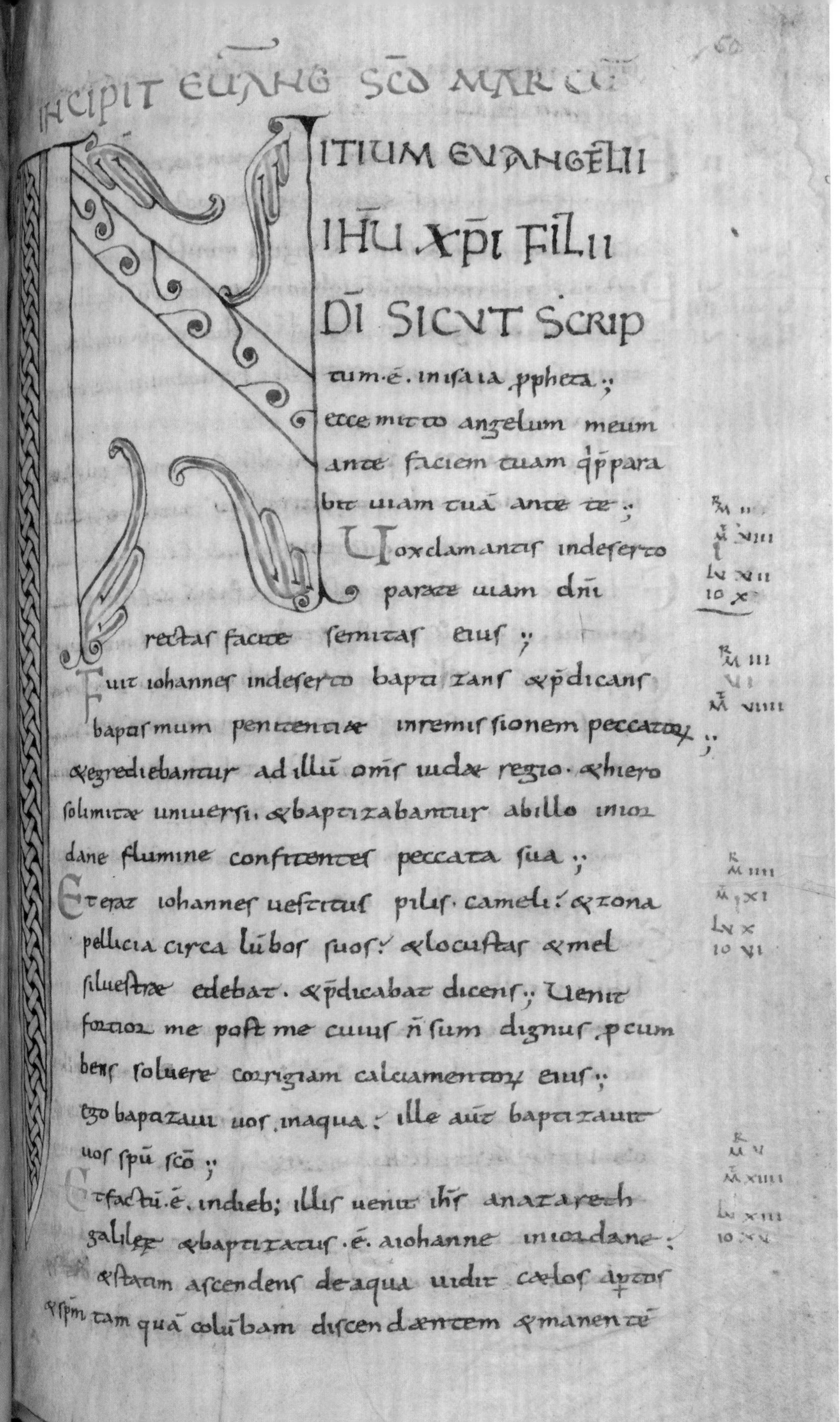

INCIPIT EUANG SCD MARCU

INITIUM EUANGELII
IHU XPI FILII
DI SICUT SCRIP
tum .e. in isaia pphéta ;
ecce mitto angelum meum
ante faciem tuam qui ppara
bit uiam tuā ante te ;
Uox clamantis in deserto
parate uiam dni
rectas facite semitas eius ;

Fuit iohannes in deserto baptizans & pdicans
baptismum penitentiae in remissionem peccatorum ;
& egrediebantur ad illū omīs iudaeae regio . & hiero
solimitae uniuersi . & baptizabantur ab illo in ior
dane flumine confitentes peccata sua ;

Et erat iohannes uestitus pilis . cameli & zona
pellicia circa lūbos suos & locustas & mel
siluestre edebat . & pdicabat dicens ; Uenit
fortior me post me cuius n̄ sum dignus pcum
bens soluere corrigiam calciamentorum eius ;
Ego baptizaui uos in aqua ; ille aūt baptizauit
uos spū scō ;

Et factū .e. in dieb; illis uenit ihs a nazareth
galileae & baptizatus .e. a iohanne in iordane ;
& statim ascendens de aqua uidit caelos aptos
& spm tam quā columbam discendentem & manentē

R M II / M VIII / L XII / IO X

R M III / M VIIII

R M IIII / M XI / L X / IO VI

R M V / M XIIII / L XIII / IO XV

Figure 14 (opposite)
The opening page of the Gospel of Mark from the 'Bodmin Gospels', a manuscript of the late 9th or early 10th century, possibly used at St Petroc's church Padstow and certainly at Bodmin later on. The interlaced decoration is typical of the period; the marginal notes are cross references to the other three gospels.

and noblemen – to control not only the law and economy of their neighbourhoods but much of the religious life as well.

Such people are the only ones in Cornwall whose religious interests we can glimpse even faintly before the Norman Conquest. Some were anxious for the well being of their souls, seeking to gain merit by a charitable act such as freeing a serf or slave. 'Byrhtflaed [a woman] freed Huna and his sister Dolo on the altar of St Petroc for the redemption of her soul.' This is one of several such records in the Bodmin Gospels. 'King Doniert's stone' at Redgate requests prayers for Doniert's soul (see Figure 3), and a standing cross at Tintagel, of about the 11th century, tells us that 'Elnat made this cross for his soul'. Lesser people too must have wished for salvation in heaven and have hoped to be remembered by those who outlived them, but only the powerful and wealthy had the means to put up memorials to display their names for many years to come.[33]

THE NORMAN CONQUEST

The Norman Conquest of 1066 led to further changes in Cornwall in respect of power and property, and therefore affected the Church. The new king, William the Conqueror (see Figure 15), took over the royal estates held by the last long-reigning Anglo-Saxon king, Edward the Confessor, as well as those belonging to his short-lived successor Harold. Some of William's followers obtained the estates that Cornish or Anglo-Saxon landowners had previously held, although some lands remained in the hands of their old owners.

William needed someone to govern Cornwall for him, and in 1076 he gave this task to his half-brother, Robert count of Mortain, along with a good deal of property in the county. Robert's wealth and royal connection made him the most powerful figure in Church affairs in Cornwall for the next 14 years until he died abroad in 1090. His power was increased by the lack of a strong bishop of Exeter. Bishop Leofric had died in 1072, and his successor Osbern was a Norman who had served the last long-standing English king, Edward the Confessor, as well as being a distant relation of King William. Osbern's time as bishop, which lasted until 1103, is an obscure one that seems to reflect a quiet man who was sometimes in poor health. He appears to have had little influence on Cornish affairs, leaving Robert with virtual freedom to do as he pleased.[34]

In 1086 William ordered a valuation to be made of all the lands and livestock in his kingdom, the valuation recorded in Domesday Book. Its section on Cornwall provides us with the earliest detailed account of the major landed estates in the county and those who held them. The valuation was chiefly concerned with lay property,

VBI HAROLD:SACRAMENTVM:FECIT:
VVILLELMO DVCI:
HIC HAROLD:DVX:

Figure 15 Harold earl of Wessex (centre) and William duke of Normandy, later William the Conqueror, from the Bayeux Tapestry. Both men had an impact on the Church in Cornwall, Harold taking property from Bodmin minster which William later returned.

but it throws light upon churches in three respects. First, it records about thirty church names, including major places like Bodmin and Launceston, and minor ones such as St Gennys, Lanreath, and Pelynt. Secondly, it tells us something about the larger churches and their landed property, topics that have been briefly mentioned already. It is from Domesday Book that we learn about the relative extent of the lands and wealth of Bodmin, St Germans, Launceston, and so on. Thirdly, it throws light on the Norman Conquest, in so far as it affected the Church in Cornwall, by estimating the income of the larger churches both in 1066, before the Conquest began, and twenty years later when the survey was made.[35]

One piece of evidence in Domesday Book shows the Conquest in a favourable light. We are told that William ordered the restoration to Bodmin of the estate that Harold had seized. Most of the larger churches, however, had seen a decline in the value of their landed property between 1066 and 1086, and some had lost part of their lands altogether. The responsibility for these losses, in every case, was ascribed to Count Robert. He had taken land or value from all of the land-holding churches except for Launceston and Probus. He had removed livestock from one of the properties of Perranzabuloe, and wrongfully subtracted four manors in the Launceston area from Tavistock Abbey. The major churches of Cornwall would have been an easy target for a powerful Norman lord intent on enriching himself and rewarding his followers. In his defence, one might point out that Robert was only following in the path of King Egbert and Earl Harold in robbing the churches of Cornwall. Moreover, Robert partly offset his ill-gotten gains with warm support for one of the Cornish churches: the minster of St Stephen-by-Launceston.[36]

Robert made Launceston the centre of his power, and built a castle there (see Figure 16). A Norman lord was accustomed to have a religious house close to his castle, whose clergy would pray for him and his family and provide for their spiritual needs. Some lords established small monasteries of French monks in England for this purpose, but Robert did not found one in Cornwall. Instead he turned to the minster of St Stephen for the religious support he required. It may be that Cornwall was seen as still too strange or unsettled to suit a community of monks from France. In 1076 the count granted a charter to St Stephen's, whose head or dean was now another Robert, probably a Norman installed by the count to ensure that the minster worked in his interests. The charter granted the church a number of lands, estimated at 8½ hides, some of which are likely to have been its existing property while others represented gifts from the count. He also gave the tithes of six of his Cornish manors for the personal use of the dean, whom he evidently wished to increase in status and wealth.[37]

As a result St Stephen's became the chief church in Cornwall to benefit from the Norman Conquest. It entered into a relationship with the lords of Launceston Castle, which outlived Robert of Mortain's family and continued through much of the 12th century. This enabled it to acquire more property and to become the best endowed and wealthiest religious house in the county. For that reason at least Count Robert deserves to be remembered as a positive figure in Cornish Church history, as well as a negative one.

Figure 16 An 18th-century engraving of Launceston Castle, originally built after 1076 by Robert, count of Mortain. For the next hundred years it was the chief centre of Norman power in Cornwall.

Chapter 2 The High Middle Ages

Figure 17 St Michael's Mount had a varied religious history in the Middle Ages. A pre-Conquest religious site, it became a Benedictine priory and after about 1420 a chantry of priests, as well as developing into the most popular shrine in Cornwall, visited by pilgrims from as far away as London and East Anglia.

FROM 1100 TO 1300

One effect of the Norman Conquest was to strengthen England's ties with continental Europe. These ties stayed strong for the next two hundred years from 1100 to 1300, the era that historians call the 'high Middle Ages'. Politically the kings of England ruled lands on both sides of the English Channel throughout this period. Religiously England was caught up in the great Church developments of Europe. These included the growing power of the pope, the crusades, and the spread of new religious organisations of monks and friars. Culturally the styles of European architecture and the writings of European scholars came to England with widespread effects. Some of these writings were in Latin; others were in French which came to be spoken, read, and written by many people in England. And what was true of England in these matters was also true of Cornwall in particular.

We shall trace some of these developments in the following chapter. How far we can trace them, however, depends on the sources available to us. Much more survives about Cornwall in the centuries between 1100 and 1300 than in the early Middle Ages. This is true both of written sources and archaeological remains, especially buildings. However, remains and sources are still limited in what they reveal. It is easier than before to make lists of monasteries and churches, chart the property they owned, and reckon its value or income. It is also easier to trace the role that important people played in the Church: the king, the bishops, and the nobility. But how most people practised their religion, whether monks, priests, or laity, remains very poorly recorded.

The evidence tends to give us a rather simplistic view of the Church, primarily of its institutions, and a rather idealistic view, since to describe institutions is to imply that they worked correctly. We cannot penetrate the complexity of people's religious practices and activities, let alone their malpractices and inactivity, as deeply as we can in later centuries. The picture of Church history in this period can only be painted with broad brushstrokes, not in photographic detail.

BISHOPS, ARCHDEACONS, AND RURAL DEANS

The power of the counts of Mortain in Cornwall ended in 1106. Count William, who had succeeded his father Robert in 1090, quarrelled with Henry I and lost his English lands and titles. This situation favoured the bishops of Exeter. The quiet Bishop Osbern died in 1103 and after a four-year interval he was replaced by William Warelwast, a Norman close to Henry and a more active man. William succeeded, although not instantly, in gaining control of five of the major churches of Cornwall. In 1123 he secured a charter from Henry restoring to his church of Exeter (and therefore to himself as well) those of Bodmin, Launceston, Perranzabuloe,

Figure 18 Lands of the bishop of Exeter, rural deaneries, and peculiars.

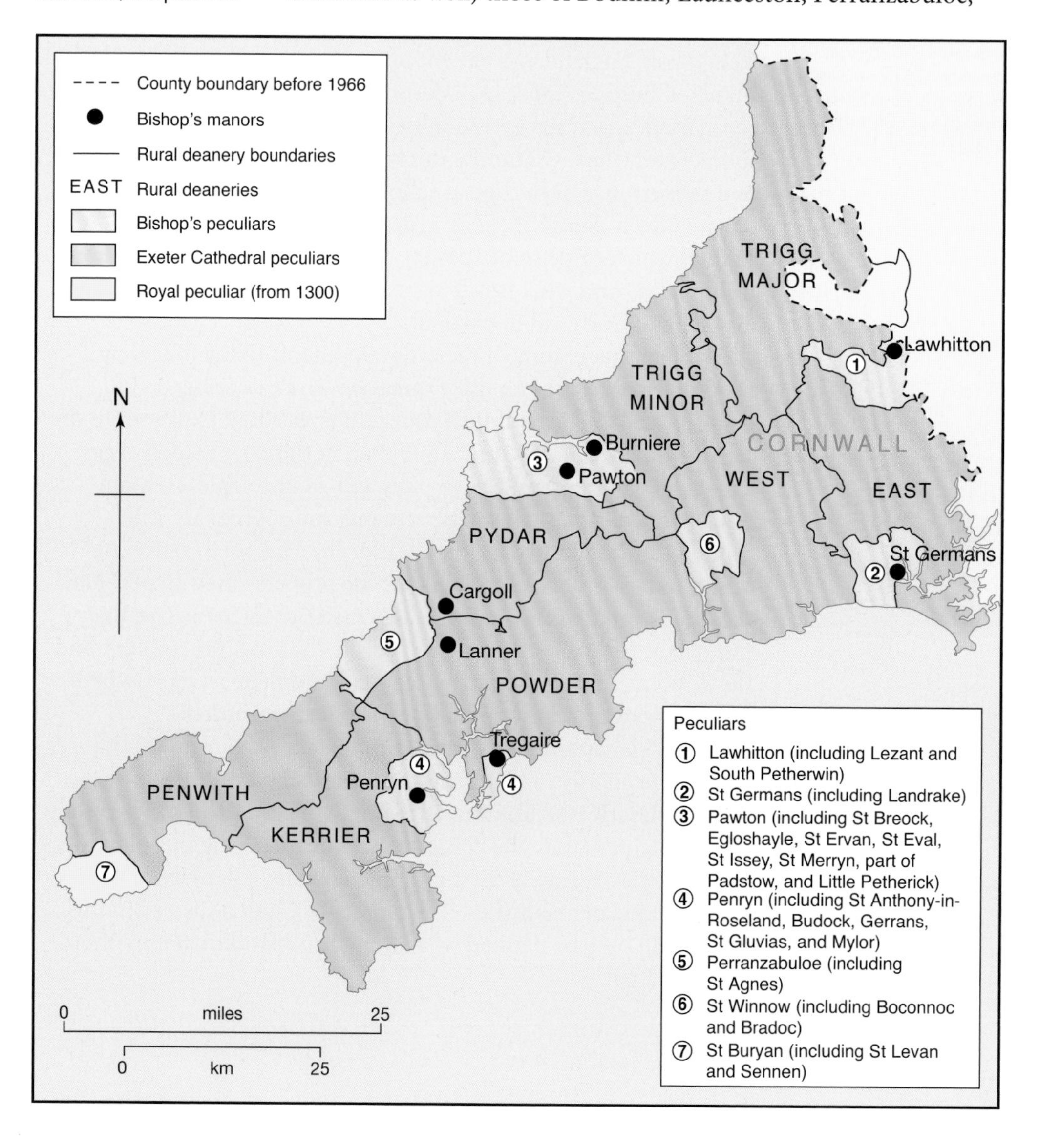

Probus, and St Kew. This enabled him to reorganise the first two and to use Perranzabuloe to endow his cathedral and St Kew to support his new foundation of Plympton Priory (Devon). For the next four hundred years the bishops of Exeter played a major part again in the affairs of the Cornish Church. They sometimes came into conflict with the king or with the later earls and dukes of Cornwall, but they were no longer sidelined to the extent that had been possible in the time of Osbern.[38]

The bishops were important landowners in Cornwall during the 12th and 13th centuries. They held six major properties in the county: Burniere in Egloshayle, St Germans, Lawhitton, Pawton in St Breock, Penryn, and Tregaire in Roseland (see Figure 18). A seventh estate, the manor of Cargoll in Newlyn East, was purchased by Bishop Walter Bronescombe in 1270 for £200, and this included Lanner, a residence in the adjoining parish of St Allen. The bishops had other lands in Devon, where they spent most of their time unless they were elsewhere in England. Most of them probably came to Cornwall only a few times during their periods of office, although Bronescombe (bishop from 1258 to 1280) made about 16 visits in 21 years (see Figure 19). For most of the time the bishops governed Cornwall by sending letters and using officers to act on their behalf. They held a court (the consistory court), which met in Exeter, dealt with crimes by the clergy and laity against the Church and its rules, and administered certain wills. Some Cornish people would have had to attend this court on business, or to deal on other matters with the bishop and his senior clergy in Devon.[39]

By 1128 the bishop had a deputy to look after his Cornish affairs: the archdeacon of Cornwall. This man was normally based at Exeter, but after 1267 he had another house at Glasney College in Penryn and could spend time there if he chose to do so. The archdeaconry covered the ancient county of Cornwall along with North Petherwin and Werrington (which lay in Devon until 1966), and St Giles-on-the-Heath nearby (which is still in Devon). The archdeacon was expected to visit and inspect its parishes once a year, to put the bishop's orders into effect, and to induct (install) new clergy to parish churches. He also held a court to deal with minor offences against Church law and to administer wills. Much of this work was done by an assistant known as his 'official', who was normally one of the Cornish parish clergy, based in the county itself. Other tasks were carried out by eight rural deans, each looking after a couple of dozen parishes (see Figure 18). The rural deans were parish clergy, chosen by the clergy of their deanery or taking their turn to serve. They were responsible for Church affairs locally and carried out orders from the bishop or archdeacon as required.[40]

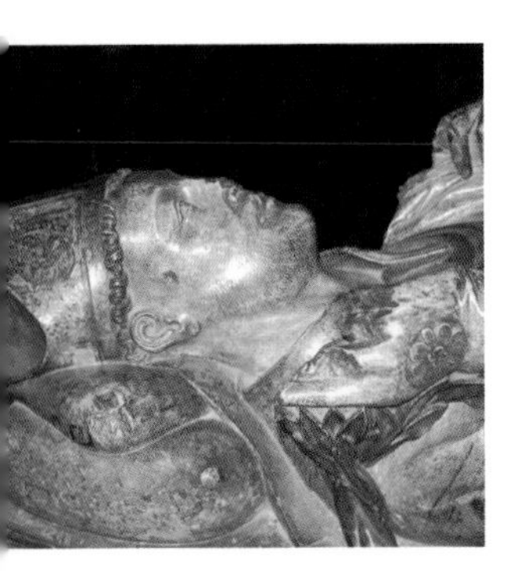

Figure 19 Walter Bronescombe, bishop of Exeter (d. 1280), as portrayed on his tomb in Exeter Cathedral. An assiduous visitor to Cornwall, he contributed greatly to its history by founding Glasney College (Penryn) in 1265.

PARISHES

The basic unit of the church in Cornwall, as in England, was the parish. In 1291, the date of the first surviving list of Cornish churches, the archdeaconry of Cornwall contained about 209 parishes or parish-like areas. About 167 of these were fully parishes. They had a parish church where every kind of religious service was available: mass, confession, baptism, marriage, funeral, and burial. The clergyman of the parish church had authority over everyone in the parish for ordinary religious purposes, and every adult in the parish was expected to attend the parish church and to pay it tithes and other dues. Some parish clergymen were rectors, others vicars, and yet others chaplains or curates – distinctions that will be considered presently.[41]

The remaining 42 units fell into two categories. Most of them (37) were places like Advent, Germoe, Lostwithiel, or Warbstow, which may be termed 'sub-parishes'. They had some of the characteristics of parishes, notably their own places of worship and probably definite boundaries within which people had duties towards them. Often they had their own chaplain to hold services. Legally, however, they were part of a larger parish: Lanteglos-by-Camelford, Breage, Lanlivery, and Treneglos in the examples just mentioned. Their place of worship was technically a chapel, not a church, and their chaplain was the employee of the clergyman of the mother church. Their parishioners paid tithes and dues to that clergyman, not to the priest of the chapel, and they were expected to attend the mother church on certain days of the year and sometimes for confessions, baptisms, and funerals.

That leaves a small group of oddities. Three were islands. The Isles of Scilly formed a parish, chiefly served by monks of Tavistock Abbey. The islands never appear in lists of Cornish churches or clergy, no doubt because of their remoteness and lack of a normal clergyman. St Michael's Mount did not belong to any other parish and was, in effect, a parish of itself, although it was run first by monks and later by an archpriest. A third island, Lammana (nowadays Looe Island), constituted another distinct area, including a strip of territory on the adjoining mainland. This, too, was first administered by monks but after 1289 by a priest of its own. A fourth parish, St Anthony-in-Roseland, was a little area served by the clergy of the priory situated there; it would have operated as a parish but is rarely mentioned in records. A fifth small district, Temple, belonged to the Knights Templars and later to the Order of St John of Jerusalem. Its church was described as a chapel in 1291, but formed an independent unit.

A further complication of Church geography was the existence of 'peculiars', short for 'peculiar jurisdictions' (see Figure 18). These were parishes taken out of the rural deaneries and the archdeaconry, and administered separately. Twenty-one churches in Cornwall, which lay on the estates of the bishop of Exeter, were his peculiars and they were organised into four small rural deaneries: St Germans, Lawhitton, Penryn, and Pawton. The cathedral had two peculiar churches and parishes: Perranzabuloe (including St Agnes) and St Winnow (including Boconnoc and Bradoc), and these (like the bishop's peculiars) had their own Church officers and courts. Monasteries and friaries also lay outside the normal system. In 1300 King Edward I removed the parish of St Buryan from the diocese altogether, along with its two daughter churches, St Levan and Sennen, and made it another peculiar, subject to royal control alone. Successive bishops of Exeter objected strongly to this encroachment and tried to reverse it, but they were not successful.[42]

A conjectural map of parishes in Cornwall in 1291 appears as Figure 20. This shows the boundaries of the areas that were fully parishes in continuous lines and those of the major sub-parishes within them in dotted lines. These boundaries are conjectural ones based on much later evidence, sometimes as late as the 1840s, but they are the best that can be drawn. As we saw in the previous chapter, the parish system in Cornwall probably grew up gradually, by at least the 900s and 1000s. Most of the Cornish parishes covered between about four and 12 square miles (1036–3108 hectares), but a few were larger or smaller for special reasons.[43]

The biggest parishes fell into two groups. Some of them belonged to churches that were staffed by groups of clergy before the Norman Conquest, like St Buryan, St Germans, and St Keverne. Here the size of the parish was linked with the superior status of the church. The other large parishes covered moorland areas, such as Altarnun, St Cleer, and Wendron; here size was not a mark of status but reflected a shortage of people to support a parish church and clergyman. The smaller parishes and sub-parishes included some in towns like St Mary Magdalene (Launceston), Lostwithiel, St Thomas-by-Launceston, Tregony, and Truro, and others in the countryside, such as St Keyne, Lammana, St Michael Caerhays, Perranuthnoe, and Temple. They are likely to have taken shape after about 1000, since they reflect the growth of the tithe system which made it easier for such areas to maintain a clergyman. The town parishes resulted from the foundation or growth of towns in the 1100s, while Lammana and Temple arose from gifts of land to religious bodies in the same period.

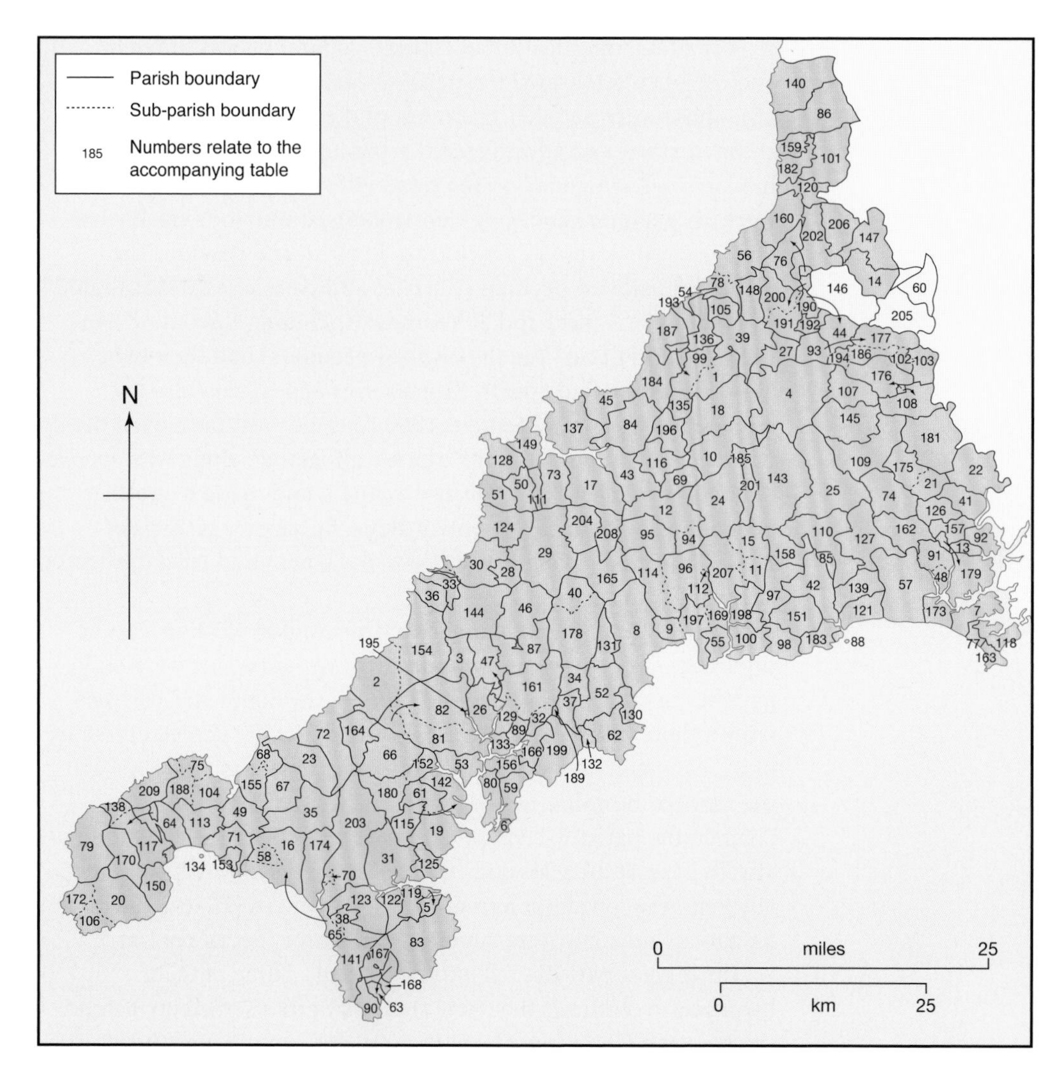

Figure 20 Parish Boundaries in Cornwall, 1291.

The varied nature of the parishes – diversified by their size, location, economy, and society – shaped the character of the Church in Cornwall as it did all over England. The income of the clergy, known as their stipends, ranged widely from parish to parish until the early 1900s, depending on the value of the tithes. Churches differed in size and adornment, according to the wealth in the parish that could be tapped to build them. We can still see these differences today in the big ornate churches of Bodmin or Launceston on the one hand, and the smaller plainer ones at Forrabury or Tremaine on the other (see Figures 65, 78, 100). This variety meant that the Church authorities had an assortment of parishes and clergy to deal with, and that there was never uniformity in how the Church operated at a local level.

PARISHES IN THE ARCHDEACONRY OF CORNWALL, 1291
Parishes were in Cornwall unless otherwise stated

1 Advent
2 Agnes
3 St Allen
4 Altarnun
5 St Anthony-in-Meneage
6 St Anthony-in-Roseland
7 Antony
8 St Austell
9 St Blazey
10 Blisland
11 Boconnoc
12 Bodmin
13 Botus Fleming
14 Boyton (partly in Devon)
15 Bradoc
16 Breage
17 St Breock
18 St Breward
19 Budock
20 St Buryan
21 Callington
22 Calstock
23 Camborne
24 Cardinham
25 St Cleer,
26 St Clement
27 St Clether
28 Colan
29 St Columb Major
30 St Columb Minor
31 Constantine
32 Cornelly
33 Crantock
34 Creed
35 Crowan
36 Cubert
37 Cuby
38 Cury
39 Davidstow
40 St Dennis
41 St Dominick
42 Duloe,
43 Egloshayle
44 Egloskerry
45 St Endellion
46 St Enoder
47 St Erme
48 St Erney
49 St Erth
50 St Ervan
51 St Eval
52 St Ewe
53 Feock
54 Forrabury
55 Fowey
56 St Gennys
57 St Germans
58 Germoe
59 Gerrans
60 St Giles-in-the-Heath (Devon)
61 St Gluvias
62 Goran
63 Grade
64 Gulval
65 Gunwalloe
66 Gwennap
67 Gwinear
68 Gwithian
69 Helland
70 Helston
71 St Hilary
72 Illogan
73 St Issey
74 St Ive
75 St Ives
76 Jacobstow
77 St John
78 St Juliot
79 St Just-in-Penwith
80 St Just-in-Roseland
81 Kea
82 Kenwyn
83 St Keverne
84 St Kew
85 St Keyne
86 Kilkhampton
87 Ladock
88 Lammana
89 Lamorran
90 Landewednack
91 Landrake
92 Landulph
93 Laneast
94 Lanhydrock
95 Lanivet
96 Lanlivery
97 Lanreath
98 Lansallos
99 Lanteglos-by-Camelford
100 Lanteglos-by-Fowey
101 Launcells
102 Launceston: St Mary Magdalene
103 Lawhitton
104 Lelant
105 Lesnewth
106 St Levan
107 Lewannick
108 Lezant
109 Linkinhorne
110 Liskeard
111 Little Petherick
112 Lostwithiel
113 Ludgvan
114 Luxulyan
115 Mabe
116 St Mabyn
117 Madron
118 Maker (partly in Devon)
119 Manaccan
120 Marhamchurch
121 St Martin-by-Looe
122 St Martin-in-Meneage
123 Mawgan-in-Meneage
124 St Mawgan-in-Pydar
125 Mawnan
126 St Mellion
127 Menheniot
128 St Merryn
129 Merther
130 Mevagissey
131 Mewan
132 St Michael Caerhays
133 St Michael Penkevil
134 St Michael's Mount
135 Michaelstow
136 Minster
137 St Minver
138 Morvah
139 Morval
140 Morwenstow
141 Mullion
142 Mylor
143 St Neot
144 Newlyn East
145 North Hill
146 North Petherwin (Devon)
147 North Tamerton
148 Otterham
149 Padstow
150 Paul
151 Pelynt
152 Perranarworthal
153 Perranuthnoe
154 Perranzabuloe
155 Phillack
156 Philleigh
157 Pillaton
158 St Pinnock
159 Poughill
160 Poundstock
161 Probus
162 Quethiock
163 Rame
164 Redruth
165 Roche
166 Ruan Lanihorne
167 Ruan Major
168 Ruan Minor
169 St Sampson (Golant)
170 Sancreed
171 Scilly
172 Sennen
173 Sheviock
174 Sithney
175 South Hill
176 South Petherwin
177 St Stephen-by-Launceston
178 St Stephen-in-Brannel
179 St Stephen-by-Saltash
180 Stithians
181 Stoke Climsland
182 Stratton
183 Talland
184 St Teath
185 Temple
186 St Thomas-by-Launceston
187 Tintagel
188 Towednack
189 Tregony
190 Tremaine
191 Treneglos
192 Tresmeer
193 Trevalga
194 Trewen
195 Truro
196 St Tudy
197 Tywardreath
198 St Veep
199 Veryan
200 Warbstow
201 Warleggan
202 Week St Mary
203 Wendron
204 St Wenn
205 Werrington (Devon)
206 Whitstone
207 St Winnow
208 Withiel
209 Zennor

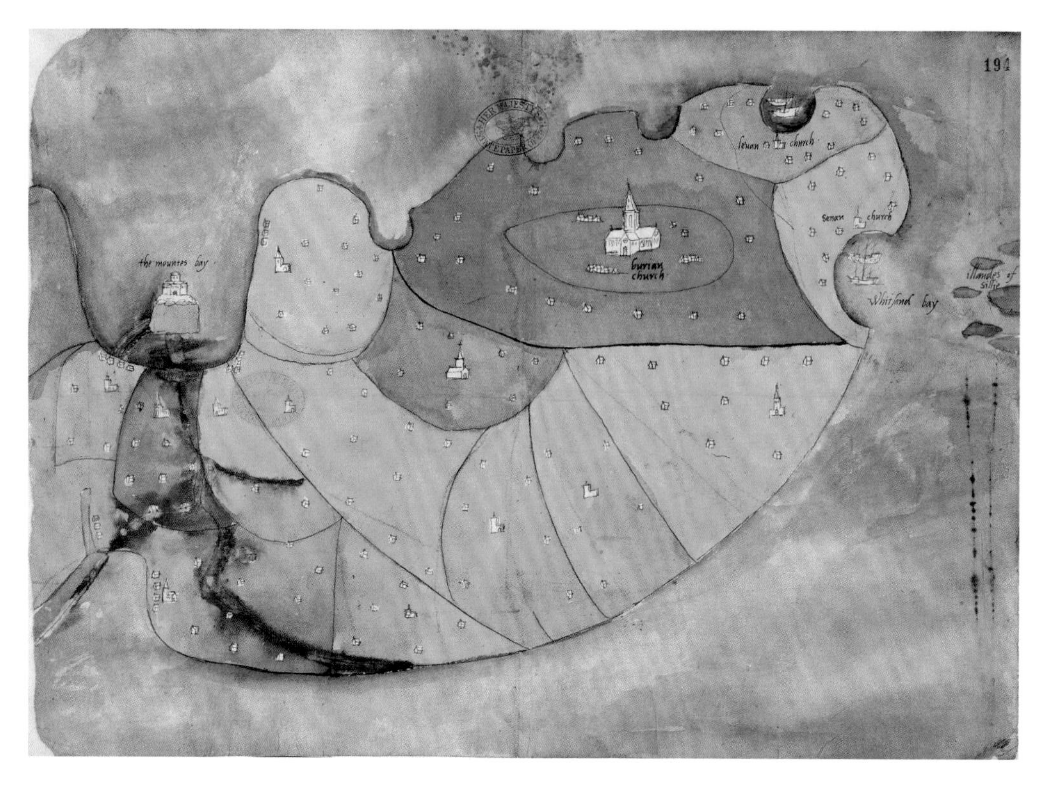

Figure 21 The oldest known map of parish boundaries in Cornwall, and one of the oldest in England. Dating from about 1574, it centres on St Buryan church and shows in a schematic way the boundaries of the parishes of west Penwith.

THE MONASTIC REVIVAL

The period from 1100 to 1300 saw a revival of monasteries in England. There were only a few dozen of them at the time of the Norman Conquest, and Cornwall, as we saw, had none at all. The Normans were stronger supporters of monks and their way of life. They began to found more monasteries after 1066, and the process grew in scale after 1100. At first the monks of these foundations were Benedictines who followed the Rule of St Benedict, but during the 12th century new kinds of monasteries developed, such as those of the Cistercian monks and the Augustinian canons.[44]

Cornwall was slower to acquire a monastery than some other parts of England. The earliest to appear (apart from the older ones that had died out by about 900) was the priory of Scilly on the island of Tresco in about 1114. This followed a grant by King Henry I of all the churches of the Isles of Scilly to Tavistock Abbey, a Benedictine house. The abbey founded the priory as a 'cell', a branch of the mother house, and sent a handful of monks there to organise worship and pastoral services on the islands. Three more Benedictine priories made their appearance in the first half of the 12th century: Tywardreath and Minster at unknown dates, and St Michael's Mount perhaps between 1135

Figure 22 St Germans. The great west doorway of the priory of Augustinian canons that had been converted from the ancient minster during the 12th century. A rare survival of large-scale Romanesque carving in Cornwall, it conveys the grandeur to which the founders of these priories aspired.

and 1144. These, too, were cells, the first two belonging to the abbey of St Serge and St Bacche at Angers and the third to Mont St Michel, both in France. All were modestly staffed: Tywardreath by seven monks and Minster by two or three, while St Michael's Mount, although apparently intended for 13, is more likely to have supported six or less.[45]

Five other cells were opened during the second half of the 12th century or the early 13th, making a total of nine. The priory of St Anthony-in-Roseland for two Augustinian canons belonged to Plympton Priory (Devon); the priory of St Carroc near Fowey for two Cluniac monks, to Montacute Priory (Somerset); the priory of Lammana on Looe Island for two Benedictine monks, to Glastonbury Abbey (Somerset); and the priory of Tregony for two or more Augustinian canons, to the abbey of Sainte-Marie-du-Val

(Normandy). A cell of Tywardreath existed for a period during the 13th century at St Mary Vale in the parish of Cardinham.

The three largest monastic foundations in Cornwall had a different origin. They were ancient minsters which were converted into Augustinian priories. In 1123–4 Bishop William Warelwast introduced Augustinian canons to Bodmin, and in 1127 he did the same at Launceston. Somewhat later, perhaps in the early 1180s, Bishop Bartholomew of Exeter followed suit at St Germans. Whereas minster clergy dwelt in separate houses with their own possessions and were free to travel about, Augustinian canons lived like monks in a single building. They slept and ate together, owned no personal property, and could not go outside the monastery walls without permission. By the early 14th century there were about 18 canons at Bodmin, perhaps as many at Launceston, and probably a dozen at St Germans. Each of the larger houses had a zone of power and influence. Bodmin's extended from Bodmin westwards and northwards towards the north coast. Launceston's occupied the east of the county between Bodmin Moor and the Tamar valley, while St Germans dominated the south-eastern corner.

The list of religious orders was completed by the arrival of the friars in the middle of the 13th century. Friars lived in a community as monks did, with common eating and sleeping arrangements, but they were not confined to their houses like monks. Instead they were required to travel outside to do pastoral work, especially preaching and hearing confessions. Whereas monks possessed lands, rents, and tithes which gave them a secure income, friars collected donations like modern charities. There were four major kinds of friars in medieval England, two of which established houses in Cornwall: the Franciscans (or Grey Friars) at Bodmin between 1240 and 1260, and the Dominicans (or Black Friars) at Truro in or shortly before 1259. A third order of friars, the Carmelites (or White Friars), established themselves just outside the county at Plymouth between 1289 and 1296, but developed links within it, especially across its eastern half. The two Cornish friaries reinforced the presence of the religious orders by at least a dozen and possibly two dozen members each, but their importance, as we shall see, was greater and more distinctive than such numbers suggest.[46]

The 12th and 13th centuries, then, saw a great monastic revival throughout England, in which Cornwall shared. This revival reflected the fact that many people saw monasteries as the best institutions for leading a Christian life. The bishops who converted the three Cornish minsters thought that in doing so they were improving the worship and other activities inside them. Not only were monasteries founded inside the county, but Cornish churches

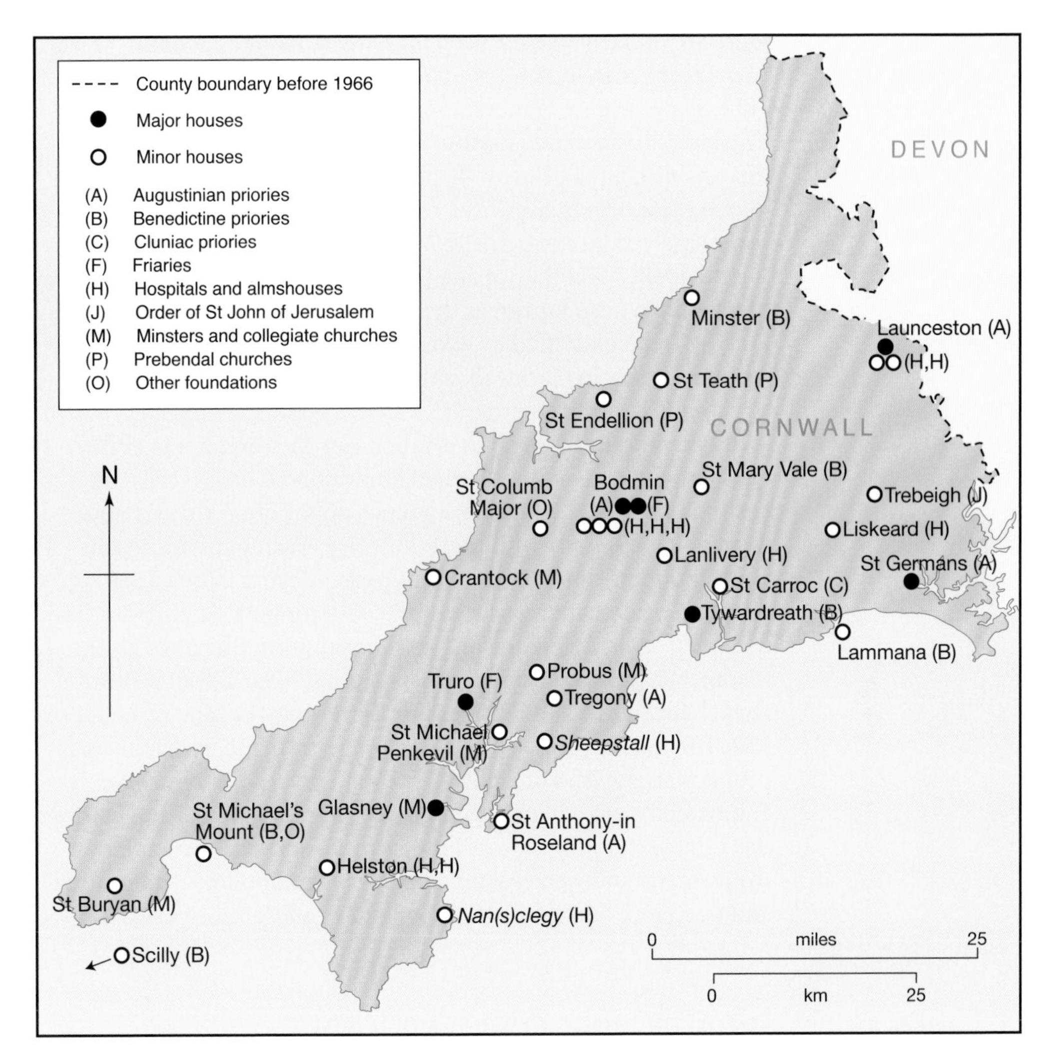

Figure 23 Religious Houses in Cornwall, 1100–1560.

and lands were granted to monasteries elsewhere in England, which administered these churches and lands without establishing cells in Cornwall. They included the monasteries of Hartland, Newenham, and Plympton (Devon), and others further afield such as Beaulieu, Mottisfont, and Wherwell (Hampshire), Hailes and Tewkesbury (Gloucestershire), Rewley (Oxford), Bridgwater, Cleeve, and Montacute (Somerset), and Wilton (Wiltshire). The longest link of all joined the church of Tintagel to Fontevrault Abbey in France.

Nevertheless, the monasteries and friaries were never as strong in Cornwall as they were in some other parts of England. Cornwall lacked wealthy nobility to give the lands that monks required to support them, and wealthy towns to provide donations for friars. At the peak of monastic numbers in the 13th century, there are unlikely to have been more than about 22 monks, 50–60 Augustinian canons, and 40–50 friars west of the Tamar. The other major orders of monks and canons who founded houses in England – Cistercians, Carthusians, and Premonstratensians – did not establish any in Cornwall, although a handful of Cornish men joined these orders elsewhere. The Knights Templars acquired some small properties, chiefly Temple on Bodmin Moor, but there is no evidence that they opened a house there. The Order of St John of Jerusalem (also known as the Hospitallers) had a single 'preceptory' at Trebeigh staffed by two or three brothers. Nor was there ever a nunnery in Cornwall, although a few Cornish women went to be nuns in other counties.[47]

By the middle of the 13th century, too, the revival was visibly weakening. Some mother houses found their Cornish cells too costly to maintain. In 1267 the French abbey of Le Val exchanged its priory of Tregony with Merton Priory (Surrey) in return for lands in France, and within twenty years Merton closed Tregony altogether. Soon afterwards, in 1289, Glastonbury Abbey withdrew its monks from Lammana and sold its property there to a local landowner. St Mary Vale must have turned from a priory into a chapel during the late 13th or early 14th centuries, and by about 1300 the monks of Tavistock Abbey were trying to exchange their property in the Isles of Scilly with King Edward I in return for endowments elsewhere, although they were not successful. During the 14th century the Cornish monasteries suffered further blows from plague and war, causing numbers of monks and canons to fall and two more houses to close soon after 1400.[48]

MINSTERS AND OTHER RELIGIOUS HOUSES

Although the popular image of a medieval religious house is that of a monastery, nunnery, or friary, there were other communities of clergy that did not belong to any of these categories. Three of the pre-Conquest minsters survived the disturbances of the 1000s and the monastic reorganisations of the 1100s. These were St Buryan, Crantock, and Probus with four, ten, and six canons respectively, the chief of whom was known as the dean, together with a few lesser clergy. The minsters were run in easy-going ways compared with the monasteries and friaries. The clergy did not even need to live near the church because they were usually allowed to receive their stipends wherever they lived, as long as they arranged for others to do their duties.

In consequence minster clergy often spent their time away from their minsters as servants of the king, the bishop, or lay lords. In

Figure 24 Crantock church as we see it today. In the Middle Ages it demonstrated its status as a religious house by being longer than usual and possessing choir aisles and a central tower. The tower fell in about 1400, and a western tower was built instead.

1268 the bishop of Exeter suppressed the office of dean of Probus and gave its endowments to the treasurer of Exeter Cathedral. Thereafter Probus was virtually only a parish church, although it continued to support five canons who rarely or never went there. St Buryan shrank into a group of lowly paid chaplains and clerks who deputised for an absent dean and canons, and only Crantock held on to some semblance of communal life. Unfortunately it was too poor and remote to have any status or influence outside its immediate neighbourhood.

More important than the ancient minsters was a new foundation in the same tradition made by Bishop Bronescombe in 1265. This was Glasney College (Penryn), one of the earliest colleges or collegiate churches in England (see Figure 45). The word college originally meant a group of clergy following a religious life; it did not imply that they were involved in education or learning. College clergy, like those of minsters, resembled parish clergy rather than monks or friars. They differed from minster clergy in possessing codes of statutes which laid down more precisely how they should work, and prevented their communities dissolving through non-residence. Bronescombe envisaged Glasney as being a smaller version of Exeter Cathedral. He probably saw its role as twofold: providing a model of worship for the Cornish parish clergy and acting as an administrative centre for Church affairs. Glasney's history was not without problems, but it realised its founder's intentions in a reasonably faithful way until it was suppressed at the Reformation.

A few more institutions call for attention. Two parish churches, St Endellion and St Teath, had multiple clergy – four prebendaries

Figure 25 A leper with his bell, asking for alms. 'Some good, my gentle master, for God's sake.' Leprosy was perceived as a serious medical and social problem between 1100 and 1300, and there was pressure to seclude lepers from the community, into remote dwellings or hospitals.

in the first case and two prebendaries and a vicar in the second – who shared their revenues and duties. One clergyman resided at each place to staff the parish, but the other posts were usually held by absentees and no communities of clergy developed at these churches. Six leper hospitals (Bodmin, Helston, Launceston, Liskeard, Maudlin in Lanlivery, and Sheepstall in Veryan) came into existence during the late 12th and 13th centuries, while a single hospital for infirm people who were not lepers emerged at Helston. A seventh leper community at *Nan(s)clegy* in St Keverne is mentioned in 1268 and may still have existed in 1481.

The number of Cornish hospitals is sometimes reckoned higher than this because, after Bishop Bitton of Exeter died in 1307, his executors (or someone on their behalf) travelled through Devon and Cornwall giving small sums of money to lepers in particular places, 22 of them in Cornwall. Six of these were the places with leper hospitals, but the others are not recorded as having had such hospitals. Here the money may have been given to lepers who were living in private houses rather than institutions.[49]

LIFE IN THE RELIGIOUS HOUSES

The religious houses of Cornwall were scattered across the county in an irregular way, reflecting the various forces that had created them. Five were in towns – Bodmin (with two), Launceston, Tregony, and Truro – while Tywardreath near Fowey was close to another. Most of the rest lay in the countryside, sometimes off main roads like Crantock, St Germans, and Minster. There were slightly more houses in the eastern half of the county, which was closer to England and mainly English-speaking, but the western, Cornish-speaking half had St Buryan, Crantock, St Michael's Mount, Glasney, and the Truro friary. Bodmin, too, had some friars who were fluent in Cornish. Nearly all the houses occupied ancient religious sites where there had been a church before. Only St Mary Vale, Tregony, and Tywardreath may have been founded in virgin locations. Remoteness was sometimes a feature, too. Three houses were built on islands (Lammana, the Mount, and Scilly) and two in secluded valleys (St Mary Vale and Minster). Such foundations point to a wish by some founders and clergy to establish religion well away from the everyday world – a wish expressed in other parts of the British Isles.

The three large monasteries in Cornwall were independent houses and recruited most of their canons locally, so they were strongly Cornish in character. At the same time they belonged to a religious order, that of the Augustinian canons, and forged links through the order with the world beyond the Tamar. The first prior of Bodmin, Guy, came from Merton Priory and the first prior of Launceston, Teoric, from the priory of Holy Trinity Aldgate (London), both Augustinian houses. In turn, Bodmin sent clergy elsewhere. Algar, its probable second prior, became bishop of Coutances (Normandy) in 1133, and 60 years later four Bodmin canons went to Ireland to start a new priory at Kells in County Kilkenny. Three of them rose to be priors of Irish monasteries and one of the three an Irish bishop, while the fourth, another Algar, was believed to have gone to Italy. Launceston did not match this achievement, but Peter of Cornwall (1139/40–1221), who was born in the town and whose family was closely linked with the priory, entered its parent house of Holy Trinity Aldgate and ended his life there as prior. He was the author of several theological works and of a large collection of evidence about visions, *Liber revelationum*, in which he included details of his family history.[50]

The smaller houses all had external connections because they were cells of houses elsewhere and their monks or canons came from outside Cornwall. Indeed, such monks and canons were mostly French in the case of St Michael's Mount, Minster, Tywardreath, and (until 1267) Tregony. Such connections brought clergy into the county from elsewhere and, although monks were meant to pray and live in seclusion, they must have come into contact with many local people, chiefly through administering property but also by running churches. St Michael's Mount drew people to its shrine, while St Anthony, Minster, Scilly, and probably Tregony were parish churches as well as monasteries.

The clergy with the most external links were the friars and the members of the Order of St John of Jerusalem – an order that

Medieval Monasteries

The best-preserved plan of a medieval monastery in Cornwall is that of the Augustinian priory of Launceston. The priory originally stood at St Stephen-by-Launceston but was moved to a new site, south of the present St Thomas church, in 1155. It was dissolved by Henry VIII in 1539, and the buildings were later demolished. The site was excavated between 1886 and 1893, and the footings of the walls were discovered over a wide area. This enabled the priory plan (shown here) to be reconstructed as it was at the end of its history in the early 16th century. The model of the church is a conjectural one by Mr Arthur Wills, but it gives a good idea of what the church probably looked like.

The church consisted of a long narrow nave, to which a north aisle was added later; a choir with aisles; and a Lady chapel at the east end of the building. South of the church were the domestic buildings of the priory. At their centre was the cloister – a rectangle of covered ways, one of which was probably used by the clergy for studying. Around the cloister stood the dormitory

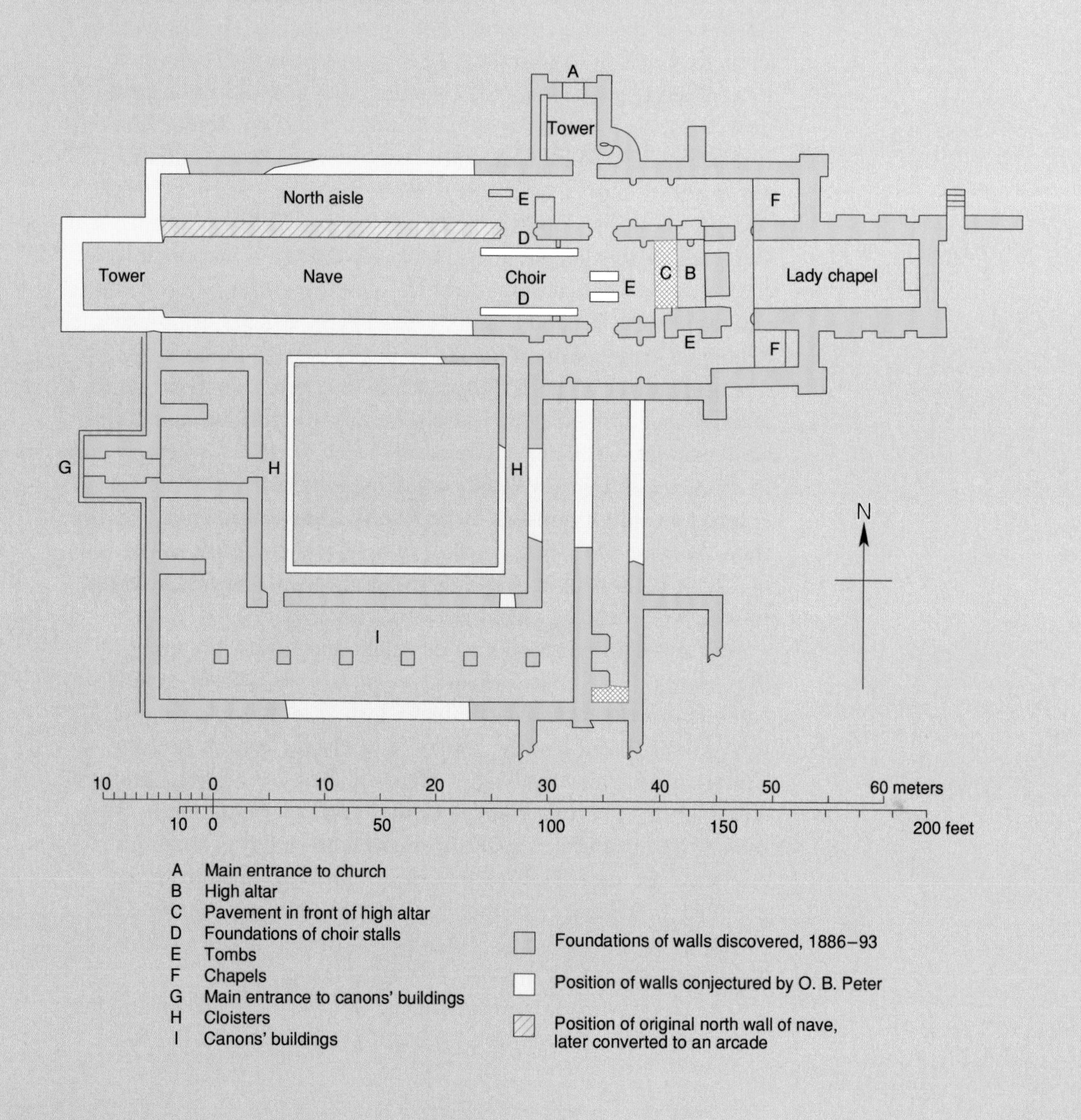

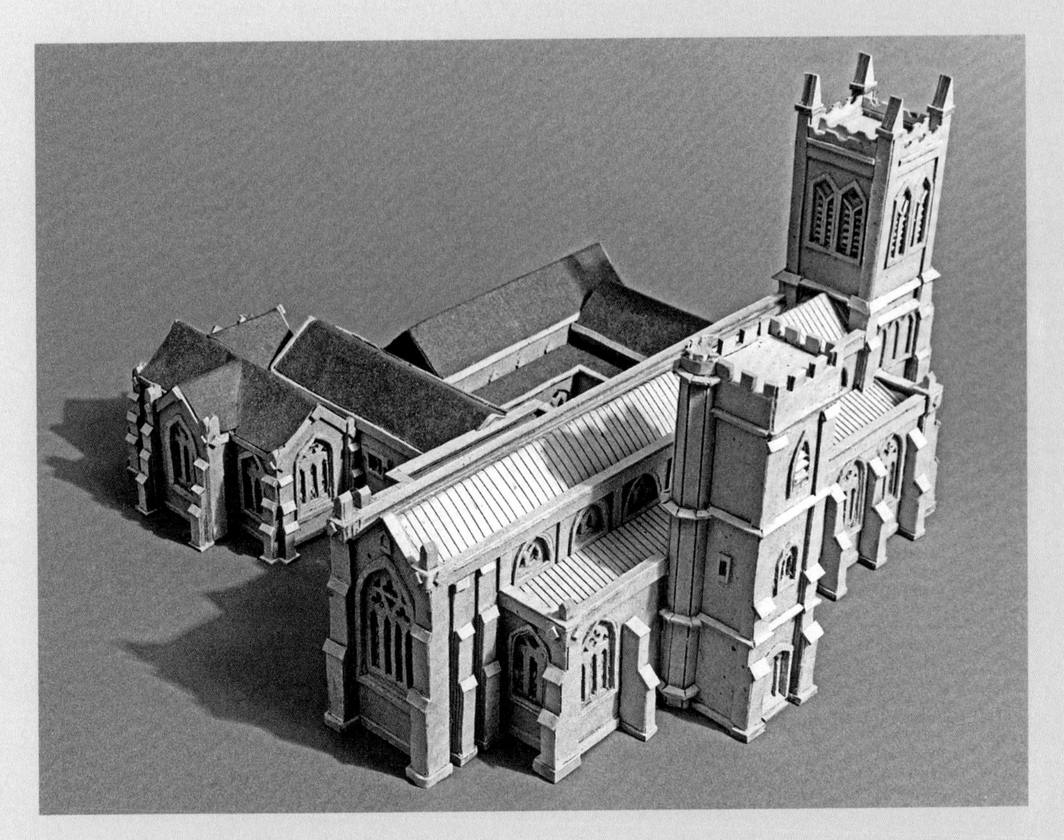

The church of Launceston Priory, a model reconstructed from the ground plan. The original long narrow 12th-century church with a cloister on its south side was enlarged and given a north aisle in the 13th or 14th century.

where the clergy slept and the refectory where they ate. Further out were a separate lodging for the prior, a hall for the feeding of servants, guests, and the poor, and accommodation for servants.

The clergy of the priory were technically known as Augustinian canons, but they lived a life similar to that of monks. Their life centred on the church, where they assembled in the choir to say eight daily services at intervals from midnight until the early evening. These services together took several hours, much of the material being said by heart because it was repeated from week to week. The nave was used for processions, and layfolk were allowed into it to pray or to listen to the services in the choir; a few privileged people may have been allowed into the choir itself.

Most of the rest of the canons' time, apart from meals and sleep, was probably spent on administrative duties. All but the most junior held responsibilities, such as the almoner (who organised the giving of food to the poor), the cellarer, chamberlain, and steward (all concerned with finance and supplies), the precentor (who directed the choir), and the sacrist (custodian of the church goods). Prior and canons together had to supervise the priory's estates and its business with the outside world. The entertainment of guests and travellers would also have needed attention. Some studying was done but the Augustinians were not an especially learned order. Nor did they work with their hands, since they kept servants to do their manual tasks.

ran hospitals, protected pilgrims, and fought crusades. Their organisations were international ones, and their members did not spend the whole of their lives in a single community like monks. If you became a friar or joined the Order of St John, you were sent from place to place to be educated or trained, and drafted about to serve in your adult life. Cornish youths recruited as friars were likely to travel to England or even to the continent, and the little house of the Order of St John at Trebeigh was staffed by men from outside Cornwall.

The friars were particularly keen on education, because a high degree of knowledge was needed to become an effective preacher or confessor. Accordingly they established houses in the university cities soon after they came to England, and some Cornish friars must have gone there to study during the 13th century. Two of them, both Franciscans, are known to have done so. The first, another Peter of Cornwall, studied logic and wrote a surviving work on the subject. The second, Richard Rufus of Cornwall, appears to have joined the friars at Paris in 1229 after which he taught at both Paris and Oxford, graduated as a doctor of divinity and wrote several works on theology. In the next chapter we shall encounter more evidence of the learning of friars in Cornwall and its impact on Cornish people.[51]

We know little about the internal life of the Cornish monasteries between 1100 and 1300, because our knowledge is largely confined to charters that tell us only about their lands and other property and those who gave them. Where their monks were recruited and how they were trained are mysterious matters. The first Peter of Cornwall, the prior of Holy Trinity Aldgate, tells us something about the relationships of the minster, and later the priory, at Launceston with the people of the neighbourhood. His grandfather Ailsi (died before 1123) was clerk of the works when the tower of

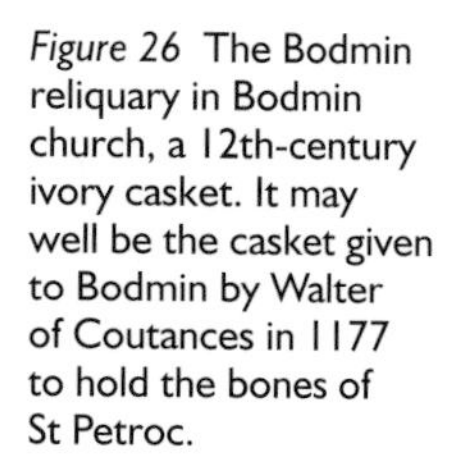

Figure 26 The Bodmin reliquary in Bodmin church, a 12th-century ivory casket. It may well be the casket given to Bodmin by Walter of Coutances in 1177 to hold the bones of St Petroc.

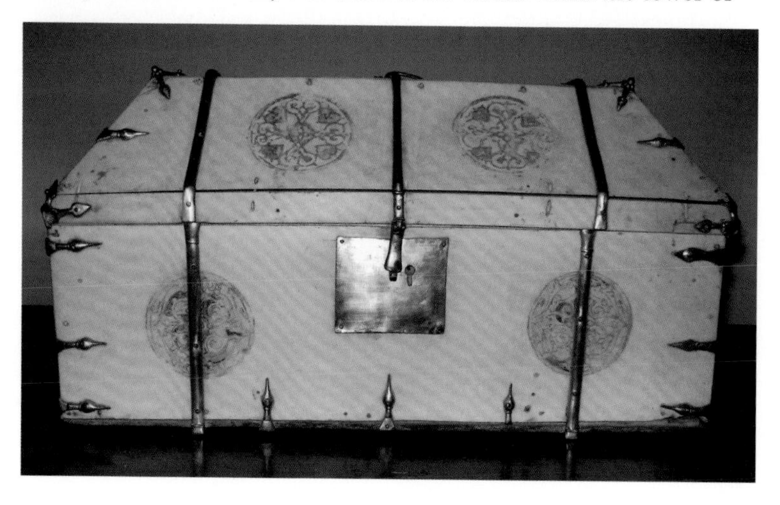

the minster was built. Ailsi had a special devotion to Stephen, the patron saint of the church, and claimed to have met the saint in a vision. Two of his sons, Bernard and Nicholas, became clergy and made gifts to the church, including a banner depicting the saint, a carpet, and an ivory casket of relics. When their brother Jordan died in about 1180 the prior of Launceston, Osbert, was present at his deathbed. The impression is given of good relations between the minster-priory and at least some local people.[52]

Launceston Priory may have benefited from the fact that the neighbouring town of Launceston (or Dunheved, as it was also known) was a self-governing borough, so that the dealings between the two were more equal and consequently more equable. In contrast Bodmin Priory ruled the town of Bodmin, an arrangement resented by its inhabitants and one that led to disputes, about, for example, who had the right to exploit the neighbouring woods and waters. Internally, however, Bodmin Priory seems to have outshone Launceston in the 12th century as a centre of Latin writing. Four works were written about its patron saint, St Petroc: a new enlarged prose Life, the so-called 'Gotha Life'; a short Life in rhymed 'goliardic' verse; a list of miracles done through Petroc's intercession; and an account of the theft and recovery of Petroc's bones in 1171. The relics were stolen by a discontented canon and taken to France, but they were recovered with the help of King Henry II and conveyed back to Cornwall with much ceremony by the bishop of Exeter and the prior of Bodmin. The episode reminds us that the status of religious houses came not only from lands and revenues but also from their patron saints and the saintly relics that drew people in to pray and seek for healing.[53]

In 1258 the bishops of Exeter started to keep registers of their activities, and these throw more light than before on life in the monasteries and other religious houses. The records are chiefly of a constitutional and disciplinary nature, such as the elections of priors and the maintenance of good order. At Launceston Bishop Bronescombe did battle with the prior, Robert Fissacre, in 1259 over Robert's poor management of the priory. Two years later Fissacre resigned. The election of his successor caused deep divisions, causing the bishop to quash the election and appoint one of the two rival candidates. At Bodmin Bronescombe excommunicated Prior Richard in about 1274 for associating with people who had themselves been excommunicated. When the prior agreed to submit to the bishop, he was ordered to hold services in his church in a simple and muted way until the excommunications were lifted.[54]

This was not the last of Richard's offences. In 1277 he was, or had been, in dispute with the archdeacon of Bodmin over tithes and other things, and in 1284, after he had incurred a further

Figure 27 The church of St Anthony-in-Roseland. Built on a cross plan in the 12th and 13th centuries, it acted as both a priory church for two canons sent from Plympton Priory and a parish church for a small adjoining area.

excommunication, the Crown was asked to arrest him. Two years later one of his canons, William of Plympton, was imprisoned by the bishop for rebellion and disobedience. Conflicts like these were common between bishops and monasteries during the Middle Ages, and are sometimes seen as evidence of the decline of monastic life. They were certainly one aspect of that life, but not the whole of it.[55]

THE PARISH CLERGY

The majority of Cornish clergy between 1100 and 1300 worked in the parishes. At least two hundred of them served the 209 parish churches and important chapels of the county, far more than those in the monasteries and friaries. By 1300 there may have been another two hundred or more clergy working as assistant curates, chantry priests praying for the dead, and chaplains in private households. The education and recruitment of these clergy are also obscure topics as far as Cornwall is concerned. There was no organised system for training them. A would-be priest had to acquire the necessary learning for Church work by attending a school or through private tuition from a clergyman. Both these means were probably available in Cornwall before 1300 but they have left hardly any record. Education involved mastering Latin in the sense of reading, pronouncing, and understanding it correctly so that one could perform the church services, as well as learning how to sing services to plainsong melodies.[56]

Figure 28 A parish clerk (left) helping his priest, who is saying mass at an altar.

The cost of education was usually a private matter for the learner's family or for some other person willing to sponsor his studies. All that the Church did in a public way to assist those without wealth or support was to encourage the existing clergy to employ them as parish clerks. The parish clerk, or holy-water clerk as he was usually called in the 13th century, was an adolescent or young adult, often someone training to be a priest. He rang the church bells, prepared the altar, served the priest at mass, said the responses in the service, and read the epistle (see Figure 28). He accompanied the priest to baptisms, weddings, and funerals, and dispensed holy water, for which he gained small fees. In 1287 Bishop Quinil of Exeter ordered that the post of clerk should always be given to a scholar in parishes within ten miles of the cathedral and the 'castles' of the diocese. He probably had in mind that they would attend the cathedral school in Exeter or schools in the larger towns with castles, such as Launceston.[57]

Our sole record of what was taught in a school in Cornwall between 1100 and 1300 is the so-called 'Cornish Vocabulary', recorded in a single manuscript written in about 1100 (see Figure 29). It is a list of Latin words with their equivalents in the Cornish language, arranged by subjects: God, heaven, earth, mankind, birds, animals, plants, houses, and furniture. This work was modelled on a similar Latin and English vocabulary compiled by Ælfric of Eynsham in the 990s, and shows that Latin was being learnt in the Cornish-speaking area of the county. Apart from being able to read and understand Latin in order to carry out Church services, parish clergy were not expected to study the Bible or theology. In 1287 Bishop Quinil told them only that they should know about the Ten Commandments, the Seven Sacraments, the Seven Deadly Sins, and the articles of the Christian faith enshrined in the creeds. He also ordered every parish church to acquire a short handbook that he had produced in Latin as a practical guide to a clergyman's daily work.[58]

A minority of Cornish clergy took their studies further. These were chiefly sons of the gentry or wealthy townspeople, who had the means to travel to centres of learning outside the county. The emergence of universities at Paris, Oxford, and Cambridge between 1150 and 1200 offered the opportunity to study the liberal arts, chiefly made up of logic, philosophy, and science. This was a lengthy procedure which, in England, required seven years to gain the degree of master of arts (MA), with a further two years of 'regency' during which an MA graduate was expected to act as a university teacher. Besides the liberal arts four other studies developed with their own degrees: medicine, civil (i.e. Roman) law, canon (i.e. Church) law, and theology.[59]

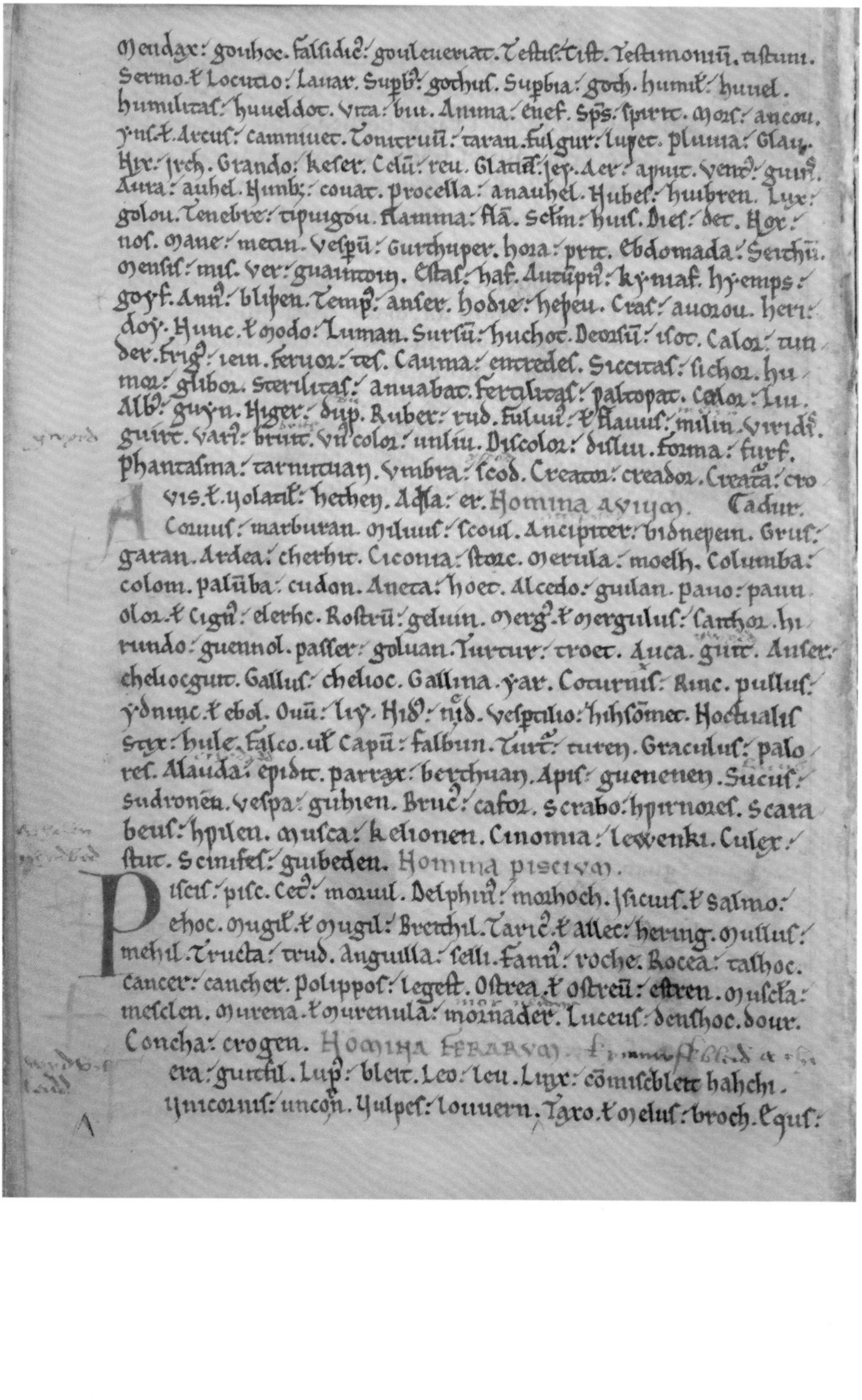

Figure 29 (opposite) The 'Cornish Vocabulary' of about 1100. It lists Latin words, each followed by its Cornish equivalent, in a logical arrangement of topics. The three headings on this page refer to 'Names of Birds', 'Names of Fishes', and 'Names of Wild Animals'.

One of the earliest known university teachers at Oxford was a Cornishman, John of Cornwall. He began his university studies at Paris in the 1150s under the great Biblical commentator Peter Lombard, and duly achieved the rank of MA. After leaving Paris, he taught theology or law at Oxford where he is named as a 'master' in the late 1170s. Three of his works on theology survive together with a Latin poetical version of Geoffrey of Monmouth's 'Prophecies of Merlin'. John mentions Cornwall several times in the poem and in a commentary attached to it, as well as referring specifically to Fowey (now Bodmin) Moor, the River Tamar, Tintagel, and other places. He was proud of his native region and wished to emphasise its place in British history. Indeed he may have spoken Cornish, since he gives the Cornish name for Fowey Moor as *Goen Bren,* and in 1173 he was recommended to Henry II in 1173 as a suitable person to be made bishop of St David's because he knew Welsh, but he was not selected.[60]

John had close connections with Walter of Coutances, who was also a native of Cornwall, probably from a wealthy Anglo-Norman family. Walter studied at Paris, became the deputy to the chancellor of Henry II, archdeacon of Oxford, bishop of Lincoln, and finally archbishop of Rouen. Other men from Cornwall rose to middle-ranking posts in the English Church during the 13th century, but it is difficult to know how common this was. Two Oxford scholars named Richard of Cornwall gained promotion as cathedral canons of Lincoln and York respectively. Master John of St Goran was appointed a canon of Exeter and put in charge of the bishop's consistory court, while Master Philip of St Austell was made archdeacon of Winchester. A more literary figure, Michael of Cornwall, appears to have studied university subjects in England, including rhetoric under the eminent Latin poet Henry of Avranches. One of his Latin works, which unfortunately has not survived, was a *Praise of Cornwall.* Education took all these men away from Cornwall, but they made important contributions to religion and culture elsewhere.[61]

Figure 30 A bishop ordains clergy. Ordinations were customarily held four times a year, and in Exeter diocese they generally took place in Devon. There were five main grades of ordination, all but the first two of which were normally conferred on separate occasions.

Education prepared one for life as a clergyman, but entry to that life was gained through ordination (Figure 30). In Cornwall this meant going to Exeter for the purpose, or even further, except on the rare occasions when the bishop crossed the Tamar. There were stages of ordination, beginning with the 'first tonsure', which could be conferred at the age of seven, and the order of acolyte at fourteen. These two orders were 'minor orders', which gave you clerical status but left you free to take up work as a layman and marry. Higher than these were the grades of subdeacon (for which you had to be at least 17), deacon (at least 19), and priest (at least 24). By about the 12th century taking these 'major orders' required a permanent commitment to clerical life, including a vow of celibacy.

PATRONS AND BENEFICES

Ordination as a priest enabled you to perform all the religious functions required in parishes. Gaining a post in the Church was a further process, just as getting a qualification today does not guarantee you a job. As we have seen, the rector or vicar of a parish church was nominated by the patron who held the advowson. By the 13th century the bishop insisted on his right of vetting such nominations, so that the patron 'presented' a candidate to the bishop who then 'instituted' or 'admitted' him to office. The bishop could refuse to institute a candidate unsuitable by education, morals, or lack of ordination, and after 1258 the institutions of most clergy to churches were recorded in the bishop's register. A further ceremony, 'induction', gave the new rector or vicar possession of his church, from which he could not be ousted until he died or voluntarily resigned it, except for very serious misdemeanours for which the bishop might deprive him – but deprivations were rare.

There was a wide variety of patrons in Cornwall after the Norman Conquest. A majority (97) of the 167 benefices (rectories or vicarages) in the county in 1291 belonged to patrons who were clergy. The bishop owned 11, the cathedral 13, and religious houses (inside and outside Cornwall) 73. Lay people held the rest. Nine were in the gift of the earl of Cornwall; these subsequently came into the hands of the king and, at times, to the king's eldest son as duke of Cornwall. Sixty-one belonged to other lay patrons, generally local lords of the manor. It followed that, to become a rector or vicar, one needed the support of a patron – support likely to go to men with higher rank, distinction in learning, or powerful friends to press their case. Most clergy lacked such backing, at least to begin with, and had to take more lowly work as curates, chaplains, and chantry priests. They worked for modest wages without security of tenure and, in the case of some of the chantry priests, for fixed periods of time.[62]

Figure 31 Churches often commemorated their patrons by displaying their coats of arms. This tile shows the arms of Richard earl of Cornwall (died 1272), patron of several churches in Cornwall.

The parish clergy, then, were not a uniform group. As well as the distinction just outlined, between the 'beneficed clergy' (rectors and vicars) and the 'unbeneficed' (wage-earning chaplains and chantry priests), the beneficed clergy differed among themselves in terms of their income and where it came from. The wide range in the size and therefore the wealth of parishes led to a corresponding span of clergy stipends from glebe, tithes, and other revenues. In 1291 the richest Cornish clergyman, the rector of St Columb Major, was estimating as receiving £17 a year and the poorest, the vicar of Colan, as getting only 6s. 8d. These were underestimates by 100 per cent or more, and the vicar may have earned about £3, but his neighbour at St Columb could well have been ten times richer.[63]

Another important distinction between the beneficed clergy related to rectors and vicars. The rector of a benefice received all the income of the benefice. By the 12th century, however, it became popular for patrons of benefices to give their advowsons to religious houses such as cathedrals and monasteries. One motive for this was to endow the houses concerned. When a religious house acquired an advowson, it could, with the bishop's agreement, appoint itself as rector on a permanent basis and receive the rector's income. This process is known as 'appropriation' and such benefices as 'appropriated benefices' or 'vicarages'. Since a parish church still had to be served by a clergyman, the religious house appointed a 'vicar' (a term meaning deputy) to act in its place. A vicar was identical with a rector in being presented to the benefice by the patron, instituted by the bishop, appointed for an indefinite period, and charged with similar spiritual duties. He differed in receiving only a partial share of the benefice income.

By the second half of the 13th century, this share was usually 'taxed' (assessed and fixed) by the bishop to ensure that it was adequate. The religious house was usually allocated the tithes of grain, known as the 'great tithes', because these tithes were the most valuable, the easiest to collect, and the least perishable, so that they could be stored, transported, or sold. The vicar was generally given the rector's house, the glebe, and what was called the 'altarage': the offerings that people made in church and the 'small tithes' of the parish – hay, animals, and so on. Quinil laid down that every vicar should receive a stipend of at least £3 6s. 8d. per annum. In practice this amount was often exceeded, but it is worth remembering that rectors' and vicars' stipends came only partly in cash and mainly in kind. Tithes had to be collected, their value fluctuated with good and bad seasons, and a clergyman might not be able to extract all the income to which he was entitled. Moreover, rectors and vicars were expected to give some hospitality to travellers and alms to the poor.[64]

Some appropriators made even greater inroads into parish income. The priories of Bodmin, St Carroc, and Tywardreath saved money by lodging their local vicars in their monasteries, feeding them there, and paying them small stipends in cash. The priories then took the whole of the parish tithes. Several of the parishes belonging to Launceston Priory were not even served by vicars. This was the case at Boyton, Egloskerry, St Giles-on-the-Heath, Laneast, North Tamerton, Tremaine, Tresmeer, Werrington, and the three churches of Launceston itself. Here the priory merely appointed a chaplain who was not presented to the bishop for

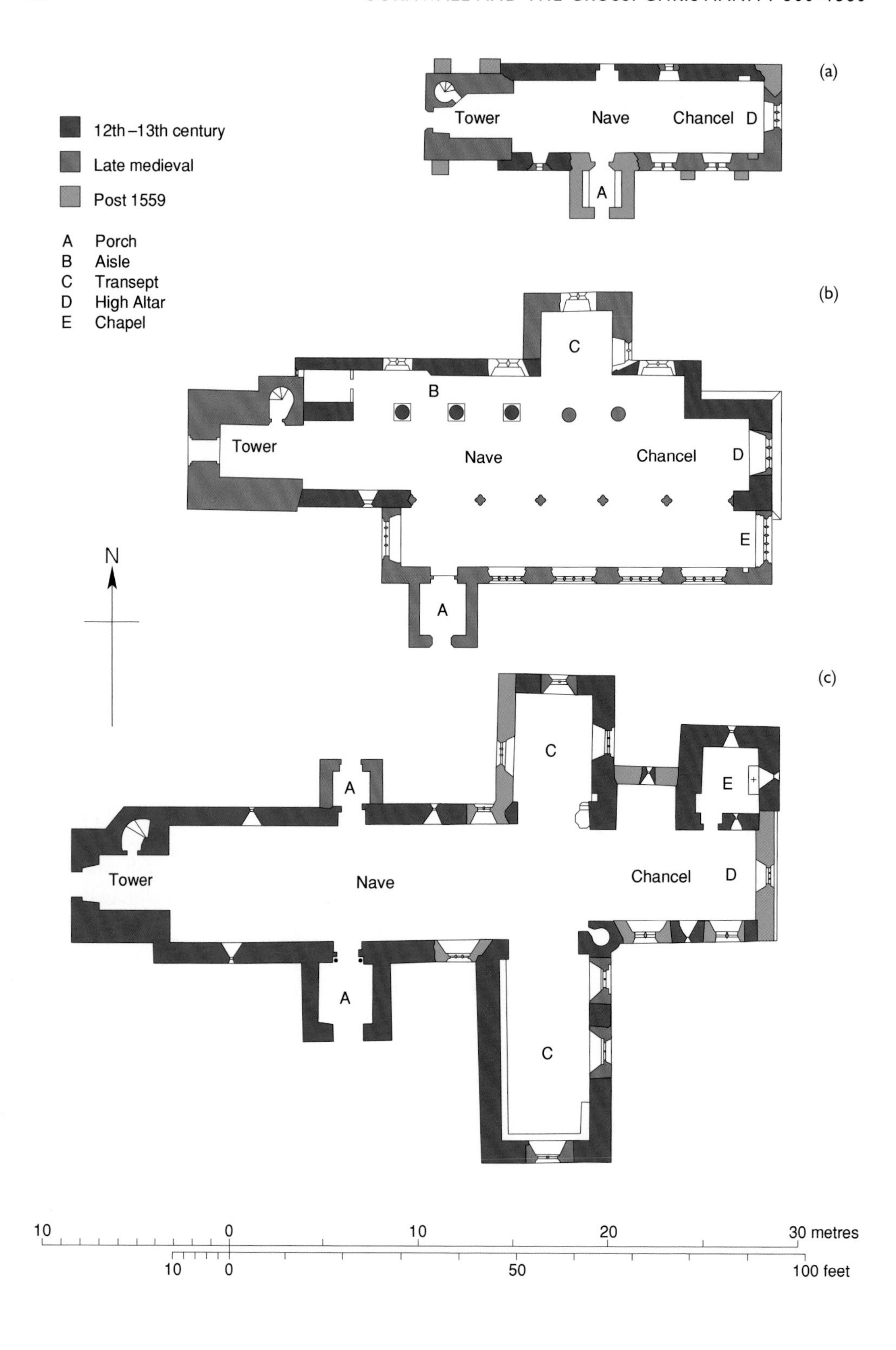

12th–13th century
Late medieval
Post 1559
A Porch
B Aisle
C Transept
D High Altar
E Chapel
(a)
Tower
Nave
Chancel
D
A
(b)
B
C
Tower
Nave
Chancel
D
E
A
N
(c)
C
A
E
Tower
Nave
Chancel
D
A
C
10
0
10
20
30 metres
10
0
50
100 feet

Figure 32 (opposite) Parish church plans of the 12th and 13th centuries. (a) Tremaine, a simple oblong divided into chancel and nave. (b) St Breward, where a narrow aisle was built alongside the nave, probably for processions. (c) Tintagel, with long unequal transepts attached to the nave, perhaps for use as private chapels.

institution and did not have tenure for life, although it is possible that such clergy held office for long periods. The same happened in the parishes of St Germans and Minster, where there were also priory churches. Bishop Brewer ordered that chaplains serving in parishes should receive at least £2 per annum, which Quinil increased to £2 10*s*. – less than the £3 6*s*. 8*d*. allowed to vicars. It is likely that this £2 rate also held good for chantry priests and domestic chaplains, but it was only just enough on which to live.[65]

CHURCH BUILDINGS

Every church was a building, and the history of church buildings has long been a subject of interest because so many of them are still around us. Unfortunately, very little has survived about this history before about 1400, either in written documents or in surviving remains. Most of the ancient Cornish churches that stand today were rebuilt in the 15th and early 16th centuries, and the religious houses were mostly destroyed at the Reformation.

The evidence that survives suggests that the largest and most ornate church structures in Cornwall between 1100 and 1300 were those of the monasteries and other religious houses. Parish churches were generally smaller. Local stone from the neighbourhood appears to have been commonly used for building (the large-scale quarrying of granite of later times had not yet developed), but stone from outside Cornwall was sometimes imported for high-grade projects. Caen stone from Normandy can still be seen in the fabrics of St Anthony-in-Roseland and Mylor, and the west doorway of St Germans seems to be built of Hurdwick stone from Tavistock.

St Germans is also the best preserved example of a monastery from this period. It was an imposing building with two western towers flanking the grand west doorway into the nave (Figure 22). The nave had north and south aisles along which clergy could go in procession, and east of it lay the chancel (or choir), apparently lacking such aisles. There may have been transepts, but this is not clear. Bodmin Priory seems to have had a similar main entrance on the west, leading to a nave and chancel each with aisles on both sides. Launceston Priory appears to have been first built as a long aisleless nave and chancel. Eventually the nave included a north aisle and the chancel north and south aisles, parts or all of which may have been added to the original building (see Panel 2).[66]

Glasney, the largest and wealthiest of the collegiate or minster churches, was similar in size to Bodmin and Launceston. There were a nave and chancel both possessing aisles, and a crossing with transepts surmounted by a central tower (see Figure 45). Crantock, an older and poorer minster, had an aisleless nave, a crossing with transepts, and a chancel with narrow aisles on either side. Later it, too, possessed a central tower, but this collapsed in about 1400 so its origin cannot be dated. The Franciscan church at Bodmin, probably the larger of the two Cornish friaries, was a further narrow aisleless building. Its distinguishing feature was a high roof, probably topped by a little tower and spire supported on walls between the nave and chancel (see Figure 44). The lesser religious houses were smaller and had little to distinguish them from ordinary parish churches. St Anthony had a nave, chancel, and transepts (see Figure 27), but St Michael's Mount had only the first two of these elements (see Figure 36) and Minster and Scilly were probably fairly similar.

Many Cornish parish churches still contain portions of fabric in the Norman style of architecture, dating from between about 1100 and 1220. This suggests that they, like the monasteries, experienced large-scale construction or reconstruction at that time. The basic plan of a Norman parish church in Cornwall consisted of a nave and a chancel, best preserved today at St John and Tremaine (see Figure 32). Naves and chancels were usually separated from one another by a wall pierced by an open chancel arch, giving a restricted view from the nave to the altar in the chancel. Parishioners gained access to the nave through a doorway, usually placed on the south side of the nave and often decorated with carving around it or on a tympanum above it. Some churches, like Egloskerry and Tintagel, had an additional north entrance, generally less elaborate. All parish churches possessed a font for baptisms, and this was an important sign of status since fonts were normally forbidden in lesser religious buildings such as chapels. Ancient fonts were frequently kept in use, perhaps for this reason, and Cornwall possesses many that were fashioned in Norman times.[67]

There were three ways of improving on the basic church plan. One was to build a tower where bells could be hung and rung. Towers from the Norman period survive on the north sides of Bodmin parish church and St Enodoc chapel, and at the west ends of St Gennys and St John. Lawhitton has a south tower of the 13th century, while Crantock and Glasney, as we have seen, were topped with central towers. Another improvement was to flank the nave with one aisle or two dividing aisles from the nave by a series of arches carried on piers or columns to form an arcade. Aisles survive or can be traced on the north side of the naves of St Breward, Morwenstow (see Figure 32), North Petherwin, and a few other churches, and may have existed on the south side of

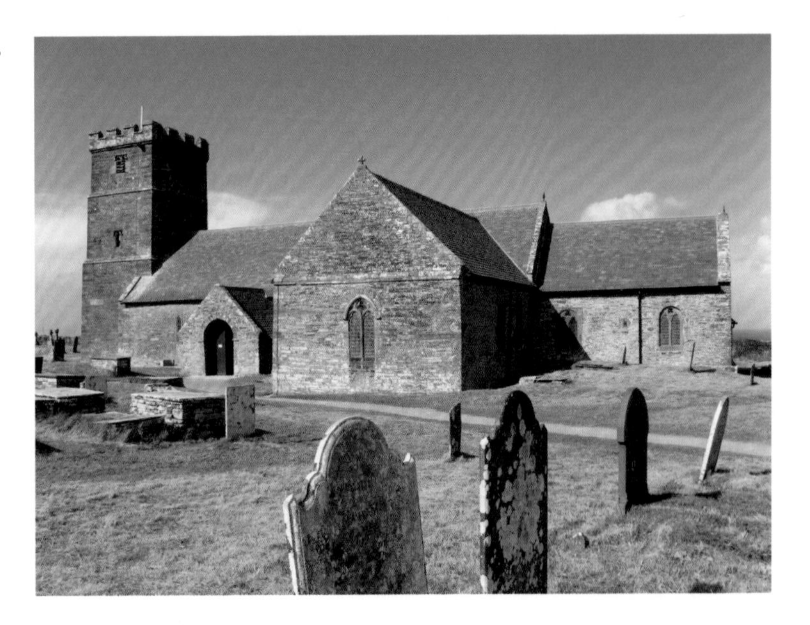
Figure 33 Tintagel church, showing the distinctive long transepts typical of many churches in the 12th and 13th centuries.

those naves as well. Norman aisles of this kind appear to have been long and narrow. They were probably designed as processional ways, not because parish churches had many clergy, clerks, and altar boys to stage processions but to give such churches status by copying the processional nave aisles of the larger religious houses.

The third way of enlarging a church was to attach one or more transepts to the east end of the nave, as can be seen at St Enoder and Tintagel. Transepts were long and narrow lateral wings, sometimes on one side of the church, sometimes on both, and in the latter case (as at Tintagel) not always equal in length (Figure 32). It is sometimes supposed that Cornish churches of the Norman period were commonly built in a cross or 'cruciform' shape with transepts. However, the transepts that survive or are recorded may equally well be later additions to the basic church plan, often made after about 1200. Transepts also gave status to a church by increasing its size, and are likely to have originated as chapels and burial areas for important families, such as lords of the manor. One at Creed has a Norman piscina pointing to the presence of an altar.

CHURCH FURNISHINGS

During the 13th century two of the bishops of Exeter held synods of their clergy, at which statutes were passed regulating the clergy's duties and lives. William Brewer's statutes date from an unknown year between 1225 and 1237 (they do not survive in a complete form), and Peter Quinil's from 1287, a lengthy and detailed document. Both sets of statutes gave instructions about church services, the functions and behaviour of the clergy, and the duties of the laity to the Church. This shows us how the authorities wished the Church to work and, more obliquely, how it worked in practice.[68]

The statutes give us glimpses of the interiors and workings of Cornish churches by saying what each should possess in terms of equipment. Quinil ordered that chancels and naves should have glass windows, and forbade church buildings to be used for holding courts or markets. Brewer had already prohibited 'scotales' in churches, meaning ale feasts held to raise money. Each church was expected to have a set of ornaments and books for services, and Quinil stipulated as many as 52 items. The high altar was to be dressed in a frontal cloth and to have a canopy above it, from which hung a locked capsule or 'pyx' containing a consecrated wafer of bread. An image of the patron saint was to stand on the north side of the altar and one of the Virgin Mary on the south side.

Churches were required to provide clothes for the priest (two surplices) as well as a rochet (a linen robe like a surplice, perhaps for the parish clerk), a silver chalice for mass, a silver cup for sick communions, corporal cloths for use on the altar at mass, cruets for wine and water, a thurible for burning incense (see Figure 34), and vessels to contain incense and holy water. A large veil was to hang in front of the altar during Lent, and a big standing candlestick was to hold a candle to burn at Eastertide. Small bells were required for ringing during mass or while taking communion to the sick, a cross and banners for processions, a woman's veil for

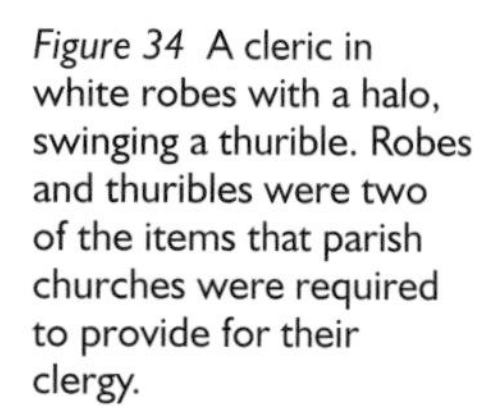

Figure 34 A cleric in white robes with a halo, swinging a thurible. Robes and thuribles were two of the items that parish churches were required to provide for their clergy.

marriages, a pall to cover bodies at funerals, and a font with a cover and lock. The font was to be kept full of water, changed once a week in case it was needed for a baptism, the lock ensuring that the water was protected. Finally, 12 books were specified, some of which may have been contained within a single volume. They enabled the priest to say and sing the daily services, the service of mass or holy communion, and the pastoral services like baptisms, marriages, and funerals.

This tells us what the authorities wanted churches to have, not what they had. The earliest evidence of real conditions in Cornwall comes from a report of 1281 by two clergy of Exeter Cathedral on the state of eight churches and one chapel that belonged to the cathedral. This records the condition of the chancels, the state of the ornaments and books, and the nature and value of the church endowments. The clergy did not take notice of naves or nave furnishings, however, since these were the responsibility of the parishioners and came under the archdeacon's supervision.

Six of the chancels were in good order: well roofed and provided with windows. Veryan is mentioned as being whitewashed. Altarnun and St Erth had defective roofs, St Breward's windows were unsatisfactory and made the chancel dark, while one window at St Erth needed repair; its chancel was also censured for not being whitewashed. All the churches in 1281 had most of the ornaments and books that Quinil was to require six years later, but there was usually some deficiency. A few of the items were missing or were old and in a decrepit condition. Even when sound, the articles were often simple in form. Chalices indeed accorded with the bishop's statutes in being of silver, sometimes gilded, but cruets and candlesticks were commonly of tin.[69]

A similar visitation took place in 1331, encompassing 14 churches and three chapels. This painted much the same picture, although there were deteriorations in some places. Only two churches, St Breward and Gwinear, were judged to be more or less satisfactory in all respects. Altarnun, Gwennap, and St Issey each had structural defects in the roofs, walls, or windows of their chancels, and Veryan was now criticised for its darkness. Most of the others were lacking in some of their ornaments and books. Such visitations warn us against assuming that there was ever a golden age of well-maintained churches and devout clergy and parishioners. Indeed, we are told that thieves had entered the church of St Erth through the chancel windows and stolen the chalice, books, wax, and other things. Nevertheless, the evidence shows that clergy and parishioners were not too far adrift from what they were supposed to provide, and that the authorities tried, at least occasionally, to keep them up to the mark.[70]

Beyond this we are obliged to conjecture the layout and furnishings of Cornish churches from what is known in England as a whole. The chancel contained the high (chief) altar. In the larger religious houses with several priests there may have been lesser altars in other parts of the building, but this is likely to have been rare in most parish churches before the 13th century. The font was probably situated in the nave near the principal doorway, as was the case in later centuries. Lay people were allowed to enter and use the nave, but the chancel was reserved for the priest (or clergy) and parish clerk, with the likelihood that church patrons or local knights and their families were admitted there as well. There was seating in the chancel for the clergy and probably for the important laity, and some churches had seats in the nave by Quinil's time. Drawing attention to disputes that had arisen about such seats, he forbade anyone to claim a right to a seat except for members of the *nobilitas* (nobility and gentry). Floors in religious houses might be paved or tiled, but those in ordinary churches might be of bare earth sprinkled with rushes.[71]

In the religious communities – monasteries, friaries, and collegiate churches – a cycle of daily services was performed in the chancel by the adult clergy. This began with matins at about midnight, and continued at intervals until compline in the early evening. At least one daily mass was celebrated at mid-morning by the clergy at the high altar, and those of the clergy who were priests might celebrate additional masses at lesser altars. The priests who served the ordinary parish churches were also expected to say the daily services, but it was left to them to decide whether they did so in church or in their houses, at least on ordinary days. On Sundays and major festivals, however, they were required to say matins in church in the morning followed by a mass for parishioners, with evensong in the mid-afternoon. What services in church were like will be explained in Chapter 4.

THE RELIGION OF THE PEOPLE

The bishops' statutes tell us a little about what the Church required of ordinary people. All children had to be baptised, a ceremony that was normally done after about 1100 on the day of their birth. Immediate baptism was so common that the statutes do not even mention it. They merely order that the older Christian practice of baptising only at Easter and Pentecost should be followed when a baby was born in the week immediately before these festivals. Both festivals involved baptising babies on the previous Saturday, and recently born ones were used for that purpose. We sometimes

Figure 35 A parish priest at work. Here he is shown at one of his largest tasks: the confessions of all adult parishioners, held at the beginning of Lent. The priest sits with his hood pulled over his head, while a parishioner kneels before him. Others await their turn at a distance. (Stained glass window from St Michael's, Doddiscombsleigh, Devon.)

encounter boys and girls named Pascow ('Easter') or Pentecost, some of whom may have been baptised on these occasions.[72]

Children could be confirmed at any age after baptism, but confirmation had to be done by a bishop, who was not easily to be found in Cornwall. Although both Brewer and Quinil ordered the parish clergy to compel parents to have their children confirmed, both accepted that remoteness from a bishop was an excuse. In practice many people may have reached adulthood without being confirmed. This did not matter much, because after about 1200 there was no linkage between confirmation and admission to the bread and wine of communion. Children who were confirmed were not allowed communion until they reached puberty, and those who reached it without being confirmed were probably allowed it anyway.[73]

Everyone was expected to learn three basic prayers in Latin during childhood: the Paternoster (Lord's Prayer), Credo (Apostles' Creed), and Ave Maria (Hail Mary). Brewer told the clergy to teach these prayers and call children into church for the purpose, but it was probably more usual for such teaching to be done by parents or godparents. You grew up, in the eyes of the Church, at puberty: 12 for girls, 14 for boys. Before that time you were regarded as a minor: innocent of sins and free of most Church obligations. At puberty you were believed to gain adult knowledge and capabilities, including the power to sin, making it appropriate for you to start going to confession (see Figure 35), receiving communion, and paying church dues.[74]

Religion was closely linked with the calendar, and there was an annual cycle of observances, ranging from feasts to fasts. These will be outlined in Chapter 4. Most of what we know about the religion of ordinary people in Cornwall comes from the later Middle Ages, especially after 1400, but there is no reason why it should not have been equally rich and diverse in the 12th and 13th centuries when it is hidden from us by lack of evidence. The network of parish churches already existed, and they were already supplemented by numerous chapels, some of them at ancient religious sites and others (such as West Looe) serving new settlements. Guilds or fraternities, devoted to fellowship and worship, existed in the rural parishes around Exeter by about 1100, and may have done so in Cornwall. The earliest clear record of one relates to a guild of St Nicholas at Truro of about 1278, and another may have existed at Nancekuke in Illogan by the same period.[75]

Pilgrimages were already taking place. St Michael's Mount appears to have been a well-known holy place by the 11th century, and we are told of three miracles experienced by pilgrims there in 1262. In 1238 Bishop Brewer granted an indulgence of 40 days of exemption from penance to those who visited St Buryan church on the anniversary of its dedication, and some other churches are likely to have had similar privileges. There is also one rare and valuable glimpse of popular religious enthusiasm at the time of the Third Crusade of 1188. In the previous year the Saracens recaptured Jerusalem from the Christians, causing consternation throughout western Europe. It appears that numerous people in Cornwall, as elsewhere, vowed to join the campaign to recover the city and were marked with a cross by a priest as a sign of their promise, a process known as 'taking the cross'.[76]

In about 1200 the Church authorities in England became aware that not all those who had made vows had fulfilled them. Enquiries were made, and a list of 44 defaulters was forwarded from Cornwall. Their owners came from seven of the eight rural

Figure 36 The church of St Michael's Mount. From the 11th until the 16th centuries, this is the most often recorded centre of pilgrimage in Cornwall. Pilgrims came to venerate an image of St Michael, and a legend grew up that he had made one of his three earthly appearances at the Mount.

deaneries, and seem to have been mostly people of middling importance, chiefly from towns. The episode shows that the crusade had an impact on people in Cornwall but that not all those who rallied to the cause sustained their initial fervour towards it. As with the theft at St Erth, we are reminded that the Middle Ages was not a simple era of faith. People then, like people today, ranged widely in their religious commitment from pious devotion to unreliability, indifference, and even criminality.

Chapter 3 The Later Middle Ages: The Clergy

Figure 37 A medieval funeral of the kind staged for gentlemen, merchants, or their wives. In the distance a priest celebrates the mass for the dead. Left of the deceased person are mourners in black robes and hoods, and on the right hand clergy are reading psalms.

THE LATER MIDDLE AGES

We have now reached the period from 1300 to 1500 that historians call 'the later Middle Ages'. During this period England retained many ties with the Continent. The kings of England and France fought a long intermittent struggle, 'The Hundred Years War', and the English held lands in France until 1558. The Church in England continued to be part of the western Catholic Church, under the headship of the pope. There were trading and cultural links between England and her continental neighbours, including links between Cornwall and Brittany. At the same time some of the international bonds of the past were weakening. The power of the popes in England, still strong until about the 1370s, decreased in some respects thereafter. Crusading waned in popularity. The French abbeys lost the lands that the Normans had given them in England and control of the cells that stood upon these lands. New religious orders and fashions no longer spread across the English Channel as easily as they had done before. The use of the French language in England fell into decline both in speech and in writing.

As a result the Church in England became even more distinctly English than it had been before. The English language (always the spoken tongue of most people) began to invade the sphere of reading and writing at the expense of French and Latin. Architecture developed a distinctive English style that we know as 'Perpendicular' (see Figure 38). Education became more insular, with schooling taking on a more local colour (especially in terms of the textbooks that taught boys Latin), while scholars of higher education went to Oxford and Cambridge rather than Paris. Cornwall shared in these changes in all the above respects; indeed, two Cornishmen played key roles in promoting the reading and writing of English. There was also a distinctive Cornish twist to the process, in that the Cornish language came to be written more, or at least has survived to a greater extent, especially in the form of religious plays.

The period from 1300 to 1500 is different in terms of surviving evidence, too. Far more of the religious heritage of Cornwall exists than before as documents, buildings, and works of art. We can see further into the lives of ordinary people, especially after 1400, thanks to the existence of churchwardens' accounts, wills,

Figure 38 Breage church, rebuilt in the Perpendicular style during the 15th century. The style takes its name from the upright tracery panels used in both buildings and furnishings; they give a vertical effect particularly to the windows. The size of the church reflects its status as the mother church of four parishes: Breage, Cury, Germoe, and Gunwalloe.

and legal documents. The volume of such sources rises sharply, so that the period requires two chapters to do it justice. This chapter centres on the clergy of Cornwall, and the next will consider their lay parishioners.

CHANGES AND CRISES

The later Middle Ages are well known for a series of crises, although it must be remembered that these were rare events and often limited in their effects. The Black Death, a major epidemic of the plague, arrived in England in about the summer of 1348, and raged in Cornwall and Devon during the early months of 1349. Some of its greatest damage was done at Bodmin where 1,500 people were later said to have died, and where the prior and all but two of the community of about 15–18 canons were dead by 17 March.[77]

Most of what we know about the effects of the plague on the Cornish Church comes from the register of John Grandisson, the bishop at that time. During the five years from 1343 to 1347 the average number of clergy recorded as being instituted to rectories and vicarages in Cornwall was nine per annum. The total in 1348 was 14, and in 1349 it rose to 85. Within 1349 the recorded figures were: 1 (January), 2 (February), 6 (March), 11 (April), 14 (May), 14 (June), 15 (July), 5 (August), 7 (September), 4 (October), 5 (November), and 1 (December). There were 17 institutions in 1350, five in 1351, and 11 in 1352. Not all these institutions followed deaths. Some were due to the previous clergyman changing benefices, but there must have been more deaths than usual. We can probably backdate the deaths from the institutions by two or three months, because it might take that long for the patron of a benefice to find a new candidate, especially if there was a shortage of clergy.[78]

Making that allowance suggests that most of the deaths of rectors and vicars took place in the early months of the year, as was the case at Bodmin. How many clergy died in Cornwall, or what percentage of the whole, cannot be known. Nor do we know if the plague brought about a religious revival, or a decline of religion due to despair or scepticism. In general, the framework of people's religious lives appears to have continued much as before. Changes indeed took place to that framework during the 14th and 15th centuries, but they were gradual ones caused by various social and cultural processes of which the plague was but one. The greatest change was a decrease in the size of the population. During the 14th century the number of people in England fell from as much as five or six million people in about 1300 to two or three million a hundred years later. Cornwall shared in some of this decline. Records show that in and after 1350 some settlements on the lands of the duchy of Cornwall were depopulated, tenements left vacant, and rents reduced in value.[79]

Some people gained from population decline. Labourers' wages increased as labour grew scarcer. Others lost, and this was especially true of the clergy. Income from tithes fell while wages and prices rose. Monasteries in particular could not afford to maintain their former numbers of inmates. Fewer clergy were now willing to do lowly paid jobs as chaplains, chantry priests, or vicars choral and, although such clergy continued to exist, they were less numerous by 1400 than they had been a century before. Indeed, it is possible that the flourishing of lay activity in the Church, which we shall study in the next chapter, was partly stimulated by a shortage of clergy.

There were some other notable crises in late medieval England of a political and religious nature, but these were of less importance for Cornwall. The Peasants' Revolt of May and June 1381, which centred on London, encouraged some Cornish people to make an attack on the property of Bodmin Priory, but the Revolt had no wider effects. In the following year the radical religious views of the Oxford scholar John Wycliffe inspired the formation of a Wycliffite or Lollard movement in religion, which survived in covert groups of followers until the Reformation. One Cornishman, Laurence Stephen, fellow of Exeter College (Oxford), was an early disciple of Wycliffe's, and during the summer of 1382 he travelled through Cornwall preaching his master's ideas. The Church authorities took swift action against him. He was arrested and persuaded to recant his beliefs; later he was given the rectory of Lifton in Devon.

Figure 39 Temple church. The Knights Templars were a casualty of the 14th century, suppressed by the pope in 1312. They had only small properties in Cornwall, chiefly an estate on Bodmin Moor which came to be known as Temple after them. There is no evidence that they maintained a house or community there, but the estate acquired its own church, rebuilt in the 19th century.

Lollardy did not establish itself in Cornwall as it did in other parts of England. By the 1540s the Cornish were to be notorious for their religious conservatism.[80]

The Wars of the Roses disrupted English political and social life at intervals between the 1450s and the 1490s, but they too largely happened away from Cornwall. There were small-scale disorders in 1473 when the earl of Oxford briefly occupied St Michael's Mount, in 1483 when some local gentry tried to defy Richard III, and more seriously in 1497 when the Cornish twice rebelled against Henry VII, once over taxation and once in support of the pretender Perkin Warbeck. None of these events, however, had significant effects upon religion.

THE DIOCESE AND THE BISHOPS

The diocese of Exeter in Cornwall experienced little change in its structure between 1291 and the Reformation. Two parishes, Tregony and Cuby, had been joined together as one benefice under a single incumbent in 1286, but they remained separate parishes and Tregony kept its parish church until the 16th century. Three sub-parishes that had been served by chaplains gained recognition as parishes and benefices in their own right: Bradoc as a rectory and Lostwithiel and Luxulyan as vicarages. About ten benefices that belonged to lay patrons in 1291 were subsequently given by these patrons to religious houses, so that by the end of the Middle Ages about 94 (59 per cent) of the 160 parishes served by a rector or vicar in Cornwall were in the hands of the bishop, cathedral, and religious houses. The number of parishes in which the tithes were appropriated to religious houses and the clergyman was a vicar rather than a rector also increased by about 19 after 1291, so that well over half of the parishes in Cornwall came into this category by 1500.[81]

Fourteen bishops ruled the diocese of Exeter between 1300 and 1500. Five of them are notable for the length of their time in office – Walter Stapledon (1308–26), John Grandisson (1327–69), Thomas Brantingham (1370–94), Edmund Stafford (1395–1419), and Edmund Lacy (1420–55) – and these five are the easiest to study because their activities were recorded in registers that have been edited and published. The bishops of this period travelled incessantly until they grew too old to do so. Their travels took them to London, Exeter, their manors in Devon and Cornwall, and occasionally more widely around the two counties. Not surprisingly they came to Cornwall less often than Devon. The usual pattern was for a new bishop to make a tour through the county early in his reign, during which he would visit his major properties and go to St Michael's Mount.[82]

The bishops varied in the extent of their subsequent visits. Stapledon did the best, coming 14 times in 19 years, while Grandisson managed only six times in 42 years, Brantingham eight times in 25 years, Stafford four times in 25 years, and Lacy eight times in 35 years. This relative infrequency reflected the long, expensive, and fatiguing task of travelling with a household and of organising food and accommodation. Even in Cornwall the bishops did not always get further west than Glasney, and as age wore them out they ceased to be able to cope with the journey at all. In his early years Grandisson beat most other bishops by going as far as St Just-in-Penwith, but he did not repeat that visit and during the last 26 years of his reign he crossed the Tamar only once, just to Lawhitton. Lacy, too, made but a single visit in his own last 15 years. But this does not mean that the bishops neglected Cornwall. They kept in touch with it by letters and officials, and there were large areas of Devon and elsewhere in England where bishops went with equal rarity.

Figure 40 A bishop confirms a baby boy, presented to him by the baby's sponsor, by anointing his brow with holy oil carried by an attendant. (Stained glass window from St Michael's, Doddiscombsleigh, Devon.)

The absence of the bishop was partly filled by a new functionary, the suffragan bishop, who travelled round the diocese on an occasional basis to confirm children, ordain clergy (especially clerks who only needed tonsuring), and consecrate churches, chapels, and churchyards. There was no permanent post of suffragan bishop in the Middle Ages; bishops hired such men when they wanted them. The earliest recorded suffragans in Exeter diocese were clergy from Ireland: Thomas, bishop of Leighlin, in 1275 and Robert Le Petit, bishop of Clonfert, in 1324. Later bishops of Exeter employed a series of such men, some of them bishops from Ireland while others were appointed by the pope to non-existent dioceses around the Mediterranean Sea like Selymbria and Tenos. Both kinds of suffragan were often monks or friars, and it was common to pay them by appointing them as rectors or vicars of parish churches.[83]

The bishop's other chief lieutenant in Cornwall continued to be the archdeacon, about 27 of whom held office between 1300 and the Reformation. Most of them had studied at university, generally law. There was no special policy of employing Cornishmen in the post.

Only four archdeacons in this period fell into that category: William of Bodrigan (by 1297–1308), Richard Penels (1418–19), Walter Trengofe (1436–45), and Henry Trevilian (1446–9), and their terms of office were not long. How much time they spent in Cornwall is uncertain, since they continued to appoint an 'official' from among the local clergy to deputise for them, and the bishop often addressed his letters on Cornish matters to 'the archdeacon or his official'. Other duties in Cornwall continued to be done by the rural deans and the officials of the peculiars, and the clergy and people remained liable to visit the bishop on important spiritual matters wherever he was staying, or to attend his consistory court at Exeter.[84]

THE MONASTERIES

In 1300 the religious houses of Cornwall fell into four groups (see Figure 23). The monasteries, a little depleted in number after the closure of two or three houses in the 13th century, now totalled nine. These were the three independent foundations (Bodmin, St Germans, and Launceston) and six smaller cells (St Anthony, St Carroc, St Michael's Mount, Minster, Scilly, and Tywardreath). With the monasteries we may group the preceptory of the Order of St John of Jerusalem at Trebeigh in St Ive. During the 1310s or '20s this house acquired the property of the Knights Templars at Temple, following their suppression in 1312. The friars continued to run their houses at Bodmin and Truro, and three collegiate churches still remained: two old minsters at St Buryan and Crantock, and the new foundation of Glasney. Finally there was the handful of small hospitals with some other less formal communities of lepers.

This situation changed somewhat between 1300 and 1500. The Hundred Years War caused short-term harm to some of the religious houses on the coast through attacks by the French and, in the case of Scilly, by the king of England's forces as well. It also brought about major alterations to the cells of the French abbeys in England – the 'alien priories' as they are known – represented in Cornwall by St Carroc, St Michael's Mount, Minster, and Tywardreath. From 1294 onwards, at times of war with France, the Crown took control of all such priories in England. The priories were not closed but their activities were restricted. Many of their revenues and moveable assets were confiscated to ensure that the king of England got the benefit, not the French. Eventually the French abbeys were prevented from even appointing priors and monks to their English cells, and in 1378 foreign monks (except for heads of houses) were ordered to leave the kingdom.[85]

Figure 41 A victim of the Hundred Years War, the priory of Minster was severed from its French mother church and later closed as a priory. The church was reshaped as the present parish church in the 15th century.

The alien priories struggled to survive in these constraints, not altogether unsuccessfully. St Michael's Mount had a French prior until about 1380, Minster until about 1382, and Tywardreath until 1433. After foreign monks were expelled in 1378, however, the task of maintaining a monastic community became almost impossible. By the 1380s it is doubtful whether any monks other than the prior remained at the three houses mentioned, and the daily services were probably done by Cornish chaplains hired for wages. Minster was the first house to lose its monastic character completely. In 1408 the king gave it to a parish priest with the title of rector, turning it into an ordinary parish church. The Mount fell next, between 1417 and 1420, when Henry V granted it and its possessions to his new abbey of Syon (Middx.). Thereafter its church became a chapel, served by a trio of English chaplains.[86]

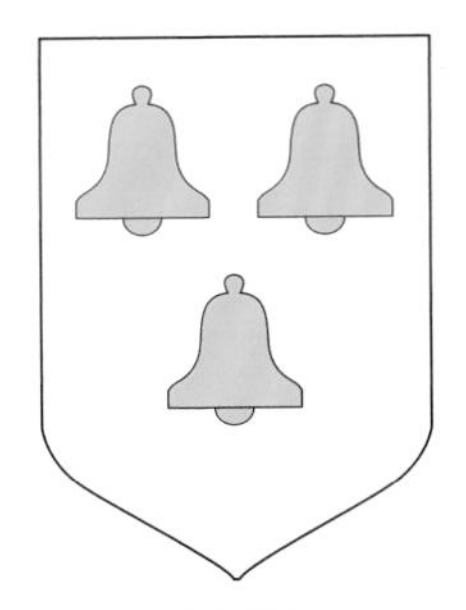

Figure 42 Monasteries adopted coats of arms in the later Middle Ages to assert their equality with the nobility and gentry. The coats of arms shown above are schematic representations drawn from documentary sources. From top: St Germans, Tywardreath, Bodmin and Launceston.

The other two alien priories were luckier. St Carroc survived because, in 1407, its English mother house, Montacute Priory, itself a French dependency, acquired 'denizen' status and ranked thereafter as an English monastery. Tywardreath, too, lived on, partly because its last French prior, John Roger, seems to have made himself useful to Henry V. In 1416 he, too, gained recognition of the priory as an independent denizen house. When Roger resigned in 1433, the next king, Henry VI, appointed a prior of English birth, John Brentyngham, who began to recruit English monks and gradually rebuilt a community. Under his successor the industrious Walter Barnecote, a Cornishman, the priory energetically pursued its claims to lapsed or lost property and regained its original staffing of seven monks. Far from being a run-down and doomed house, as is sometimes suggested, Tywardreath staged a remarkable recovery in the 15th century that made it the one success among the four Cornish alien priories.

There were two further losses of religious houses in the 15th century. The preceptory of Trebeigh was still fully functioning in the 1370s and 1380s, but by the early 15th century the preceptors who ran the houses of the Order of St John were allowed to hold more than one simultaneously and by about the 1430s Trebeigh became permanently linked with the preceptory of Ansty (Wilts.). After this the order's Cornish affairs were managed from Ansty, and the staff of Trebeigh was reduced to a chaplain and perhaps a few servants. The priory of Scilly was abandoned for a time between the 1340s and the 1360s, because of the Hundred Years War and, although the monks later went back, the islands remained a lawless and dangerous place. The mother house, Tavistock Abbey, seems to have disbanded the priory during the second half of the 15th century, and by 1492 its affairs were managed by a single monk in the islands.

More information survives about the Cornish monasteries after 1300 than before but, as in much of England, it covers only parts of monastic life. At the beginning of the 14th century Bodmin had 18 canons, making it likely that Launceston had about the same number and St Germans perhaps about twelve. After the Black Death all three places had fewer clergy, as was commonly so throughout England. It was harder to recruit monks, due to the fall in the population, and more expensive to run a monastery. By 1381 Launceston housed about 13 canons, Bodmin 11, and St Germans eight, totals that were generally sustained in the 15th century although they fell lower at times. In 1500 there were probably about 30 canons in the three large houses, seven monks at Tywardreath, two canons or monks each at St Anthony and St Carroc, and one in the Scillies – a total of just over forty.

Figure 43 A 14th-century bishop on a roof boss in Exeter Cathedral. It probably symbolises Bishop Grandisson, the reigning bishop when the boss was manufactured.

The bishops' registers contain numerous records of the elections of priors, visitations, and disciplinary problems but, by tending to centre on disputes and breaches of procedure, they show us the least attractive sides of monastic life. The canons of Launceston had some unhappy feuds. In 1430 the election of a prior led to a bitter contest between John Yerle and William Shyre, the bishop apparently favouring Yerle, for whom the older canons voted, while Shyre had the support of the younger canons who formed the majority. Shyre was declared elected, but the bishop refused to confirm the election. The canons defied the bishop, appealed to the archbishop of Canterbury and the Crown, and spread rumours that Yerle had helped to poison the previous prior. The bishop was forced to give way, but he took revenge later by forcing Shyre to make a public retraction of slanders against him and to promise him obedience. There was to be another disputed election in 1534.[87]

The management and discipline of the three larger houses was also a cause of concern from time to time. Bishop Grandisson fought a series of battles to improve what he considered to be the unsatisfactory state of Launceston under Prior Adam of Knolle (1327–46). Grandisson charged Adam with spending time outside the monastery with secular persons, some of them women. He was keeping too many servants, and impoverishing the monastery. He had stopped giving alms to the poor. The canons were drinking too much in their refectory as well as in private. They were keeping dogs and hawks, presumably for hunting. In 1344 the bishop removed the prior from practical control of the monastery and appointed two canons to govern it. The canons began to carry out reforms, but Adam resisted. He assigned other people to do the administration, abstracted money, and continued to spend time with a married woman friend.

The angry bishop denounced the prior as 'a son of damnation', a man 'who has for many years led a life detestable to God and man, scorning and undermining our commands, punishments, and sentences with damnable audacity'. Adam managed to hold out for a couple more years, but in the end the bishop was too strong for him and on 19 June 1346 he was forced to agree to resign. In the following year the bishop turned his attention to Bodmin. Its affairs were little better. The canons were wearing secular clothes such as buttoned and hooded tunics, thigh boots, and pointed shoes. They were playing dice, backgammon, and chess, and talking to women. Some of them were living in private rooms, dogs were being kept, and the monastery was badly in debt.[88]

These kinds of problems surface in one bishop's register after another, all over England. They arose because the larger monasteries were independent bodies with complex affairs. A prior was expected to live in some style, to entertain visiting bishops, judges, and gentlemen, and to show favours both to the powerful and to those who depended on the monastery as tenants and neighbours. The prior of Bodmin had country residences: one at St Margaret's outside Bodmin and another at Rialton near Newquay. The rest of the canons needed servants to enable them to concentrate on their religious tasks. All these commitments ate into a monastery's resources, and sometimes weakened its purpose.

It is easy to overestimate the negative evidence about monasteries. On the positive side we know that many lay people thought well of them and gave them some support. In 1274 visitors to Bodmin on days of county court business are said to have attended services in the priory, and it is likely that they went to the shrine of St Petroc there as well as to the nearby Lady Chapel, where offerings were made to an image of the Virgin Mary. St Germans acquired a relic of its patron saint in the 14th century, and miracles were claimed as a result. Tywardreath, despite its small size and comparative remoteness, established a confraternity or group of supporters that included men and women from all over Cornwall. They included families of the gentry such as the Bevills of Killigarth, the Grenvilles of Stowe, the Treffrys of Fowey, and the Tregians of Golden. The members of this confraternity assisted the monastery with gifts, and it held obits for them (masses of requiem) on the anniversaries of their deaths.[89]

The larger Cornish monasteries were not without books. In about 1300 the Franciscan friars of Oxford set out to compile a union catalogue of standard theological works, indicating the places in England where copies existed. The friars' enquiries produced a report of 41 titles held by Launceston and 52 by Bodmin, which we would otherwise not know about. How often these books were used is not recorded, but some canons certainly took an interest in literature of a less difficult or more practical kind. John Bowyer of Bodmin compiled an anthology of religious and moral poems in English during the late 15th century, part of which survives in the British Library. At about the time that Bowyer lived, in 1478, the antiquary William Worcester passed through Bodmin on his way to St Michael's Mount. He met and talked to two canons, William John (later prior) and John Stevyns, who were interested in 'physic' (what we would call natural science, especially medicine). John showed Worcester 'several ancient books' on the subject.[90]

Occasionally canons and monks went to university, but this was probably rare and we know of only four canons and one monk from the Cornish houses who received permission to do so. They were Alan Kenegy of Bodmin in 1405, William Shyre of Launceston in 1428, William Vivian of Bodmin in 1445, Walter Barnecote of

Figure 44 The church of the Franciscan friary at Bodmin in 1716, after it had been turned into a two-storeyed civic building. The church building was long and narrow, and probably had tall narrow Gothic windows and a small bell-tower on the roof.

Tywardreath in 1455, and Thomas Fort of Bodmin in about the 1480s. The usual period of study allowed was three years, and the university was generally Oxford, although Vivian's permission was for Cambridge and Fort also studied there after moving from Bodmin to become head of the Augustinian priory of Huntingdon.[91]

THE FRIARS

The friaries resemble the monasteries in being better recorded after 1300, but still imperfectly so. No details of their staffing survive until the Reformation, but it is possible that the two Cornish houses each contained about two dozen inmates before the Black Death, after which numbers of friars in England declined like those of monks and canons. The friars managed to maintain their national and international links longer than monasteries did: men with Germanic surnames were recorded being ordained from the Bodmin friary in the 15th century.

Some of these links were connected with education, which the friars continued to embrace with enthusiasm. Novices were taught grammar in their own friaries, if necessary, and went to regional centres to learn basic and practical theology. A few of the most promising friar students were sent to Oxford or Cambridge to study the liberal arts and theology, graduating in some cases as bachelors and doctors of theology. But the learning of the friars was not confined to the universities; it also went on in the local friaries. We hear of a lecturer at Bodmin in 1328 and one at Truro in 1397, who probably provided 'continuing education' for the adult friars, and a few distinguished scholars are known to have been based at the Cornish houses during the 14th and 15th centuries. John Somer, famous for his astronomical work on the calendar, was briefly the warden or presiding officer of Bodmin in the early 1380s, while Truro was home to Benedict Lugans and Thomas Truro in the same period, both graduates in theology.[92]

The bishops of Exeter valued the learning of the Cornish friars, and appointed some of them to hear confessions in Cornwall with the power to deal with serious sins and crimes that normally belonged to the bishop. One of the attractions of friars for this purpose was that they included men who could speak the Cornish language. In 1331 Grandisson authorised the Bodmin friar Alfred of 'Drefe' to act as a confessor throughout Cornwall, in view of his skill 'in the idiom of those parts'. Drefe is the modern Drift in Sancreed parish, and Alfred was evidently a native speaker of Cornish from the far west of Cornwall. Later, in 1355, Grandisson appointed another Bodmin friar, John, as a confessor 'to those in Cornwall who know either language', and Roger Tyrel from the Truro friary to hold the same office 'for the merely Cornish [speakers] who do not know English'. It is likely that Cornish was known and spoken in both friaries during the 14th century, and some of the friars must have been among the most learned members of the Cornish-speaking community.[93]

Critics of the friars attacked their tendency to associate with the rich rather than the poor. The Cornish houses certainly enjoyed the support of important people. When William Worcester visited Cornwall in 1478, he transcribed the names of 26 'nobility and gentry in the calendar of the friars of Bodmin', who would have been prayed for on the anniversaries of their deaths. At Truro he noted the names of seven members of the county gentry who were buried or commemorated in the friary church. The illegitimate brother of Sir John Arundell of Lanherne (d. 1435), named William Clerk, entered the Carmelite order and was rewarded (against the spirit of the order) with the family's rectory of St Columb Major. Our information is distorted, however, because the sources available to us favour the wealthy. The relationship of the friars with lesser folk has left little trace, but their ability to recruit members from all over Cornwall including the Cornish-speaking area suggests that they had good will among the general population from whom such members came. Two friars are even mentioned working as parish chaplains in 1474: the Dominican Philip Arundell at Penzance and a certain Friar Adam at Poundstock.[94]

PANEL 3

The Friars in Cornwall

A Franciscan friar preaching in a pulpit, wearing a robe of coarse cloth tied with a knotted rope girdle (see opposite), illustrates the humble dress of this order. This was part of their claim to live more strictly and holier than monks or parish clergy, and closer to Christ and his disciples. They did not own lands or churches, but lived from donations of food or money. Friars had no permanent home, and might be drafted from one friary to another at any time. As well as keeping the religious life and saying daily services, they worked pastorally among lay people, hearing confessions and preaching sermons, from their bases at Bodmin, Plymouth, and Truro.

Friars are often underrated in local history because they have left fewer records than monks, and hardly any of their buildings survived the Reformation. And whereas monks in a monastery came from the neighbourhood and rarely left it, friars had wider careers. Their Cornish recruits were sent to study or serve elsewhere, and other men were brought from elsewhere to Cornwall. Much still needs to be done to list the friars who lived and worked in the county, and to discover where they came from and went to.

Friars emphasised education more than most other clergy, and their members were expected to attend lectures and study books. Early in the 14th century Henry, dean of Crantock, gave a copy of Peter Comestor's *Historia Scholastica* to the friars of Bodmin, and Truro's 14th-century copy of Witelo's treatise on perspective is now in Cambridge University Library. Distinguished friars who worked in Cornwall included John Somer, famous for his astronomical work on the calendar, at Bodmin in the early 1380s, and Benedict Lugans and Thomas Truro, both graduates in theology, at Truro in the same period. In the 1530s the canons of Bodmin employed the learned Dominican friar John de Coloribus as a preacher or lecturer, and those of Launceston did the same to Alexander Barclay and John Taylor, leading members of the Franciscan order.

Not surprisingly with such high ideals, friars easily became the target of critics who claimed that they did not live up to their promises. They were accused of seeking the company of the rich rather than the poor, and of wearing finer clothes, eating finer food, and building finer churches than their rules of life allowed. Other charges claimed that they forgave sins too easily and even did so in return for money. The famous late 14th-century English poem *Piers Plowman* is particularly hostile to friars. Here (below), in a scene from the poem, Lady Meed (who symbolises corrupt wealth) is absolved from her sins by a friar, in return for a handsome donation. Chaucer's *Canterbury Tales*, written a few years later, makes similar allegations, but does so more covertly and comically.

MINSTERS, HOSPITALS, AND HERMITS

Unlike friaries which were units of international organisations, minsters, collegiate, and prebendal churches were individual and local in character. St Buryan, Crantock, and Probus continued to rub along, largely as parish churches, most of their clergy being absent elsewhere. The only important place of this kind in Cornwall was Glasney (see Figure 45). Its church was one of the biggest in the county, it had a larger clerical staff than most other religious houses in the county, and its endowments exceeded those of any foundation apart from the four largest priories. There were 13 canons headed by a provost, 13 vicars choral, and smaller numbers of chantry priests, clerks, and boys.

The Glasney canons did not all reside continuously. Many held parish benefices or did duties for the bishop, and they were allowed to stay away for half of the year and still receive their stipends. Nevertheless, the resident members of the college must have numbered at least twenty men and boys, and this allowed them – perhaps uniquely in Cornwall – to stage the newly fashionable Church music called polyphony, sung in harmony by different voices. In 1438 one of the canons, John Michell, owned a booklet of 'songs of music', and by 1548 the college employed a clerk of the Lady Chapel who may well have taught and directed the

Figure 45 Glasney College, a 19th-century reconstruction based on a lost plan of c.1580–1640. The church was one of the largest in Cornwall and its precinct was fortified against attack from the sea. Beyond the church to the south lay the houses of the canons and other clergy.

polyphony. The college was also a centre of learned men. Some of the canons were graduates who owned or studied books, and by the Reformation one of the vicars choral was teaching at a grammar school for the public, but when the school originated is not known.[95]

The Cornish hospitals were the smallest and poorest of the religious foundations. There were still seven of them in 1300: six for lepers at Bodmin, St Mary Magdalene (Helston), Lanlivery, Launceston, Liskeard, and Sheepstall in Veryan, and one for non-lepers at St John Baptist (Helston). All probably offered long-term care, rather than short-term medical help like their modern successors. They usually had small endowments of land or income which they supplemented from donations. Hospitals were characteristically sited outside towns (because of their links with disease) but on major roads, often by bridges where traffic slowed and passers-by could be waylaid for alms. After about 1300, leprosy grew rarer among the population, and some foundations for lepers closed or turned into places for other kinds of infirm or elderly people. At least two of the Cornish leper hospitals, St Mary Magdalene (Helston) and Sheepstall, appear to have shut down during the 15th century, and Lanlivery may have been a third. Bodmin, Launceston, and Liskeard continued to provide care for 'lazars' until at least the mid-16th century, but it is not clear whether that word, by that time, meant only lepers or included other kinds of sick people.[96]

Figure 46 A knight encounters a hermit in a forest, in an illustration to a romance. Cornwall had similar hermits living in wooded parks at Liskeard and Restormel.

During the 15th century a new fashion developed in England for founding almshouses, a word that is a coinage of that period. Almshouses shared some of the characteristics of earlier hospitals, but differed in usually ministering to people suffering conditions other than leprosy, especially old age, and in providing individual dwellings in the form of a row of small cottages, rather than communal buildings. Three almshouses were founded in Cornwall after 1400: one at Launceston by 1446, and two in Bodmin (St Anthony and St George) by 1492. Launceston's appears to have been created by the borough corporation of Dunheved, while at Bodmin (where the corporation had less power) the initiative was due to two local guilds, each of which maintained a chapel and added an almshouse to it. Launceston is mentioned as having six inmates, and the others may have been of similar size.[97]

A few people followed a religious vocation without joining a community, yet withdrawing from everyday life to a greater or lesser extent. Some (always men) became hermits, living a simple life alone in a dwelling. The dwelling was usually a secluded one not far from a town or place of resort: thus in Cornwall hermits are recorded living in the deer parks near Launceston and Lostwithiel, as well as at St Michael's Mount. Some may have lived from people's alms, but the more fortunate were paid small stipends by noblemen or, in the case of the Mount, by Syon Abbey. Little is known of what they did, but the hermit of the Mount carried out some small administrative tasks on behalf of his church.

More austere than the hermit was the anchorite, who left the world altogether to follow a life of prayer and contemplation in an enclosed dwelling. Such men or women often acquired high reputations for holiness and were visited by people seeking spiritual counsel. One, Cecily or Lucy Moys, received permission from the bishop of Exeter to live in a house in the churchyard of Marhamchurch in 1403. Another, named Margaret, was based at Bodmin in the same period, and both were well-enough known for a canon of Exeter to bequeath them each £2 in 1406. There may have been a few widows known as 'vowesses' who lived a life of chastity and prayer while living in the world. Such women, along with the anchoresses, were the nearest that Cornwall came to having nuns within its borders.[98]

Figure 47 A simplified picture of an English grammar school in the 1490s. The schoolmaster (here a layman, sometimes a priest) presides from a high seat. A schoolboy comes out before him to be 'apposed' or examined. Other boys sit round the edge of the schoolroom, facing inwards. Usually they sat on forms without desks, holding their books and writing materials on their laps.

THE PARISH CLERGY: EDUCATION

On 21 December 1308 Walter Stapledon, who had just arrived in his diocese for the first time as bishop, made his way to Crediton where a huge crowd of clergy was awaiting him. They had come to be ordained from all over Cornwall and Devon, and there were 1,005 of them: the largest ordination ever recorded in the diocese. The Cornish were well represented, 106 receiving tonsures and 326 being made acolytes. These were probably schoolboys, boys who helped in church services, and parish clerks. A further 116 were young adults: 74 ordained as subdeacons, 22 as deacons, and six as priests, together with 14 who were already parish clergy and needed one or other of these orders to qualify. The numbers partly reflected the fact that there had been no ordination for some time, but they also mirrored the society of the day. At a time when the population was high and work was limited, becoming a priest was a rational choice of career although most priests only received low wages.[99]

How such candidates for ordination were educated is little clearer after 1300 than before. Knowledge of reading, song, and some Latin grammar continued to be needed for admission as subdeacon or above, and bishops are occasionally found rejecting candidates until they were fully qualified. Yet there was still little systematic help for those who wished to acquire such knowledge. As before, young men had to learn grammar at their family's expense in a town school or through private tuition. A few religious houses – Crantock, Glasney, and possibly the larger Cornish monasteries – provided board, lodging, and some education for a few boys who acted as servers or choristers, but such places were likely to be given to kinsfolk of the clergy in those houses, or to sons of their friends and tenants. The ancient practice of appointing students as parish clerks continued during the 14th century, but weakened in the 15th as such posts came to be held by older men for longer periods. Education continued to be most accessible to the wealthy and the well connected, and as in previous centuries they were also the best placed to find a patron to give them a rectory or vicarage.[100]

Most of the parish clergy after 1300 were probably educated inside the county, but an important minority followed the practice of going to university that had developed in the 13th century. Such travel was now centred largely on Oxford (see Figure 48), while Paris fell out of favour, another example of English insularity. Some of the Cornish students at Oxford came from wealthy families. They went there when they were about eighteen after going to school elsewhere, and followed university courses during their late teens and early twenties. Others delayed going until they had gained a rectory or vicarage rather than doing so before this happened as we would consider appropriate. Church benefices gave them an income to pay for their higher education, and the bishop would give them permission to be absent from their parishes to study. The Cornish at Oxford came from both the English-speaking east of the county and from the Cornish-speaking west. Five men

Figure 48 Oxford in the 14th and 15th centuries. The map shows places associated with the Cornish, including Exeter College, some of the halls that were run by Cornish principals, and John Cornwall's grammar school.

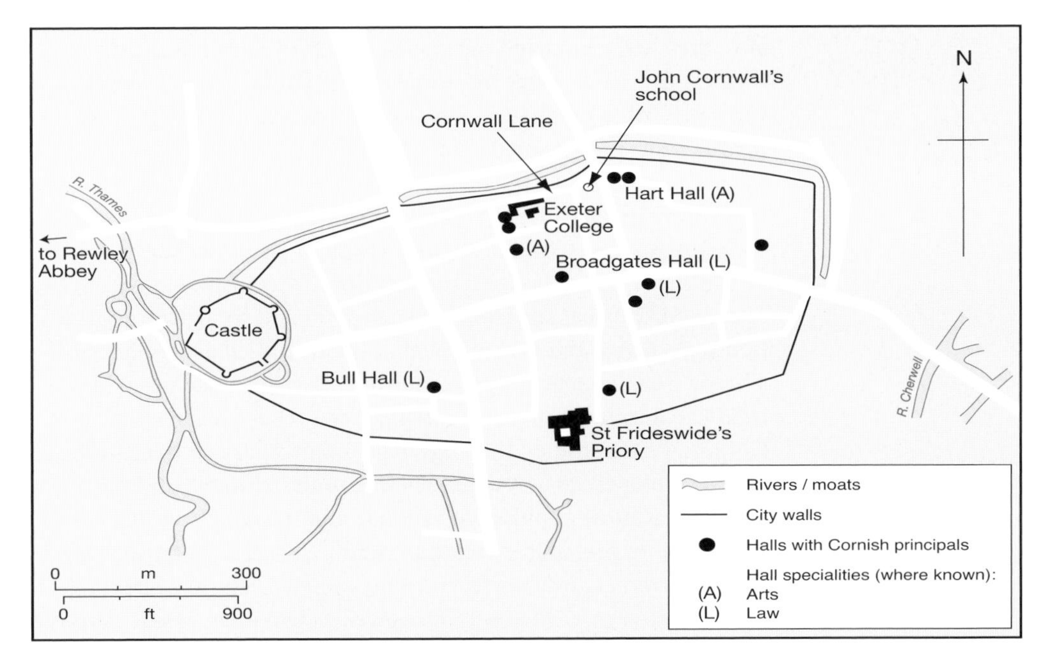

from Camborne alone are known to have gone there during the 15th century, and a number of other students are recorded with surnames taken from places in the western parishes.[101]

Students in Oxford up to about 1500 usually shared a room in a university hall, which was simply a rented house managed by a principal appointed by the university authorities. The principal, a graduate in his twenties or thereabouts, had charge of a dozen, two dozen, or three dozen students who paid for their board and lodging. He might also act as their guardian, keeping their money and arranging for their tuition. Halls tended to gather students according to the degrees for which they were reading (arts, law, or theology) and from particular regions of the country. One hall, St Edmund, may have attracted Cornishmen in the early 14th century when it was ruled by two scholars from the county in succession. Another, Hart Hall on the site of the present-day Hertford College, was purchased by Bishop Stapledon at about the same time and given to Exeter College which he had founded. It was later rented out by the college and became a popular lodging place for west-of-England students.[102]

After the 1260s the halls were gradually supplemented by colleges offering free board and lodging, but the colleges were small in size and numbers until the 1380s and catered chiefly for postgraduates. They, too, favoured entrants from particular counties or dioceses. The college for men from the South West of England was Stapledon's foundation of 1314: Stapledon Hall as it was first known, later Exeter College (see Figure 49). It provided places for eight men from Devon and four from Cornwall to study the arts course, but only after they had completed the first two years of the course at their own expense. They were then housed and fed for the five remaining years needed to graduate as a master of arts and for two or three further years of regency during which they acted as lecturers. This made the college, like the halls, a community of young men in their twenties, apart from a thirteenth older scholar who acted as chaplain and was required to study theology or canon law.[103]

It is likely that at least a couple of dozen Cornishmen were to be found in Oxford at any time between 1300 and 1550, totalling a few hundreds across the period. Most of them studied arts which gave a broad liberal education, or canon and civil law which provided legal and administrative skills, helpful to forward a career in the Church. Fewer studied theology, because ordinary students were expected to gain an MA degree before undertaking it, and the subject was most popular with monks and friars who were allowed to do so after preparatory work in their own religious houses. We hear of several Cornish scholars who gained doctoral degrees at Oxford between 1300 and 1500, as well as two men – John Nans

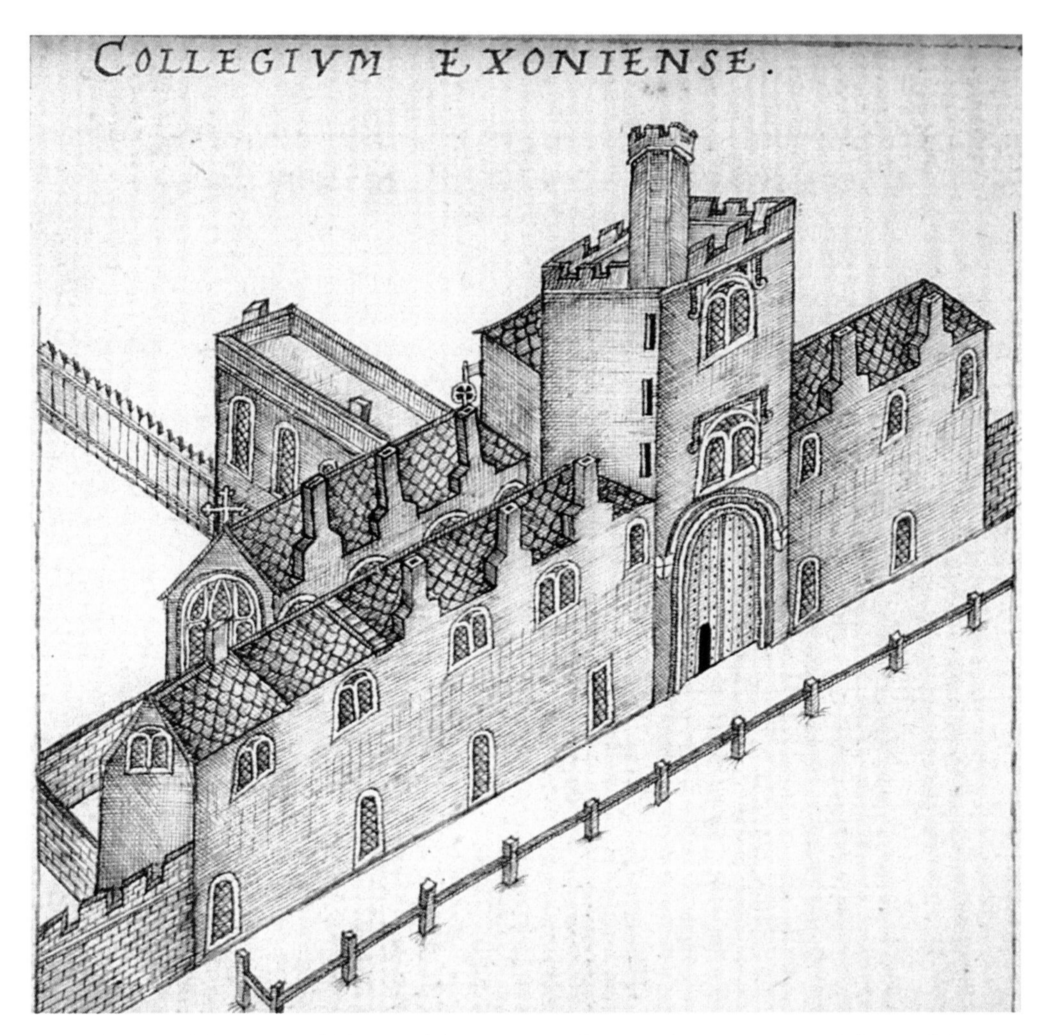

Figure 49 Exeter College Oxford, founded by Bishop Walter Stapledon, as it was in the 16th century. The lane in front of the college was sometimes known as Cornwall Lane, but it has since been closed and the approach to the college rearranged.

and Thomas Tomyowe – who struck out a new path by studying law at Bologna in Italy during the early 1480s. Three men from Cornwall even rose to be chancellors of Oxford, the highest office in the university: these were William Polmorva (1350–2), Ralph Redruth (1391–3), and Walter Trengoff (1419–21). Two others, John Landreyne and Ralph Tregrisiow, were eminent enough to be consulted about the condemnation of John Wycliffe's writings between 1380 and 1382.

One other Cornish graduate merits mention as an oddity: Ralph Tremur, rector of the small moorland parish of Warleggan. He was already described as 'Master' when in 1331 the bishop (Grandisson) allowed him to leave his benefice for three years to study at Oxford on condition that he was ordained, an example of the practice by which ordination and study might follow the acquisition of a benefice. In 1334 Tremur resigned from Warleggan and became, in Grandisson's words, a fugitive and wanderer in the diocese and elsewhere in England. A year later the bishop was horrified to hear that Tremur had developed heretical opinions which he was secretly teaching to others, notably that the communion bread and wine, when consecrated, did not become in substance the body and blood of Christ.

Grandisson ordered Tremur to be excommunicated, but the errant cleric appears to have fled to London, prompting Grandisson to warn its bishop about his activities. He conceded that Tremur was a distinguished man: a master of arts, learned in grammar and in four languages. The man's opinions, however, were detestable. He taught that only manual work was truly good and that priests achieved nothing by merely opening their mouths and digesting communion wafers. He had called St Peter 'a bad, hollow rustic' and St John the Evangelist 'a liar'. Finally he had stolen a pyx from a church containing a consecrated wafer, thrown the wafer into a fire, and absconded with the pyx. Reformer or eccentric? It is hard to be sure, since we have only Grandisson's charges on record, but the communion, priests, and saints were to become the targets of Wycliffe and the Lollards some 25 years later. Tremur may have anticipated some of the views that they were to express more rationally and effectively.[104]

Some university men came back to Cornwall after their studies. About one fifth of the rectors and vicars instituted to parishes in the county under Bishop Lacy (1420–55) were graduates, either natives or incomers. The provosts of Glasney College after 1427 were generally Cornishmen who had graduated or at least studied at university. Other such men found employment in Devon rather than Cornwall, sometimes serving the bishops of Exeter. There was usually at least one Cornish canon of Exeter Cathedral and three or four held posts there at the same time for a period around 1400. Three became deans of the cathedral: Ralph Tregrisiow from Creed (1384–1415), John Cobbethorn from Launceston (1419–58), and John Arundell junior of Lanherne (*c*.1482–96). Other Cornish graduates followed careers away from the South West. William Polmorva scored an early success by becoming a royal clerk and confessor to Philippa, queen of Edward III, until his death in 1362. Tregrisiow's uncle, Stephen Pempel, rose to be dean of Wells (1361–79), and John Gentill gained a senior post in the royal court of admiralty (1428–35).[105]

Figure 50 The east end of St Ive church, embellished in the early 14th century with decorative work carved in Beer stone from Devon, in the style of Exeter Cathedral. The work was probably paid for by Bartholomew de Castro, a long serving rector with links to Exeter.

Most notable is a group of graduates that formed at the court of Henry VI and his queen, Margaret of Anjou. It included John Arundell senior (died 1477), probably from the Lanherne branch of the family, Henry's chaplain and physician, later bishop of Chichester; Walter Lyhert (died 1472) from Lanteglos-by-Fowey,

Figure 51 A medieval Cornish rector: Thomas Awmarle of Cardinham, who died in about 1400. Proud of his gentry ancestry, he displays his family coat of arms and wears a sword, the latter against the strict code of clerical life. He addresses onlookers directly, saying (in translation) 'I ask our brothers for me to pray, and I will for you as much as I may'.

Margaret's confessor and subsequently bishop of Norwich; John Stanbury (died 1474) from Morwenstow, Henry's confessor, bishop of Bangor and afterwards of Hereford; and Michael Tregury (died 1471) from St Wenn, also close to Margaret, sometime rector of the university of Caen and later archbishop of Dublin. Such achievements became rarer in the second half of the century, but posts of distinction were gained by Thomas Fort (died *c.*1503), canon of Bodmin, bishop of Achonry in Ireland, and later prior of Huntingdon, while John Arundell junior of Lanherne (died 1504) became a chaplain to Edward IV and chancellor of Prince Arthur, son of Henry VII. After serving as bishop of Lichfield, he was translated to Exeter, the only medieval Cornishman (except perhaps for Leofric) to hold the senior post in the diocese.[106]

THE PARISH CLERGY: DAILY LIFE

The everyday life of the parish clergy, like that of monks and friars, centred on saying the eight daily services. There was no requirement to say them in church except on Sundays and festivals, and many parish clergy may have done so in their houses. Baptisms, visits to the sick, and funerals might be required at any time, since baptism took place on the day of birth and a funeral on the day of death or soon afterwards. The year was punctuated by the sequence of feasts and fasts and by the collection of tithes and offerings. The parish was not a unit of local government until Tudor times, but a medieval rector or vicar had to supervise the affairs of his church and might become rural dean or be assigned by the bishop to investigate, for example, a dispute over church patronage or a crime that had been committed against Church law.

Parish life was not always a calm routine. There could be tensions between the clergy and their parishioners over refusals to pay tithes, attend church, or keep the Church's moral code. In 1342 the archdeacon of Cornwall, Adam Carleton, petitioned the bishop to allow him to exchange the post for a parish in Huntingdonshire,

Figure 52 A parish priest's duties: visiting the sick. The priest hears the sick person's confession, and anoints him with holy oil from a box. (Stained glass window from St Michael's, Doddiscombsleigh, Devon.)

complaining that his health was inadequate to deal with 'a people … so extraordinary, rebellious, and difficult to teach and correct.' A more powerful man than himself, he thought, was needed to handle them. Occasionally clergy were victims of crimes. A clerk of Poundstock was wounded in his church in 1357 and the provost of Glasney in his precinct in 1375. The dean of Crantock was dragged from his church in 1382, and a priest of Penryn was violently attacked in the town in the following year. The rector of Whitstone died mysteriously by murder or suicide in 1359, a priest of St Hilary was stabbed and beheaded in 1380, and the vicar of Linkinhorne was killed in 1411 after falling out with local people. Such events underline the importance of not regarding all medieval Cornish people as good Catholics.[107]

Each parish contained a house for the rector or vicar, which he was expected to keep in repair. If he let it become dilapidated, he or his heirs might be pursued for costs. The earliest house of which a record survives is St Neot's in 1314, which was described as having a hall and chamber linked by a door, with other buildings. Veryan's in 1331 included a hall, chamber, *garderoba* (which might mean a store room or privy), cellar, and kitchen. The incumbent would have had one or more male servants, depending on his wealth, and sometimes a chaplain to assist him. We know little of the lives of rectors and vicars, since we lack their personal records except for a few wills and even the latter only after 1400. Those of the Cornish clergy mention modest possessions: gowns, bedding, a few pieces of silver (cups, bowls, and spoons), and livestock such as sheep and cattle. This reflects the fact that many rectors and vicars were involved in agriculture, usually through servants or tenants rather than personally.[108]

A few clergy refer to their books, generally Latin ones: prayer books, grammars, books on canon law, and the occasional work of theology. One priest's book is still extant: a breviary owned by Thomas Greke of the parish of Lanteglos-by-Fowey, in which he noted the names of his family members. There is no direct evidence that the Cornish clergy were authors of books, but it is possible that they helped produce some of the Latin Lives of Cornish saints or the plays in Cornish that feature Bible stories and saintly legends. Some of the saint cults introduced into parish churches were probably due to them, too. John Waryn of Menheniot, for example, was a devotee of St Anne, and left money in 1426 to build a chapel and found a guild in her honour in his parish church.[109]

The lowest clergy of all were the chaplains and chantry priests. Shortage of clergy after the Black Death caused their wages to rise, but this left them only slightly better off. The rises were paralleled by increases in prices, and successive governments tried to stop wages rising. In 1351 the Statute of Labourers fixed the earnings of lay workers, and this was followed by similar measures aimed at the lesser clergy. In 1362 stipends for chantry priests were set at £3 6s. 8d. and those for parish chaplains at £4, figures that were raised to £4 13s. 4d. and £5 6s. 8d. respectively in 1414. As there was limited scope for employment as a priest in Cornwall, some of the poorer Cornish clergy sought careers in Devon or elsewhere in England. A fortunate few were able to join the staff of Exeter Cathedral as vicars choral or perpetual chantry priests: posts that were better paid, had security of tenure, and sometimes led to promotion as parish rectors or vicars. Several clergy with Cornish surnames held such posts.[110]

Chaplains and chantry priests in Cornwall are little recorded until after the Black Death and the total of two hundred or more that we have postulated before that event can only be a conjecture. The earliest list of them comes from the poll-tax records of 1381, when there were 157, a figure that stayed much the same until the

Figure 53 Trevalga church, lonely on the cliffs of the north coast. it was one of the many churches in Cornwall owned by religious bodies elsewhere: first Tewkesbury Abbey and later Exeter Cathedral.

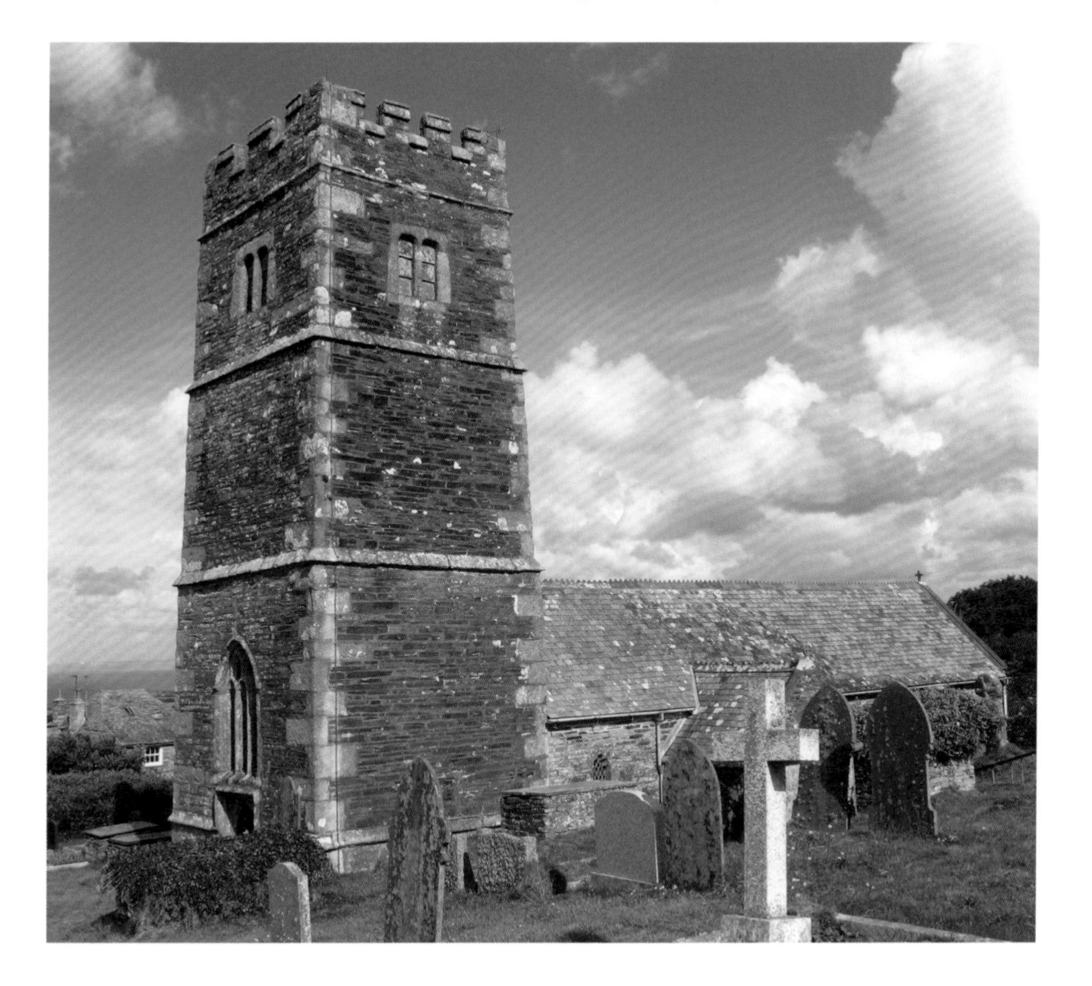

Reformation, so that they formed about half of the parish clergy. The relative shortage of chaplains after 1349 was irksome to rectors and vicars who wished to employ such people as assistants in their parishes. By the 15th century, if a clergyman could not find a chaplain willing to work for him, he might ask the bishop to order one to do so, such as a priest who prayed for the dead. In 1438, for example, the rector of Trevalga, who wished to live away from his parish, got the bishop to issue a 'compulsion' to John Gregory, a chaplain of Tintagel. Gregory was told to serve Trevalga parish in return for an adequate salary, and to present himself before the bishop within twelve days if he had any objection to doing so.[111]

Chantry priests were of two kinds. Some were hired by the year to say masses for the dead, causing their masses to be known as 'annuals' and themselves as 'annuellars'. They would establish themselves in the church of the dead person's parish and say their masses at an altar there. Others served perpetual chantries endowed by a wealthy person or supported by a religious guild, and received a salary for as long as they held the post. In that respect they were better off than their temporary colleagues, and some of them were formally instituted to their posts by the bishop like rectors and vicars. In 1548, when chantries were abolished in England, there were about 27 perpetual chantries in Cornwall, employing about 31 priests; the number of annuellars is not known, but may perhaps have been about the same. Some chantry priests were expected to help run the church or the nearby parish, and a few served chapels of ease such as Boscastle and Penzance. By the 1540s a handful taught schools as well, but there is no evidence as yet that any did so in Cornwall before 1500.[112]

The poll-tax records of 1381 also contain the names of 81 clerks. A few of these were junior clergy in monasteries or collegiate churches, but most were probably parish clerks. There is a problem here in that Cornwall's 209 parishes would each have needed at least one clerk and possibly more. In 1427 John Walle, rector of Sheviock, left bequests in his will to the clerk of the 'town', meaning the settlement by the church, and to the clerks 'on the land', signifying the rural parts of the parish, implying that there were at least three at that time in a parish of medium size. Many such clerks may have done the duty as a part-time supplement to a lay career, however, and may have paid the poll tax as laymen. The 81 clerks of 1381 are likely to have been young men intending to follow careers as priests, and some of them can be identified with clergy who were ordained in the following years.[113]

OLD AGE AND DEATH

Contemporaries tended to envisage the clergy as youthful men (like Chaucer's Clerk of Oxford) or mature ones (such as his Parson). In reality there were also those who developed infirmities and disabilities (especially blindness or lameness), or grew into an old age that made it hard for them to work. The solution usually adopted in the early 14th century was for an elderly or infirm rector or vicar to ask the bishop to appoint him a coadjutor or assistant, or for the bishop to appoint such a person on his own initiative. The coadjutor might be a neighbouring clergyman, or a chaplain who moved into the incumbent's house and helped run his affairs. In the early 15th century it became more common for rectors and vicars to resign their benefices in return for receiving a proportion of the income as a pension. Such an arrangement had to be sanctioned by the bishop, who approved the amount (usually a third of the income) and made their successors promise to pay it.[114]

This system worked well for rich clergy but not for those who were poor. A rector or vicar with a small stipend faced difficulty in negotiating a pension, because the stipend could not support both him and his replacement. Hired chaplains or chantry priests

Figure 54 The splendid tomb of Prior Thomas Vivian of Bodmin (died 1533). Originally placed in the priory church, it was moved to the parish church at the Reformation.

who became too old or ill to work had no resources to fall back on. If they became destitute the bishop had to take responsibility for them. In 1309–12 Bishop Stapledon addressed this problem by founding a hospital at Clyst Gabriel, east of Exeter, for infirm priests who had no livelihood. A few of the priests admitted to the hospital had Cornish names and probably came from the under-class of poor hired clergy. What happened to the majority of such clergy when they grew sick or old is not recorded.[115]

When death came, status ruled as it did in life. The grandees of the Cornish Church – the priors of the monasteries – were given elaborate funerals and monuments inside their churches. John Leland, visiting Cornwall in 1542, noticed the tomb of Thomas Vivian, prior of Bodmin and titular bishop of Megara (see Figure 54), and those of Roger of Horton and Stephen Tredidan, priors of Launceston. The prosperous middling clergy, rectors and vicars, made their wills and told their executors to hold funerals for them, sometimes defining the masses to be said for their souls and the alms to be paid to the poor. They claimed the privilege of burial in their chancels, usually beneath a ledger stone flush with the floor and inscribed with their name, their date of their death, and a prayer to God for mercy on their souls. As for the poor unbeneficed clergy, they rarely had a burial inside church and little money for funeral or prayers. Their destiny was to lie in the open air, like the majority of the population, under unmarked grassy mounds in parish churchyards.[116]

The ledger stones of the wealthier clergy were sometimes deco-rated with an inlaid brass memorial, showing a priest in vestments:

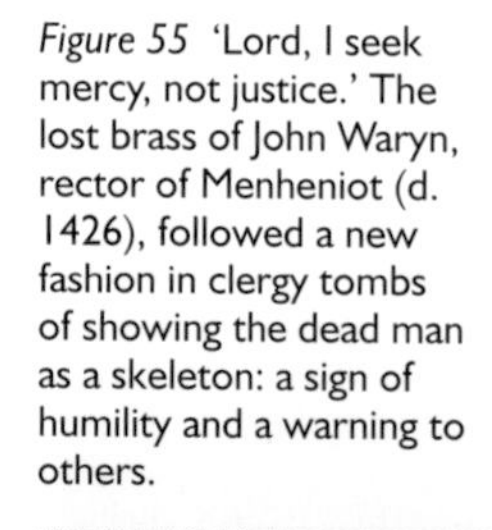

Figure 55 'Lord, I seek mercy, not justice.' The lost brass of John Waryn, rector of Menheniot (d. 1426), followed a new fashion in clergy tombs of showing the dead man as a skeleton: a sign of humility and a warning to others.

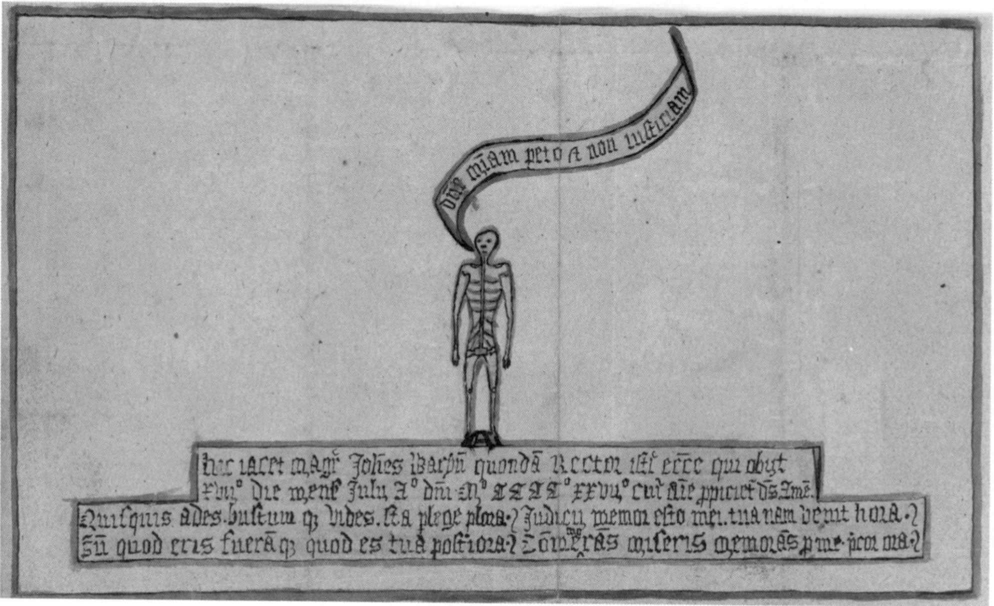

not a lifelike portrait but a conventional image supplied by a workshop. We still possess a few of these portrait brasses, including those of Thomas Awmarle (*c.*1401) at Cardinham (see Figure 51), John Balsam (1410) at Blisland, and John Trembras (1515) at St Michael Penkevil. Some of these brasses, like Aumarle's and Trembras's, display their owners' status as gentlemen by showing their coats of arms. John Waryn of Menheniot (1426), on the other hand, sought to teach passers-by rather than to proclaim his own importance. His brass, no longer extant, followed a fashion popular with some clergy in 15th-century England by depicting himself as a skeleton (see Figure 55). The Latin inscription warned those able to read it, 'I am what you will be, and I was what you are.'[117]

Chapter 4 The Later Middle Ages: The People

Figure 56 Christ's entry into Jerusalem, one of the colourful scenes in the early Tudor Passion window in the church of St Docco and St Kewa at St Kew. Christ is identified by his red robe.

THE PARISH CHURCHES

Everyone in England during the later Middle Ages made a journey on the day of their birth. They were taken from their mother's breast by the midwife and their family, and carried to the parish church to be named and baptised. Like it or not, they joined the Church at birth, and they were expected to support it (and the church of whichever parish they came to live in) for the rest of their lives. For most of them 'the Church' meant not the pope, the bishop, or the diocese, but the parish church. There they attended services, at least occasionally. There they were christened, confessed, married, and buried. They had to help maintain the building, and sometimes they felt a pride in it and a desire to embellish and improve it.

This desire led to the widespread rebuilding or restoration of churches in Cornwall during the later Middle Ages. Some were remodelled during the 14th century. The south transept of St Germans (see Figure 7) and the east end of the chancel of St Ive (see Figure 50) contain examples of fittings in Beer stone from Devon, probably shaped by masons of Exeter Cathedral, and the now-vanished church of Glasney used similar stone. The majority of projects, however, took place in the 15th and early 16th centuries, making this one of the greatest periods of church rebuilding in Cornish history. Rebuilding obliterated most of the fabric of churches that had existed previously, making it hard to recapture what they had been like. More positively, it filled the county with a distinct and often uniform kind of church, which we today regard as typically medieval but which actually dates from the very end of the Middle Ages.

The typical rebuilt church of the 15th and early 16th centuries was made of granite, or 'moorstone' as it was known. This was evidently a fashionable material, gathered or quarried on the moors of the county and probably replacing what had previously been a wider variety of stone from more local sources. Granite is hard and often coarse, making it difficult to carve satisfactorily, so that the mouldings of windows, doors, and piers generally had to be simple. Only wealthy churches like St Mary Magdalene (Launceston) and Truro could afford suitable granite and expert craftsmanship to enable their buildings to be ornately carved (see Figure 78). Finer kinds of stone from inside Cornwall, such as elvan and catacleuse, were sometimes used for decorative features or for tombs. Good examples of these survive as the carved holy-water stoups and probable saint's shrines at St Endellion (see Figure 12) and at St Issey, both apparently the work of the same master craftsman.[118]

The late medieval rebuilding work generally made Cornish churches larger and more striking visually (Figures 38, 75, 78 and 82). Externally towers, usually of three stages with buttresses and battlements, were added or existing towers were enlarged. Porches were provided or extended for reasons to be mentioned presently. Aisles were built alongside many naves: sometimes a single aisle, sometimes one on each side; sometimes they were completely new and sometimes developments of earlier ones. In the most ambitious schemes, as at Bodmin, St Columb Major, and St Endellion, the aisles extended alongside the chancel as well.

The aisles of late medieval churches were wider than those of the 12th and 13th centuries (Figures 57, 75) and often incorporated the north-south transepts of earlier periods. Chancel aisles served as chapels devoted to saints, especially the Virgin Mary. Lady chapels in her honour became popular in religious houses during the 13th century. Launceston Priory had one by 1312 and Bodmin Priory by 1343, and this provision was probably imitated in the larger parish churches during the 14th and 15th centuries. Nave aisles provided further space for images and altars at their east ends, and seats for the congregation further west. By leaving an alley alongside the seats, the aisles could also be used as processional ways.[119]

The energy and resources for church building and decoration came from various sources. Rectors, as we have seen, were responsible for chancels, and this included religious foundations which became rectors and appropriated parish tithes. Exeter Cathedral paid just over £30 to rebuild the chancel of St Merryn in 1422, the cost including masonry, rafters, tiling, and four glazed windows. Gentry might contribute to the general improvement of a church, or build a transept, aisle, or chapel in which they would worship and be buried. Some wealthy Cornishmen with interests in tin mining gave profits from their mines, or even mines themselves, to churches, chapels, or religious houses. The early 16th-century stained-glass windows of St Neot included a picture of a miner, perhaps acknowledging that the glass was partly funded from the mines where such men worked, or from their wages.[120]

Not all churches were so lucky. Parishioners might struggle to maintain their naves, or try to avoid the task. In 1377 the bishop had to order the people of Crantock to contribute to repairing the central tower and, when the tower fell, damaging the nave, another bishop granted an indulgence to help the parishioners, remarking that they were too poor to afford the repairs (see Figure 24). At other times the people of a parish joined in heroic efforts to raise money for ambitious building projects. Such efforts are most fully recorded at Bodmin, whose church was rebuilt between 1469 and 1472 to create the structure that exists today (see Figure 67). The work cost £268, not counting gifts of materials and labour. Some £24 of this came from a levy, agreed by the community, under which certain people paid 1d. or ½d. per week, but most of the money was donated voluntarily by the craft and religious guilds of the town, the congregations of the outlying chapels, and 447 individual men and women, including servants. The sums given ranged from 1d. to 13s. 4d.[121]

Nor did expenses end with building works. Churches had also to be furnished, and much care and money was spent in doing so. During the 13th century it became fashionable to have a larger

Figure 57 Altarnun church, like many late-medieval church interiors, had no wall between nave and chancel. Instead, a wide rood screen separates the nave and aisles from the chancel and chancel aisles, and the nave is filled with benches whose ends are elaborately carved.

opening between the nave and the chancel, framed by a chancel arch, and by the end of the century such openings were coming to be filled with a wooden screen with a 'rood' or crucifix above it, nowadays known as a 'rood screen'. The origin of rood screens in Cornwall is hard to date. Bishop Quinil's statutes of 1287 do not refer to them, nor do the visitations of the Cornish churches belonging to Exeter Cathedral in 1330. This suggests that if they existed at this time they were not obligatory, but they probably became common during the 14th century. Rood screens were panelled up to a height of about four feet and had open windows above, with a door or doors in the middle. Above the windows was a loft or gallery on which stood the rood.[122] The screen formed a conspicuous boundary between the clergy in the chancel and the people in the nave, but it also gave the people a relatively good view of the service – probably better than in the old churches with narrow chancel openings. This visibility is particularly striking at Altarnun (see Figure 57).

The parishioners were responsible for the screen because it stood in the nave and, since it was the principal object that they looked at, they often aspired to make it as splendid as possible. Its woodwork might be elaborately carved and painted, and saints be shown in paintings on its panels or in sculpted images on or near the screen. In 1531, for example, the parishioners of Stratton contracted with two 'carvers', John Dow of Lawhitton and John Parys of North Lew (Devon), to provide a rood screen right across the church, in the manner of the screen at St Kew. Standing upon it were to be figures of Christ, Mary, and John the Evangelist, modelled on those of Liskeard, with windows over Christ, as at Week St Mary. An altar was to be placed at either end of the screen, on the nave side, with statues of St Armel and the Virgin Mary respectively, and two further screens called 'intercloses' were to divide the chancel from the chapels that flanked it, in the style of St Columb Major.[123]

The nave of the church continued to be the laity's area. We have noticed that some of them had (or claimed to have) seats in the nave as early as the 13th century, and by the 15th the ambitions of parishioners to have a well-furnished church extended to installing seating for everyone or to improving the seating that existed already. In 1491 the parishioners of Bodmin commissioned Matthy More, 'carpenter', to fit chairs and seats in four 'renges' or blocks like those of Plympton St Mary (Devon). A pulpit was to be built replicating that of Moretonhampstead (Devon), and the whole work was to take four years and to cost £92, the church providing the timber. Seating usually took the form of benches with backs, whose ends alongside the alleys were often carved. Sometimes the

Figure 58 St Christopher, a popular subject for wall paintings in medieval churches. It was often placed, as it is here in Breage church, on the north wall opposite the church entrance. Some people believed that seeing the painted image of St Christopher would save you from sudden death on that day.

carvings showed the instruments associated with the Crucifixion, such as the lance, nails, and crown of thorns. Alternatively scenes of daily life were portrayed and, by the 16th century, initials and coats of arms became popular, probably commemorating those who sat in those seats or paid for their installation (see Figure 60).[124]

Walls, windows, and floors might also be decorated. It would be hazardous to say that such decoration was universal or always very elaborate, but it took well-developed forms in some places. A tympanum or partition across the upper half of the chancel arch, above the screen and behind the rood, might carry a picture of the Last Judgment. No such picture survives in Cornwall, but a few wall paintings are still visible. One favourite subject was St Christopher carrying the infant Christ, as may be seen at Breage (see Figure 58), St Keverne, and Poughill. Another depicted the 'Sunday Christ', a motif popular in England from about the mid-14th century and often known as 'St Sunday', and there are four Cornish churches still containing these paintings. They show Christ's body wounded by the tools and playthings of people who spent Sunday at work or in sport, and seek to warn people to keep the Lord's Day piously.

Floors might have tiles, especially in churches that were also religious houses and therefore wealthier. These might show symbols of Christ or the Virgin Mary, or coats of arms of bishops or local gentry. Stained-glass windows were also common, reaching their acme at St Neot in the early 16th century, where a complete series was installed showing Christ, saints, the donors of the work, and scenes from the Life of the church's patron saint (see Figure 1). The windows still commemorate not only the gentry who contributed to them individually but the young men, 'sisters', and wives of the parish who did so as groups.[125]

SUNDAY WORSHIP

Public worship in parish churches centred on Sunday mornings, when the priest and clerk would read matins in the early hours of daylight, celebrate mass in the middle of the morning, and read evensong in the afternoon. The chief of these services was the Latin mass, and we can visualise its shape in the 14th and 15th centuries from prayer books and from the ways in which churches were built and furnished. By this period most parish clergy in southern England were using prayer books of the 'Use of Sarum', which contained the forms of the services followed at Salisbury Cathedral. This applied to the material of the service; the way in which it was done was simpler in a parish church than a cathedral, reflecting the single priest and clerk who performed it. The priest said or

Figure 59 Mass being celebrated at an altar by a priest attended by two clergy acting as deacon and subdeacon, with other people watching. For simplicity, no screen is shown between the clergy and the people.

sang most of the mass while the clerk made the responses, and no spoken words were required from anyone else. Indeed the rood screen made the point that the congregation were spectators, not performers, of the worship.[126]

The first part of the mass consisted of prayers and Bible readings (an epistle and a gospel). After the gospel there was an opportunity to preach a sermon, but it is unlikely that most parish clergy did so, although they were told to teach their flocks from time to time the meaning of the Lord's Prayer, Hail Mary, and Apostles' Creed, and (as in Quinil's time) to warn them about sins and urge them to cultivate the virtues and to do works of charity. More usually the priest would come to the screen, or to a separate pulpit, to ask the parishioners to pray for particular causes, or to announce bishops' letters, indulgences, or excommunications. A common practice by the 15th century was to keep a parish 'bead roll' on which people paid to have their names inscribed. This was read by the priest on Sundays, often from a pulpit which may have been used for this purpose more often than for preaching. Several Cornish parishes are recorded possessing bead rolls, and a prayer list survives from Camborne that may have been copied from one.[127]

The second half of the mass centred on recalling Christ's Last Supper and on consecrating a wafer of bread and a small chalice of wine. This part of the service was so holy that the priest muttered the words inaudibly, and the congregation was alerted to the progress of the service by his actions. When the wafer had been consecrated, he held it above his head, and likewise the chalice. At this, the holiest moment of the mass, men were expected to remove their headgear (as they did in the presence of a social superior), and it is likely that people tried to get a glimpse of the wafer and chalice – Christ's real body and blood, as the Church taught – so that they could receive his power and blessing. Windows, nowadays known as hagioscopes or squints, were sometimes cut through the walls of side chapels or transepts to extend the view to those parts. The priest who celebrated mass consumed the wafer and wine by himself, even if there were other clergy present.

The congregation did not normally receive communion. Instead they exchanged a greeting of peace in the form of the pax – a small disk of ivory or metal with a Christian symbol upon it. This was kissed by the priest at the altar after he had consecrated the wafer and chalice, and taken by the clerk around the congregation who kissed it in turn. When mass had finished there was another ceremony. The priest came to the screen door and read in Latin the opening words of the Gospel of John: 'In the beginning was the Word'. The clerk sprinkled the congregation with holy water, and the priest blessed a loaf of bread and distributed it to the people. The loaf was provided by households in turn, and was merely blessed, not consecrated like the wafer. Parishioners received communion in church only at Easter, and then only if they had reached the age of puberty. They came to the screen, probably in order of rank, knelt, and had a consecrated wafer put into their mouths. The consecrated wine was considered too precious to give them, in case it was spilt, so they received a sip of ordinary wine.

Parish worship, then, was different from that of most modern churches. It was not educational. Little attempt was made to teach parishioners about the Bible or Christian behaviour beyond the basic matters mentioned above. Rather worship was medicinal. It offered spiritual benefit, especially at mass when Christ became

Figure 60 Early Tudor carved bench ends from Altarnun. Unusually the upper one includes the name of the carver, Robert Daye.

present, healing your sins and afflictions. The laity were not involved in saying the services, but they were capable of joining in emotionally, just as we do when we watch a concert or a sporting event. Since they were physically shut off from the service, they did not have to copy what the priest did and had some freedom to follow their own inclinations.

Some wealthy people took Latin prayer books to church and read them during the services. Those who could not read or did not own books were recommended to say the three basic prayers in Latin, as in previous centuries. Yet others were young or inattentive, and sometimes complaints were voiced about the disturbances caused by such people. If a church lacked much seating, it was easy for the congregation to stand, form groups, or walk about, as it chose. As benches and pews became common during the 15th and early 16th centuries, however, they restricted people's movements and encouraged them to act in similar ways. This development anticipated the Reformation, when more deliberate attempts were made to make congregations behave in a uniform way by standing, sitting, or kneeling all together.

There could be variety, then, in what the congregation did, even at formal services, and variety, too, in how the church was used at other times. Parish churches were not only places of formal worship led by clergy. In most of them the organised services occupied only a few hours of the week. For the rest of the time the church might only have witnessed people's private devotions. Every parish church contained some images and these were present so that people could venerate them. As well as the rood with its figures, there were statues of the patron saint on the north side of the high altar and the Virgin Mary on the south side. Other statues stood by lesser altars or in prominent positions elsewhere, and saints and religious scenes were painted on walls. Although so many Cornish churches were dedicated to Brittonic saints, most of the images inside them, by the 15th and early 16th centuries, honoured the well-known saints of Catholic Christendom.[128]

SACRED SPACE AND SOCIAL SPACE

Parish churches were built not only to be impressive and beautiful but also to be practical. Their plans reflected the uses to which they were put. A church was not a single space but a series of rooms of greater or lesser holiness. The outermost, the porch, was used for the ceremonies that brought people out of secular life into the arms of Holy Church. The baptism service began here by exorcising the baby to make it capable of entering the church to be christened. Marriages took place in the porch, and so did 'churching', the leading of mothers back into the church by the priest after childbirth. Passing from the porch people entered the nave, often sanctifying themselves with drops of water from a holy-water stoup by the nave door. The nave was holier than the porch. It contained the font near the door, the rood screen at the east end, the wall paintings, and the images mentioned above.

Holier still was the chancel and, in many churches, the chapels that lay on either side of it or in the transepts or elsewhere. The rood screen closed off the chancel, and only special people, or people on special occasions, went through its door. The first group included the priest and his clerk, the male choir maintained in a few large churches, and the patron of the church (if such a person lived locally) with his or her family. The second group consisted of married couples receiving their wedding blessing and adults confessing their sins. Chapels, too, were often private places, reserved for wealthy people or for guild members. Chancels and chapels were also holier because the Church's prayers were offered in them and mass was celebrated. In the view of the Catholic Church, when the priest consecrated the wafer of bread and chalice of wine during mass they became, in substance, the real body and blood of Christ. This called for the consecration to happen in a special area, removed from ordinary people and fit for Christ to manifest himself.

A Cornish church between 1300 and 1500 was a miniature of the Church as a whole. Visually it proclaimed its allegiance to Christ, both on the cross and presiding at Judgment Day, as well as to his mother and the saints. It was a church not only of the living but the dead, or at least the more important dead who were buried beneath its floors or named in its bead roll. It was a mirror of society, with the clergy in the holiest part, the patron or other gentry in privileged places, and the congregation almost certainly arranged in social order, especially after seating was installed. It was a developing, not a static church, which underwent rebuilding and embraced new religious cults. During the later Middle Ages several Cornish churches acquired images or services in honour of the Name of Jesus, St Anne the mother of the Virgin Mary, St Roche the patron of plague victims, St Syth the patroness of servants, keys, and lost objects, and the murdered King Henry VI.[129]

Many images had organisations dedicated to supporting them. These were of three kinds: stores, companies, and guilds. Stores were simply funds in the form of money, sheep, cattle, or bees. The parish church itself had a store, often named after the patron saint, such as the 'store of St Ervan' or 'of St Mawgan', and there were stores belonging to the individual images. William Trenowyth, a peasant farmer of St Cleer in 1400, bequeathed two

PANEL 4

Devotion to Jesus

The Passion of Christ is depicted in a late 15th-century stained glass window in the north-east chapel of the church of St James at St Kew. The story is told in 12 scenes from Jesus entering Jerusalem riding on an ass to his betrayal, death and resurrection (below). Four scenes (right) show how the artist has captured the drama of each episode.

Although we think of the medieval Church as venerating saints, its chief veneration was given to God, especially in the person of Jesus. His image, sitting on a rainbow in judgment, was often painted above the chancel arch in churches. A sculpture of him hanging on the Cross stood on the rood screen, or was suspended above it, in every parish church. Most solemnly of all, when a priest celebrated mass, the bread and wine used in the celebration were believed to become his real body and blood – holier than anything else in the world.

Devotion to Jesus perhaps became even stronger during the 14th and 15th centuries. Chapels were dedicated to him as Christ, Jesus, or the Saviour. In Cornwall these included ones at Padstow and Polruan near Fowey. His name, in the Greek form IHS, was often painted on walls, and special masses of the Name of Jesus, sometimes with musical material, were celebrated in his honour in some churches, especially on Fridays.

FACING PAGE

Top left: The Last Supper of Jesus and his disciples. Jesus, in red, takes bread and prepares to cut it with a knife. Under his arm, wearing green, is St John the Evangelist, shown as younger than the other disciples.

Top right: The Betrayal. Jesus and his disciples are in the Garden of Gethsemane. Judas (in blue) leads soldiers to them and identifies Jesus (in faded red) by kissing him. Peter (in green) tries to resist and draws his sword.

Bottom left: The Trial. The soldiers bring Jesus to Pontius Pilate (sitting on a throne) who reluctantly agrees to his execution, but washes his hands of the matter.

Bottom right: The Flagellation. Jesus is tied to a pillar and flogged by men with whips, before being taken to execution.

sheep to the store of St Mary in his parish church, and one each to the stores of the Holy Cross and St James. A store had one or more wardens to look after the offerings made to its image and to pay for a light in front of it, but the supporters of the store did not necessarily form a society.[130]

A company possessed a stronger social framework, and there were three kinds of these: the young men, the maidens, and the wives. They reflected the fact that people were expected to attend church and contribute to its maintenance once they reached puberty. The young men and maidens were the unmarried in the parish, aged from the early teens up to about the mid-twenties, when most people wed. The wives were the married women or widows. Each company raised money during the year through social events like ale feasts, money collections (notably on Hock Monday and Tuesday, in the second week after Easter), or the keeping of sheep or bees. This money was given to the maintenance of the church, and sometimes to an image or light supported by the members.

Guilds (also known as fraternities) were social groups as well. We have already noticed their first recorded appearance in Cornwall in 1278, and they were very common between the 14th and early 16th centuries. Mentions survive of four guilds in the churches of Liskeard, Poughill, and South Petherwin, five

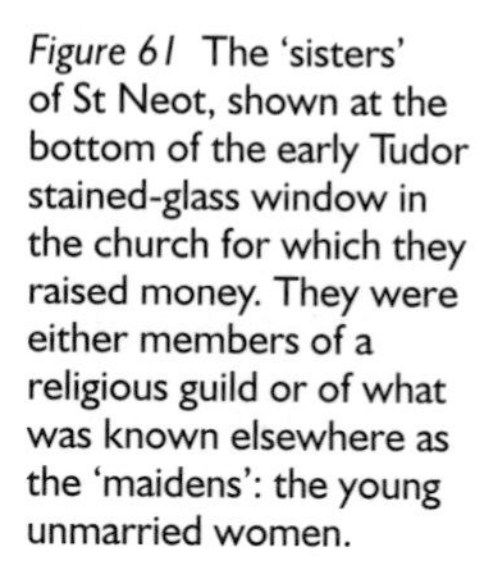
Figure 61 The 'sisters' of St Neot, shown at the bottom of the early Tudor stained-glass window in the church for which they raised money. They were either members of a religious guild or of what was known elsewhere as the 'maidens': the young unmarried women.

at Stratton, eight at St Mary Magdalene (Launceston), and ten at Antony and Camborne. The larger numbers suggest that the smaller ones may sometimes be selections rather than totals. Bodmin, one of the most populous parishes in Cornwall, may have had as many as 29 guilds.

Little is known about their membership. Adult men may have dominated many of them in view of the formation of companies to cater for other social groups. Some guilds, especially in towns, were restricted to particular kinds of people. The minstrels of Launceston, for example, formed a guild by 1440, while Bodmin, about thirty years later, had guilds of cordwainers (i.e. shoemakers), millers, and skinners together with glovers. Guilds like these were both craft guilds, regulating their members' work, and religious guilds, maintaining an image in a church or chapel and paying for prayers for dead members. People in a neighbourhood might also form a guild. In Bodmin there were guilds based in Bore Street, Fore Street, and Pole Street, while the rural chapel of Gwarnick in St Allen had a guild of supporters, doubtless of those who lived near.[131]

The medieval parish church, then, was a church with several focuses, not one. Although the chancel was important, there were also the rood screen with its images; the aisles and chapels for additional masses; the nave for announcements, processions, and baptisms; the porch for services of introduction; and the tower for ringing bells to send messages from the church to the world. These subdivisions reflected the fact that the Catholic Church itself was complex and offered a good deal of choice. True, it demanded obedience to certain doctrines, duties, and modes of behaviour. But it also provided a range of options: various places in which to worship, an array of saints to venerate, different guilds and companies to join, and a huge assortment of good practices to follow and causes to support. We shall now explore some of these options and how the people of Cornwall chose between them.

CHAPELS

By the late Anglo-Saxon period parish churches were supplemented, in England generally and in Cornwall particularly, by chapels in the sense of buildings independent of the parish churches and often located far from them. Some chapels were ancient religious places which failed to gain full parochial status or, perhaps, lost it in early times. These were often dedicated to a unique saint, like many parish churches, and functioned as what was later known as chapels of ease. They served local communities

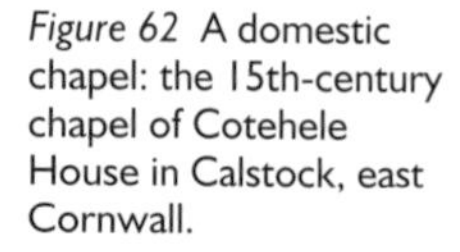
Figure 62 A domestic chapel: the 15th-century chapel of Cotehele House in Calstock, east Cornwall.

who lived at a distance from the parish church, and some of them, as we saw in Chapter 2, were virtually parish churches with full-time chaplains, although they were legally under the control of a neighbouring parish church and its rector or vicar.[132]

After the Norman Conquest evidence survives about other chapels. A few of these were built in or alongside castles like Launceston, Restormel, and Tintagel, and eventually they became common in Cornish manor houses. Others were chapels of ease, 'ease' meaning that they existed for the convenience of people who lived a long way from a parish church, especially in the new towns founded in Cornwall after 1100. Camelford, Grampound, East and West Looe, Launceston, Mitchell, Penzance, and Wadebridge all came to acquire such chapels. A further type of chapel was the cult chapel. Its primary purpose was to maintain the worship of the Trinity, Christ, an angel, or a saint. It did not focus on a family or a neighbourhood like household chapels and chapels of ease, but sought to draw in people from as widely as possible. Chapels of this kind included St Mary in the Park at Liskeard, St Mary Magdalene at Cosawes in St Gluvias, and most famously St Day in Gwennap and St Michael's Mount, which we shall encounter presently.

Chapels in manor houses often formed part of the house, like the chapel at Cotehele which can still be visited (see Figure 62). This was entered from the ground floor and had a small high window inside communicating with the upper storey of the house, so that occupants could watch the service from there. Cult chapels were usually oblong freestanding buildings no higher than a one-storey house, often built of granite (see Figure 64). Inside they were divided by a screen, separating the outer 'antechapel' for the laity from the inner part with the altar, where services took place. Chapels of ease tended to be larger and some grew almost to the size of parish churches, with aisles, transepts, or towers. St Minver parish had two such chapels: St Enodoc and the chapel of St Michael at Porthilly, the modern Rock (see Figure 63).

No complete list of medieval chapels in Cornwall has yet been made, but the number was certainly large. Charles Henderson, who made a careful count of those in the 95 parishes of the western half of the county, found evidence of 188, about twice as many as there were parish churches. This would suggest a Cornish total of at least 350 chapels, and Canon J. H. Adams, a lifelong student of chapels, suggested that there may have been as many as 650–700. Adams's estimate is supported by research on chapels in Devon. A survey of its 409 parishes has discovered about 1,300 chapels, over three times as many as the parish churches, and this does not include all the evidence supplied by place names or archaeological remains which might well add to the total.[133]

Chapels, then, were numerous and ubiquitous features of the Cornish scene, urban and rural, inland and maritime, highland and lowland. The larger towns had several: Bodmin at least eight and Launceston about the same number. Padstow could boast about nine. Smaller places, like those already mentioned, acquired one or two. Nor were chapels built only in centres of population. Many were sited in isolated spots to which access was difficult, such as small

Figure 63 A chapel of ease: St Michael's chapel at Porthilly (near Rock) in St Minver parish, imitating a parish church with its chancel, nave, transepts, south chapel, and tower.

Figure 64 A cult chapel in a remote location. The well chapel in St Clether parish, probably dedicated to the saint and standing half a mile from the parish church.

islands. A voyager along the south coasts of Cornwall would have passed chapels on Looe Island, St Michael's Mount, St Clement's Island by Mousehole, and at least five on the Isles of Scilly. There were promontory chapels at St Ives, Padstow, and Polruan, possibly acting as marks for ships at sea. Some chapels stood on inland hills, such as Carn Brea, Roche rock, Michaelstow Beacon, and Rough Tor, while others were hidden from view in woodland like the parks of Liskeard and Restormel, or in secluded valleys such as St Mary Vale in Cardinham and St Illick in St Endellion. The effect of such buildings, supplemented by crosses and wells, was to make the landscape yet more Christian in nature.[134]

The foundation and running of chapels varied according to type. Nobility and gentry provided and maintained them in their houses. Groups of local people built and cared for chapels of ease, and individual devotees or groups were responsible for cult chapels. One such group occurs in relation to the ancient chapel at Chapel Amble in the parish of St Kew, where Bishop Stafford licensed Nicholas and Emmot Helygan, a neighbouring gentleman and his wife, their two children, and 11 other named people, husbands and wives, to worship in 1405. In Camborne where there were several outlying chapels – St Anne at Baripper, St Derwa at Menadarva, St Ia at Troon, St James at Treslothan, St Mary in the parish churchyard, and 'Gwynwala' (perhaps at Kehelland) – each one was run by a guild which contributed money to the parish church, money that appears in the accounts of the churchwardens. The Camborne accounts do not mention any guild officers, but these appear in another instance, the chapel of St Weras at Burlawn Eglos in St Breock. Here two 'store wardens' are mentioned, who would have been in charge of handling income and expenditure, and two 'ale wardens', who evidently looked after fund-raising.[135]

WELLS AND OTHER LANDSCAPE FEATURES

The christianisation of the landscape by churches and chapels was reinforced by other smaller structures. Holy wells (a term used here to encompass both natural springs and man-made wells) were common throughout England as well as in Cornwall, although it is difficult to compile lists and estimate numbers in the Middle Ages. The first recorded Cornish well with sacred associations is the one in the First Life of St Samson, which is said to have flowed in a cave in response to his prayer. Several more are described in saints' Lives or documentary sources before the Reformation, and others in antiquarian works on Cornish history from the 17th and 18th centuries. A great many wells regarded as holy today, however, are recorded as such only in the 19th century on the basis of local folklore or conjecture. The detailed mapping of Cornwall by the Ordnance Survey may have been one factor in establishing their reputation as ancient sites.[136]

A holy well might lie by a parish church (Whitstone), by an outlying chapel (Gwinear), by a road (St Keyne), or in a remote place such as a cave (Holywell in Cubert). Some were defined with stonework in the form of a small well house covering the spring, with a low door for visitors to reach the water. Others had larger structures, including seats where people could sit to wash themselves, as at St Constantine in St Merryn parish. The biggest surviving buildings, almost of chapel size, are those of St Cleer and Dupath, the latter in Callington parish (see Figure 95). A further development was the provision of a chapel beside the well. This was the case at St Clether (Figures 64–5), St Columb Major, Gwinear, St Issey, Madron (see Figure 8), Merther, Padstow, and Chapel Euny in Sancreed parish.

Figure 65 The well chapel at St Clether (left). Water runs through the building beneath the altar, and there is also access to the water from outside (right).

Figure 66 A fine early-medieval Cornish wheel-headed cross, now standing outside Cardinham church.

Some wells were associated with Cornish saints, who were believed to have lived at the well or to have been martyred there before their bodies were buried on the site of the parish church. One or two wells were dedicated to international cult figures: Jesus in St Minver and apparently Our Lady at Lady Nant Well in Colan. Little is recorded about how Cornish holy wells were used in the Middle Ages, or by whom, but observers writing after the Reformation tell us that some of them were visited by individuals or by groups of parishioners on certain days of the Church year. People went to Lady Nant Well on Palm Sunday, Madron on Corpus Christi Day, and Chapel Euny (Sancreed) on New Year's Eve.[137]

Healing powers were ascribed to many wells. St Cadoc's was believed to cure intestinal worms as early as the 11th century, and was still so reputed in 1478. Altarnun's was remembered in about 1600 as having been used to give therapeutic treatment to the insane. In the 18th century St Levan's well in St Levan was thought to be wholesome for the eyes and for toothache. The other attraction of Cornish wells, at least in late Tudor, Stuart, and Hanoverian times, was for divination. The people of Colan threw their palm crosses into Lady Nant well on Palm Sunday and drew conclusions from whether these floated or sank. At Gulval you could learn whether those you loved were ill or well by pronouncing their names and watching how the water bubbled up.[138]

Wells do not exhaust the list of religious objects in the landscape. Standing crosses, or pillars inscribed with crosses, were common (see Figure 66). Their principal function in historic times was to mark roads and crossroads, sometimes those leading to parish churches or holy wells, and to indicate the boundaries of glebes or parishes. A saint's chair is mentioned at Germoe, where the structure still remains in the form of a small stone arcade containing three seats (see Figure 9). There was another chair at St Mawes and a third at St Michael's Mount, where the archangel was believed to have sat in a lofty part of the rock.[139]

Trees were associated with some saints and their wells. One, alleged to have grown on the site of the martyrdom of St Gwinear, probably at Roseworthy in Gwinear, is mentioned in a Life of the saint written in about 1300. Others at the church of St Breward and by the chapel of St Illick in St Endellion were recorded by the Cornish writer Nicholas Roscarrock as having existed in the second half of the 16th century. We hear of paths associated with saints in the parishes of St Endellion and St Levan, ditches in Padstow, cliffs at St Agnes, a hill at Breage, and a rock at Camborne. In this way the aetiology of parishes – the explanation of how their features originated – came to be closely linked with the cults of local saints.[140]

THE RELIGION OF THE COMMUNITY

The Church involved people as communities and as individuals. All adults in a parish had the duty of attending church, keeping the Church's laws, and supporting the clergyman with tithes and offerings. Besides the nave of the church, they had to maintain the furnishings of the whole building and the books, ornaments, and materials needed for services. Bishop Quinil's statutes of 1287 laid down that parish churches should have a store or fund for their maintenance, administered by wardens who were to render an account of their stewardship once a year before the clergy and five or six of the parishioners. The account was to be recorded in writing and submitted to the archdeacon during his visitation. During the 13th, 14th, and 15th centuries most English parishes acquired churchwardens to carry out this duty. There were normally two wardens, chosen to serve for a year, sometimes according to a rota to ensure that all major householders took their turn. Women, if widows, might therefore hold the office.[141]

Although the statutes talk of written accounts, records of this kind do not survive in England until the late 14th century. The oldest in Cornwall are some accounts of St Mary Magdalene (Launceston), kept as part of the borough records after 1461, and an account book relating to the rebuilding of Bodmin parish church in 1469–72. Accounts survive from eight other Cornish churches before 1559. They are illuminating about how money was raised and what it was spent on. Parish income came chiefly from voluntary contributions: freewill offerings, fees for seats and for burials inside the church, sales of candles, and convivial

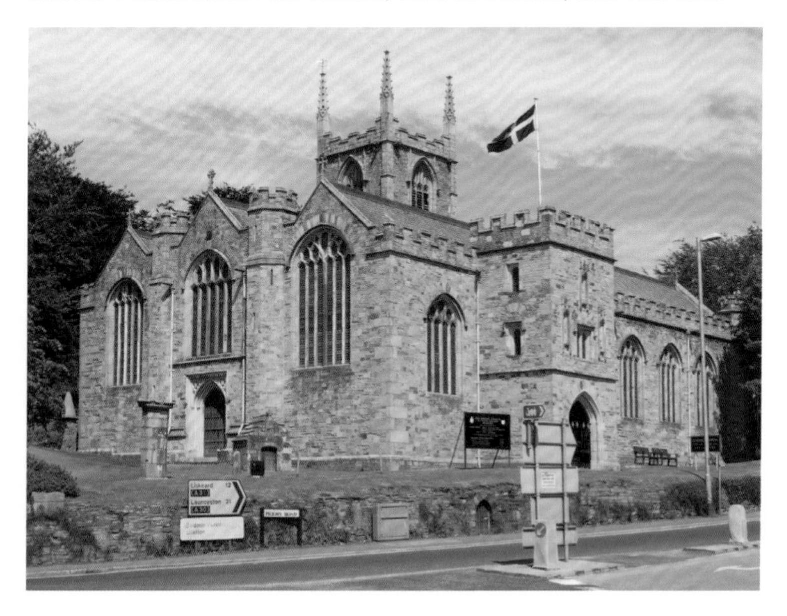

Figure 67 Bodmin parish church, the largest in Cornwall. It was built with great effort by the townspeople and their guilds, perhaps in a determination to rival the nearby priory whose power over the town was irksome to local people.

feasts known as church ales. Some parishes, by the later Middle Ages, built a church house close to the church, the best remaining example of which is at Poundstock (see Figure 68). This was used for the church's social occasions or for private functions.[142]

Church expenditure included the wages of the parish clerk and sometimes those of a sexton, the maintenance of the nave and church furnishings, and the materials used in services. By the early 16th century some larger and wealthier churches in England were financing the purchase of an organ, the payment of a director of music, and the expenses of a small choir of men and boys. These resources would be used to stage a regular mass or antiphon with polyphonic music in honour of Jesus or of Our Lady, copying what was done in the colleges and larger monasteries. The borough of Bodmin paid several pounds in 1529–30 to bring 'organs' from London by sea to Fowey, by riverboat to Lostwithiel, and thence by land, evidently for use in the parish church. A further sum was spent on an organ case, and a donor gave two books of 'pricksong' or polyphony.[143]

The communal life of a parish was framed by the calendar as well as by the upkeep of the church. Religious observances changed as the seasons passed, and everyone was expected to follow these changes. The Church year, then as now, included a cycle of events based on the life of Christ and, to a greater extent than today, feast days of saints. Advent, the four weeks before Christmas, was a time of penitence and preparation; indeed the Church authorities tried to encourage people to treat it as a Lent in terms of fasting and going to confession. Christmas Day itself was a great religious festival,

Figure 68 The late medieval church house at Poundstock, one of the best surviving examples of these popular buildings, managed by the church and used for fund-raising and social events.

Figure 69 Ash Wednesday marked the beginning of Lent. In church, the priest marked the foreheads of the people with ashes as a reminder of mortality and a call to repentance.

although it had little to distinguish it in church apart from the celebration of a midnight mass to mark the birth of the Christ child. Its festivities chiefly took place at home, especially among the wealthy.[144]

Lent, beginning in February or March, had a wider impact. On its opening day, Ash Wednesday, people came to church to be marked on the forehead with ashes (see Figure 69). During the days that followed all adults were required to go to church for confession. In 1429 there were set times for the people of Lelant to attend for this purpose, and similar arrangements are likely elsewhere. During Lent, which lasted six weeks, adults had to abstain from eating meat and dairy products. Palm Sunday, the Sunday before Easter, was the first of seven spring and summer days on which parish processions were held, in this case round the outside of the church. The following 'Holy Week', the last week of Lent, included penitential observances culminating on Good Friday when bells were not rung, mass was not celebrated, and people took part in 'creeping to the cross' – literally dragging themselves on their bellies across the church floor from the porch to the rood screen.[145]

Easter Day was a communal festival, and adults received their annual holy communion on that day or the day before. Fasting stopped and diets changed again. There were more parish processions on St Mark's Day (25 April), the Monday, Tuesday, and Wednesday of Rogation Week (the sixth week after Easter), Ascension Day (the Thursday of the same week), and Corpus Christi (the second Thursday after Pentecost). Meanwhile Pentecost or Whit Sunday (the seventh Sunday after Easter) formed the third great festival of the year, along with Christmas and Easter, commemorating the coming of the Holy Spirit to Christ's apostles and the foundation of the Christian Church.[146]

Every month had its saints' days, some of which were observed as popular festivals. Such days might include the feast day of the

In die ascensionis.

Figure 70 A diagram of the procession for Ascension Day, the Thursday of Rogation week. First goes the lion banner, then two cross banners, then the dragon. This symbolised the victory of Christ over evil (earlier in the week the dragon led the procession). Next comes the holy sacrament of communion carried in a shrine by two clergy, attended by two others holding thuribles. The 'doughnuts' are the heads of the clergy; behind them would have come the parishioners.

church's patron saint, a day in the summer (such as St John Baptist, 24 June, or St Thomas Becket, 7 July) when a parish revel was held, and days with special customs of their own. On St Clement's Day (23 November) and St Katharine's Day (25 November) children (particularly boys) dressed as priests and women, and toured the parish singing, dancing, and asking for food or money. Later a boy bishop was chosen to lead the church services on St Nicholas's Day (6 December) and Holy Innocents' Day (28 December), and this was followed by similar activities, centred again on boys.

The parish processions call for special consideration, especially those of Rogation Week (see Figure 70). During this week clergy and people travelled through the parish to its borders and sometimes met other processions by arrangement. With the procession went the church relics, banners, a cross, and a dragon. The parishioners of Perranzabuloe carried round the relics of St Piran by 1331 and did so up to the Reformation. Processions with the relics of St Buryan are mentioned in 1478, although in this case no calendar date is mentioned and the journeys apparently extended beyond the parish. The parishioners of St Hilary visited St Michael's Mount on one of the Rogation days from the 1460s onwards. Once they went with the people of Perranuthnoe, and the clergy of the Mount routinely provided refreshments for those who carried the relics and banners.[147]

Further accounts of processions come from Nicholas Roscarrock, writing after the Reformation but recalling what was done before that time. One of his anecdotes concerns the chapel of St Nectan in Newlyn East, a chapel sited on the parish boundary and used as a rendezvous by four local parishes in Rogation week. This chapel, Roscarrock tells us,

> had a yard belonging unto it in which there were four stones on a little mount or hill at the north-west corner, where the crosses and relics of St Piran, St Crantock, St Cuthbert, [and] St Newlyn were wont to be placed in the Rogation week, at which time they used to meet there and had a sermon made to the people.

In other words, the parishioners of four parishes – Crantock, Cubert, Newlyn East, and Perranzabuloe – used to journey to the chapel at Rogationtide with their crosses and relics. From one point of view we might interpret such journeys as expressions of parochial independence, promoting solidarity and the maintenance of the borders. When more than one church was involved they may have signified the opposite: the hallowing of links between communities through prayer and fellowship.[148]

THE RELIGION OF THE INDIVIDUAL

The chief events of everybody's life were blessed and validated by the Church. Birth was immediately followed by baptism, and baptism by confirmation if a bishop (usually the suffragan) came around for the purpose. At puberty adolescents were likely to make their first Lenten confessions and receive their first Easter communion. There appears to have been no special rite of passage for this; they simply joined in what the adults did. Thereafter they were expected to attend church, at least occasionally, and to pay tithes and offerings. When people were gravely ill or dying, the parish priest came to them, heard their confessions, anointed them with holy oil, and gave them communion (see Figure 52). Death was followed by a funeral at the parish church, usually on the following day, and the dead were buried in their parish churchyard. In 1387 the wife of a peasant farmer, John Keych of St Ive, claimed to have bestowed over £5 on his burial and related hospitality. The rich, as their wills show, planned to spend much larger sums.[149]

For many people these rites and duties were sufficient. Others, with greater piety, embraced their religion with more zeal. They might ask a priest to bless a new house or new well, and might decorate the house with religious art in the form of statuettes, paintings, or (after the late 15th century) printed engravings or texts. If wealthy they might have rosaries for saying prayers (see Figure 96), rings or seals depicting Christ or the saints, or religious books. Most such books were prayer books, notably the short Latin versions of the daily services known as the 'hours of the Virgin Mary' contained in the 'primer' or 'book of hours'. One book of this kind survives that appears to have belonged to a lay owner in Cornwall: a book of hours containing a reference to the dedication festival of Fowey parish church and notes of the births of seven children between 1512 and 1523.[150]

In or outside the house there were numerous other religious practices with which individuals might choose to involve themselves, or not. These included prayers, pilgrimages, the support of religious houses, donations to roads and bridges, and charity to the poor. Even crusading still had its well-wishers. The Order of St John at Trebeigh raised over £18 per annum in Cornwall in 1338 for their activities in the Mediterranean, and went on gathering money for this purpose until 1536. Many good causes were backed by indulgences (see Figure 71). Those who supported them with prayers, work, or money were offered remissions of penance, measured in days or years. Indulgences did not forgive people's sins, which could only be done by a priest after confession, but they replaced the penances due for sins. Bishops could issue indulgences worth 40 days of penance (a 'lent'), while the pope could grant multiple lents and whole years of penance, or remit all penance completely (a 'plenary indulgence'). The latter was originally given only to those undertaking crusades or pilgrimages to Rome or Jerusalem, but by the 14th century it could be obtained from the papal administration for a modest fee on condition that it was used only once, generally on the deathbed.[151]

People in Cornwall would have had the opportunity to gain a wide variety of other indulgences. Some could be had in return for prayers or church visits, without involving money. Others required monetary donations, but an amount was never specified and it was left to people's consciences and their confessors to decide if they had given enough. When Exeter Cathedral was rebuilt in the 14th century, letters were sent to churches throughout the diocese each year, offering an indulgence to contributors. Many lesser causes gained indulgences; Bishop Lacy (1420–55), for example, granted them to Padstow parish church, the chapel of St Winnols in St Germans parish, the image of St Mary Magdalene in Creed church, the guild of minstrels in Launceston, the leper hospital of Helston, a road near Liskeard, Lostwithiel bridge, Marazion

Figure 71 The indulgence of the church of St Michael Penkevil. In 1335 nine bishops who were visiting the papal court, then based at Avignon in France, were each persuaded to grant 40 days of indulgence to the church.

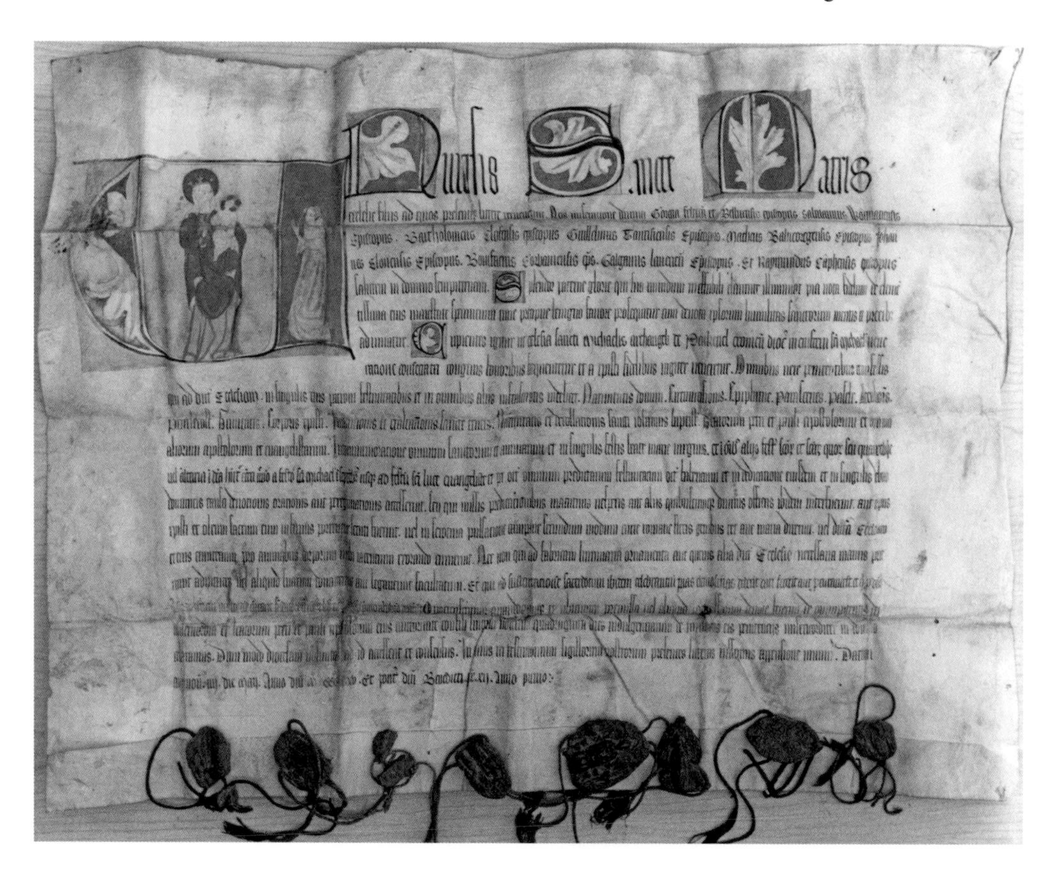

causeway, and the new quay at Newquay. In the end there were so many indulgences in circulation that they may not have had the impact hoped for by their sponsors.[152]

As has been stated, describing how institutions work implies that they work correctly. The Church in the Middle Ages did not always function properly. We have only to read the writings of Langland, Chaucer, and the Lollards in the 14th and 15th centuries to hear allegations that the clergy were ignorant or negligent and the laity slack in their religious duties. These allegations are themselves oversimplified, but they warn us against believing that the Middle Ages was simply an age of faith. There are no records of the crimes that came before the Church courts of Exeter diocese before the 16th century, but the 'significations of excommunication' survive which the bishop sent to the king about the most obstinate offenders. These were people who had refused to submit to the courts, had been excommunicated, and yet remained defiant. The king was asked to tell the sheriff to arrest and hold them until they obeyed the Church.

The offences committed by such people in Cornwall included fornication, slander, perjury and breach of contract, the misadministration of wills, failure to pay tithes or other dues, assaulting a rector, shedding blood in a church, and (in one case) pretending to be a priest. And besides those who offended, there must have been many whose religious observances were slack or intermittent. No census of church attendance exists in the periods with which this volume deals, and the surviving evidence tell us more about the devout and committed than about those who were not.[153]

PILGRIMAGE

Pilgrimage offered another array of choices. The majority of journeys to holy places were local ones, because such journeys best suited everyday life. Each religious house, parish church, chapel, and some wells had one or more festivals during the year relating to the patron saint, the dedication of the building by a bishop, or the images or altars inside. On these days visitors from the neighbourhood were likely to come to hear mass, receive the benefit of an indulgence, and take part in social festivities. Beyond this certain religious sites had a greater reputation for sanctity, embodied in relics of saints, holy images, or water. They attracted more people, sometimes from further afield.[154]

Several of the Cornish religious houses owned relics of saints, including Bodmin, St Carroc, St Germans, Launceston, St Michael's Mount, and Minster. The Mount's relics, about which we know

Figure 72 St James the Great dressed as a pilgrim, from Golant church. He has the pilgrim's traditional equipment: a broad-brimmed hat and a staff for support and protection.

most, included some milk of the Virgin Mary, a portion of her girdle, stones from the Holy Sepulchre, and bones of SS Agapitus, 'Apolina', Felix, and Mansuetus. Some of the parish churches and chapels, like Fowey, Illogan, and St Ives, claimed to have the bodies of the saints after whom they were named. Others asserted that they possessed relics of Christ, Mary, or other well-known saints, like the fragments of Christ's cross held at Grade and St Buryan. The most popular of such relics in Cornwall by the later Middle Ages were apparently those attributed to St Piran at Perranzabuloe. These included a shrine containing the saint's bones and a reliquary enclosing his head; Sir John Arundell of Lanherne bequeathed 40s. to renovate the reliquary in 1433.[155]

No one in Cornwall was canonised as a saint between the Norman Conquest and the Reformation, but one cult sprang up around a human body after the death of Richard Bovyle, rector of Whitstone, in the early spring of 1359. Local opinion seems to have been divided as to whether he was murdered or committed suicide, but his body was treated with little respect and buried in the churchyard or in unconsecrated ground. Shortly afterwards pilgrims began to frequent the burial place and miracles were claimed. The rector was reburied in the parish church, and pilgrims continued to visit his grave for the next two and a half years. The bishop ordered a report on the miracles, which stated that ten people had been cured at the rector's grave. One had been deranged, three blind, and six crippled. They had come from north Cornwall, north Devon, and in one case Plympton in south-west Devon. Five were women, three men, and one a child. None was of gentry rank or a cleric, and they give the impression of being, at best, burgesses, yeomen farmers, and craftsmen, or else inferior folk. One man is described as being a smith. Nothing else is heard of the cult and it may have withered away, since the bishop took an unsympathetic view of it.[156]

The two chief places of pilgrimage in medieval Cornwall were the chapel of the Holy Trinity at St Day in Gwennap, and the priory (later the chapel) of St Michael's Mount. The chapel of St Day is first mentioned in 1269 and contained an image of the Trinity. It received bequests in many Cornish wills and the 16th-century geographer John Norden wrote in about 1604 that 'men and women came in times past from far in pilgrimage' to go there. Some of its popularity, perhaps, came from the fact that it lay on the main route to the Mount, so that both places could be visited on a single journey. The Mount's popularity was underpinned by a document, probably fabricated in the 13th century, which alleged that pilgrims going there would be granted remission of one third of all their penance. After about 1400 it also claimed to be one

Figure 73 A bench end from St Winnow church, showing a Cornish ship at sea, blown by the wind. Small ships of this kind often set out from Cornwall carrying pilgrims to Compostella.

of only three places on earth where the Archangel Michael had appeared to living people.[157]

The Mount had a strong appeal to the Cornish in the 15th and early 16th centuries, and most surviving wills from the county made a small donation to it. Other pilgrims came to it from outside Cornwall, from as far away as London and East Anglia, and some of their names are recorded. The receipts at the shrine ranged from £17 per annum to as much as £44 in the late 15th and early 16th centuries. But not all Cornish pilgrims stayed in Cornwall. We hear of people going to Canterbury to venerate St Thomas Becket and to Windsor to the tomb of King Henry VI. Further afield there were the three great international shrines of St James at Compostella, the apostles Peter and Paul at Rome, and Jesus himself at Jerusalem. These involved longer journeys, higher expenditure, and greater dangers.

Compostella was the nearest of the three. The passage by sea was not too arduous, and numerous licences were granted for Cornish ships to carry pilgrims there – pilgrims, no doubt, from England as well as from Cornwall. In 1434, for example, seven boats from Falmouth, Fowey, Landulph, St Michael's Mount, Penzance, and Saltash were allowed to take passengers on the journey in groups of 25 to 60. The variety of ports shows that, contrary to modern belief, there was no 'pilgrim's way' through Cornwall to a single point of departure. In any case pilgrims used ordinary roads, on which they were a small part of the traffic. An occasional Cornish pilgrim can be traced as far as Rome, and one or two may even have reached Jerusalem. In 1368 John Dabernon, a wealthy gentleman of Calstock, left the large sum of £26 13s. 4d. in his will for someone else to go there on his behalf.[158]

EDUCATION, LITERACY, AND LITERATURE

Christians are a 'people of the book', and medieval Christianity (for all its visual imagery) made extensive use of education, literacy, and literature. Clergy and parish clerks had to be able to read and sing Latin, and preferably to understand what it meant. Schools came into existence to teach boys, some of whom became clergy while others remained as laity. Wealthy lay people like the gentry, the merchant class, and eventually the prosperous yeomen farmers of the countryside valued school education. It gave them the skills to keep accounts, send letters, and read books: prayer books, practical treatises, and recreational literature.

By modern standards, medieval schooling was limited in two ways. It was largely confined to boys and it was not generally free.

Figure 74 English in Cornwall: one of the inscriptions from the Passion window of St Kew church. 'Here a washys hys dycyplys' ('Here he [Jesus] washes his disciples' [feet]').

Girls from wealthier families also learnt to read, but this generally happened at home and to a more limited extent. Their knowledge of Latin was usually confined to recognising and saying the words of Latin prayer books rather than fully understanding them, and they were more fluent in reading French or English. Most boys who went to school probably started at around the age of seven. They began by learning to read the Latin alphabet, pronounce Latin words, and sing them to plainsong. This might be done in an elementary school or in the junior part of a grammar school. The 15th-century Cornish play *Bewnans Meriasek*, written for (perhaps in) the parish of Camborne, depicts a class of children learning the alphabet, suggesting that such education was familiar even in the Cornish-speaking area of the county.

Boys able to progress from reading and song learnt grammar: the study of how to read, understand, write, and speak Latin. This study usually took place in grammar schools, which existed in most English towns by the later Middle Ages, but little is recorded about them in Cornwall. Launceston appears to have had such a school by the mid-14th century, Bodmin by about 1470, and Penryn and Saltash by the 1540s. After about 1440 wealthy people endowed grammar schools to provide free schooling in England, but Cornwall lagged behind in this respect until Thomasine Percival, the Cornish widow of a lord mayor of London, founded one at Week St Mary in 1506–8 (see Figure 90).[159]

Words were carved on stones or artefacts in Roman Britain, and lay people are recorded reading books in England as early as Anglo-Saxon times. By the end of the 13th century, it was becoming fashionable for the wealthy to own prayer books such as psalters and books of hours (see Figure 76) and their tombs in churches were being provided with inscriptions. At first most books and inscriptions connected with churches were in Latin, which was felt to convey the dignity and orthodoxy proper for such places. Latin was used as late as the early Tudor period for the captions in the windows of St Neot: *Hic Dominus fecit Evam de Adam* ('Here the Lord made Eve from Adam').

Only gradually did some inscriptions use languages that would reach out to non-Latin readers. A few tombs were inscribed in French during the 13th and 14th centuries, like that of Clarice of Bolleit at St Buryan. English made its first recorded appearance in a Cornish church on the monumental brass of Nicholas Aysshton in Callington church in 1465. By 1500 or thereabouts it was possible for those who made the Passion window at St Kew to tell the story of the Passion in English dialect (see Figure 74). 'Here owr Lord rydeth ynto Jherusalem.' 'Here a [i.e. he] prayyth to the Fader.' 'Here [he] ys ybrot byfore Pilat.'[160]

Latin writings by medieval Cornishmen survive on a range of topics. We have already encountered scholars who wrote on logic, theology, and visions, as well as producing poetry. Such writing generally took place outside the county, however, and far fewer literary works can be shown to have originated locally, chiefly Lives of saints like the 11th- and 12th-century Lives of St Petroc, probably written at Bodmin. A Life of St Piran was written at Perranzabuloe or at its mother church, Exeter Cathedral, and a lost Life of Nonn of Altarnun is mentioned in 1281. In 1330 Bishop Grandisson complained about the lack of knowledge of the county's saints and ordered that such written Lives as survived should be copied for posterity. Whether or not because of this command, we hear of some more works of this kind later on. A Life of Paternus was written or copied at North Petherwin in 1510–11 and, when the Tudor historian John Leland toured Cornwall in 1542, he found and made notes from Lives of Breage and Ia, notes that imply the existence of Lives of Gwinear and of Elwen, the saint of a chapel in Sithney parish.[161]

The wide use of French in England for speaking, reading, and writing from the mid-12th century onwards also affected Cornwall. This was particularly so in the writing of documents, including letters, deeds, and financial accounts, and the archives of the Arundell family of Lanherne contain such documents until as late as 1409. Many larger works of literature or instruction were written in England in French up to the end of the 14th century, and members of the Cornish gentry and higher clergy are likely to have read them. Our chief piece of evidence on the subject is a list of six books bequeathed by Sir Ranulph Blanchminster of Week St Mary in 1348 to his two daughters and another woman.

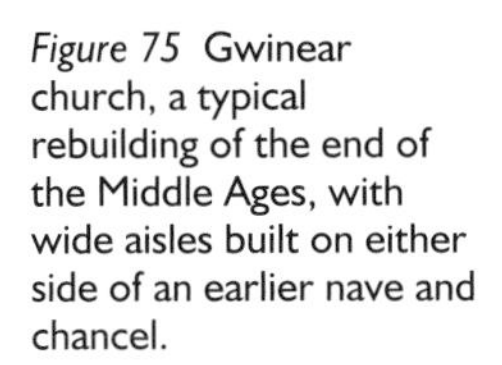
Figure 75 Gwinear church, a typical rebuilding of the end of the Middle Ages, with wide aisles built on either side of an earlier nave and chancel.

Two were secular works: *Brut* (a chronicle history of Britain) and a volume of romances. Four were religious texts: a psalter, a book of Sunday gospels, the *Apocalypse* (a version of the Biblical 'Book of Revelation'), and Peter of Peckham's theological handbook *Lumiere as Lais* ('a light for lay people'). All six books could have been written in French, although Latin is an equal possibility for the psalter and gospels, and they are typical of the writings owned and read by wealthy men and women of that period.[162]

Meanwhile the reading and writing of English had never entirely stopped in England, and after about the time of the Black Death in 1348–9 it began to overtake French in terms of numbers of works produced, the copies made of them, and the people who read them. Two Cornishmen played leading parts in this process. One, John Bryan (more usually known as John Cornwall), was a foremost teacher of Latin in Oxford until his death in 1349. He was credited with abandoning a custom by which boys were taught Latin in French and with speeding up the pace at which they learnt by teaching them in English. This judgment is probably an exaggeration, since some medieval schoolmasters are likely to have taught Latin in English long before Cornwall, but Cornwall certainly composed a grammatical treatise in Latin containing material in English, the first of its kind to survive since the Norman Conquest.[163]

Figure 76 A mother (St Anne) teaching her daughter (the Virgin Mary) to read a prayer book. Women of the wealthy classes were literate by the later Middle Ages, and read religious works and works of fiction.

The other outstanding Cornish contributor to the development of English was John Trevisa, born in about 1340 probably in the parish of St Enoder. Trevisa studied arts and theology at Oxford, entered the Church, and died in 1402 as vicar of Berkeley (Gloucs.). Thomas, Lord Berkeley, the local magnate, was interested in reading the standard Latin handbooks of the day, and commissioned Trevisa and other writers to turn them into English for his convenience. Trevisa translated the chief history of the world then read in England, the *Polychronicon* by Ranulf Higden, and one of the major medieval encyclopaedias, *On the Properties of Things* by Bartholomew the Englishman. He took the English language seriously and wrote a treatise advocating its use for translations, even of religious works. He was also proud of being Cornish. It was he who attributed to his fellow countryman, John Cornwall, the enhanced use of English in schools, and he intervened three times in the *Polychronicon* to correct or add information about his native county. His translations circulated widely, first in manuscript copies and later in printed editions.[164]

The Cornish language went on being spoken during the later Middle Ages west of a line running from Padstow through Wadebridge and Bodmin to Fowey. Stories and legends in the language probably circulated orally; the extent to which it was used for writing is not clear. There are no private letters or financial

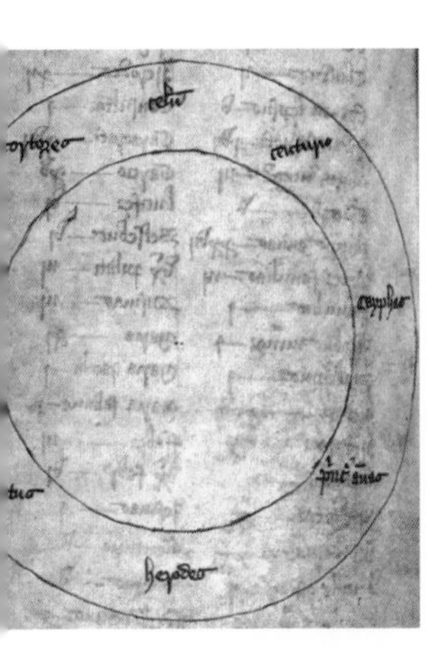

Figure 77 The staging plan of *The Passion of Christ*. Clockwise from the top, are the positions for (in translation) Heaven, the Centurion, Cayphas, Prince Annas, Herod, Pilate, the Doctors (of the Law), and the Torturers.

records in Cornish, although it is not impossible that such things were written. What exists is chiefly religious in nature and dates from about the 15th century. It includes *Pascon agan Arluth* (a poem on the Passion of Christ), five religious plays, and the so-called 'Charter Endorsement' – speeches about a marriage, perhaps from another such play. Further religious literature survives from the following century in the form of some homilies, and there was once a Life of St Columb (no longer extant) that was reported to Nicholas Roscarrock round about 1600.[165]

Three of the extant plays form a trilogy based on the Bible: *The Creation of the World*, *The Passion of Christ*, and *The Resurrection of Christ*. The other two recount the Lives of saints: *Bewnans* [i.e. *The Life of*] *Meriasek* on the patron saint of Camborne, and the recently discovered *Bewnans Ke* on the patron saint of Kea. Calling these works religious plays is insufficient, however, since they include legendary material, such as King Arthur in *Bewnans Ke*, and vignettes of secular life like the school scene in *Bewnans Meriasek*. The trilogy contains numerous references to places in Cornwall, especially in and around Penryn. This has led to the suggestion that it was composed by one or more of the clergy of Glasney College. The college owned the church of Kea and three of its provosts between 1476 and 1507 were, at one time, rectors of Camborne, so a link is possible between the college and all five plays, although firm evidence on the point is elusive. There were other clergy in western Cornwall, and possibly even lay people, capable of writing such works.[166]

People in Cornwall, then, used three or four oral and written languages at the same time during the later Middle Ages. What language they used might change with their situation or purpose. Many men and women spoke Cornish, English, or both, and some of these could write in English, a few in both. There were also a small number who knew a third language, Latin or French, or even four like Ralph Tremur. Far from being peripheral and primitive, Cornwall had a rich linguistic and literary culture that mingled its own traditions with those of the wider world.[167]

Chapter 5 The Reformation

Figure 78 The porch of St Mary Magdalene, Launceston, a splendid town church of the early 16th century. Originally only a chapel, by this time it had become the favoured church of the townspeople and was magnificently rebuilt in carved and decorated granite.

THE EARLY 16TH CENTURY

At the beginning of the 16th century, in 1501, the Church in Cornwall was still the same in major respects as it had been for the last 250 or 300 years. It still acknowledged the headship of the pope, and it still included monks, canons, friars, and chantry priests. Church services were still in Latin, and still involved their ancient ceremonies. People still venerated images, went on pilgrimages, and earned indulgences. This does not mean that the Church was fixed and unchanging. As we have seen, it constantly underwent changes of small kinds, but larger changes were gradual and organic. Most of the changes, great and small, that affected a region like Cornwall were due to the Church's leaders or to the likes and dislikes of the ordinary clergy and the laity. They did not come from the king or those who helped him run the kingdom.

Fifty years later things had changed enormously, and by sixty years later the changes were confirmed as permanent. Pope, monks, canons, friars, and chantry priests had gone. Church services were in English not Latin, and they had lost nearly all their ceremonies. Images, pilgrimages, and indulgences had all been forbidden. These changes were partly due to changes in theology, culture, and society, but they came about more quickly and dramatically than usual for political reasons. From the early 1530s until the early 1560s the English monarchs intervened dynamically in religious affairs, with immediate and obvious results. This contrast will emerge from the chapter that follows. We shall begin by surveying the still late-medieval Church in Cornwall in the first thirty years or so of the century. Then we shall follow the Reformation of the Church that took place under Henry VIII and his children Edward VI, Mary I, and Elizabeth I.

Figure 79 Hugh Oldham, bishop of Exeter (d. 1519), his head on a cushion held by an angel. When he died the Church in England seemed invincibly Catholic, yet the Reformation was already underway in Germany.

Three bishops presided over the Church in Cornwall during the first half of the 16th century. They were John Arundell, born in the county itself (1502–4), Hugh Oldham (see Figure 79) from Lancashire (1505–19), and John Veysey, a Warwickshire man (1519–51). Oldham came to Cornwall at least twice and Veysey perhaps at least once, but journeys of this kind were now unusual. Oldham lived chiefly at his Devon manors, as previous bishops had done, and Veysey was often away from the South West altogether. He was president of the Council of Wales and the Marches for a long period, and frequently stayed at his birthplace, Sutton Coldfield, where he built a house, endowed a school, and made other charitable bequests. Like bishops before them, Oldham and Veysey employed officials to do much of their administrative work and suffragan bishops to carry out confirmations and ordinations.[168]

The archdeacon of Cornwall continued to discharge his traditional duties in the county. Their scope is summarised in a valuation of his income made in 1535, which reckoned that he received £1 per annum from fees for inducting clergy to benefices, £3 14s. 8d. from fees for proving wills, and £44 5s. 7½d. from the fees paid by parishes at the annual visitations made by the archdeacon or his official. In 1537 Bishop Veysey gave the post of archdeacon to Thomas Winter, the illegitimate son of Cardinal Wolsey, who did not come to Exeter diocese but leased his rights to William Body, a gentleman usher of the king's household. Body's lease was to run for 35 years during which he would pay an annual sum of £30, leaving him free to act as archdeacon and to make what profit he could. The lease led to disputes between Winter and Body, but Body maintained his claim and, when Winter resigned the archdeaconry in 1543, he gained a fresh lease for a further 34 years from the new archdeacon, John Pollard, this time for a mere £10 per annum. Body will appear in our story later.[169]

The Church in Cornwall in the early 16th century still included six monasteries: the three Augustinian priories of Bodmin, St Germans, and Launceston, the Benedictine priory of Tywardreath, and the two small cells of St Anthony-in-Roseland and St Carroc, plus the single Benedictine monk representing Tavistock Abbey on the Isles of Scilly. There were two friaries (Bodmin and Truro), three collegiate churches (St Buryan, Crantock, and Glasney), three prebendal churches (St Endellion, Probus, and St Teath), and one former hospital, St John (Helston), now a sinecure post for a single clergyman. Three other hospitals or almshouses functioned in Bodmin, two in Launceston, and one outside Liskeard. Finally there were the parishes or parish-like areas, still 209 in number, served by a rector, vicar, or curate. As in previous centuries additional clergy served in some of the parishes: curates assisting rectors and vicars, chantry priests, and a few chaplains in the households of the gentry. All the parish clergy below the level of rectors and vicars operated largely outside the bishop's supervision, at the beck and call of those who employed them.

We can pass beyond listing these institutions to estimating the number of clergy that they supported. There were at least 61 members of the religious orders in the 1530s, all resident in Cornwall – a figure that may need to be supplemented by a few novices and

Figure 80 The church of St Endellion, staffed since the 13th century by a rector and three prebendaries. Although the clergy did not form a community, the Reformation abolished the prebendaries in 1548; they were, however, restored ten years later.

some additional friars, since the figures for the latter come from when their houses were dissolved in 1538 after possible losses of members. The largest group within the religious orders were the Augustinian canons, totalling 31, of whom Launceston had 12, Bodmin 10, St Germans seven, and St Anthony-in-Roseland two. There were 10 monks: seven at Tywardreath, two at St Carroc, and the one on the Scillies. The Franciscans of Bodmin numbered at least nine friars and the Dominicans of Truro at least eleven. The collegiate and prebendal churches had a nominal strength of 58, divided between Glasney with 23 clergy, Crantock with 13, St Buryan with eight, Probus with six, St Endellion with four, St Teath with three, and St John Helston with one. In practice the figure of 58 was more like 31, given that some of these clergy also held parish posts or lived outside Cornwall.[170]

Turning to the parishes, there were 160 beneficed clergy (rectors and vicars), of whom 15 held more than one benefice, reducing the total to about 145. Some of the 145 (at least a dozen) did not reside in Cornwall, so that the resident number may have fallen to about 130. Below them were 196 other clergy, all resident. About 28 of these were curates in charge of parishes which had no rector or vicar, 49 were curates assisting rectors or vicars or deputising for those who were absent, and 119 were chantry priests, guild priests, and domestic chaplains. This adds up to a maximum of about 350 parish clergy with a benefice or a post in Cornwall, of whom about 310 to 320 may have lived in the county for most of the time.

In 1535 the government of Henry VIII conducted an enquiry into the annual incomes of all the religious houses and beneficed clergy in England, preparatory to levying taxes on them. The result of this enquiry, the *Valor Ecclesiasticus*, provides total figures for the gross and net incomes of the chief dignitaries, monasteries, and parish clergy of Cornwall during the 1530s, with the caveat that its figures were a little underestimated, at least in the case of the monasteries. The largest net incomes were now regarded as belonging to the three biggest priories: Launceston with £354, Bodmin with £270, and St Germans with £243. Close behind came the bishop of Exeter with £235 per annum from his lands and churches in the county, while Exeter Cathedral's income was reckoned at £239, all from the tithes of its churches. Glasney was reckoned at £210, and Tywardreath at £151; in fact the latter got over £200. The rest of the religious houses were less well endowed. Crantock was deemed to have £94 per annum, St Buryan £74 (most of which went to the dean), St Anthony about £28, and St Carroc £11. No figures were recorded for the friaries or the monastic property on the Scillies. Some 16 other religious houses outside Cornwall still drew revenues from the county, although the sums were mostly fairly small.[171]

Table 1: *Stipends of Rectors and Vicars in Cornwall, 1535*

Stipends	*No. of rectors*	*No. of vicars*
Under £5	2	3
£5–£9	12	26
£10–£14	13	26
£15–£19	14	19
£20–£24	9	7
£25–£29	6	3
£30 and above	18	2
Total	74	86

The parish clergy, as in times past, ranged widely in their incomes or wages and the terms of their duties. The 160 beneficed clergy were divided between 74 rectors and 86 vicars. Five of them received no more than hired chaplains: these were the rectors of Forrabury and Ruan Minor and the vicars of St Anthony-in-Meneage and Manaccan, each with just under £5, while the vicar of Lostwithiel was reported as having only £2 13s. 4d., perhaps an underestimate. A further 12 rectors and 26 vicars with between £5 and £9 were little better off, because a comfortable salary began at about £10 in the 1530s. As in the 13th century, vicarages tended to be more uniform in value than rectories, so that most vicars got between £5 and £19 and very few more than £20, whereas 31 rectors enjoyed more than the latter figure. The two wealthiest vicars were those of Breage with £33 and Madron with £50. There were nearly twenty rectories worth over £30, the richest of all being

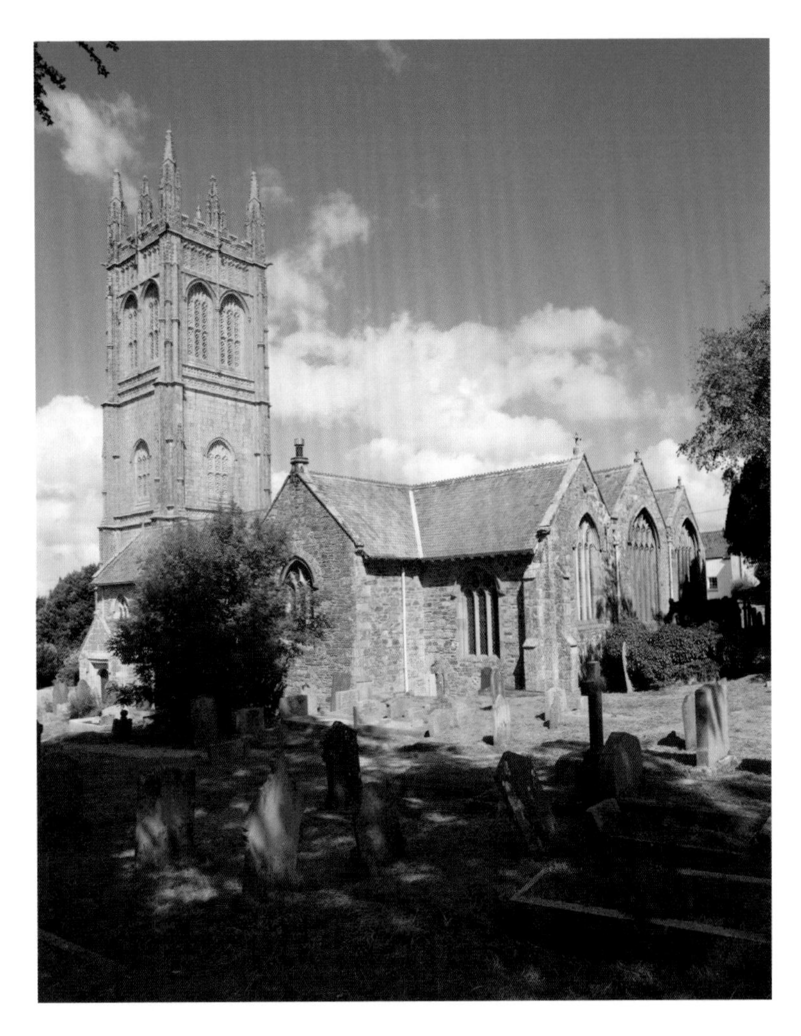

Figure 81 The fine tower of Probus church, built in about the 1520s when enthusiasm for church building and beautification was still strong.

St Columb Major with £53 and the deanery of St Buryan, effectively the rectory of that parish, with £58. Not all of this was profit, however. Both Breage and St Buryan had chapels of ease within their parishes, and the rector or vicar had to pay the stipends of the priests who served them.[172]

The other half of the clergy, the non-beneficed chaplains and chantry priests, still fared poorly in their salaries and sometimes in their conditions of employment. The most fortunate were the curates in charge of parishes that were part of a larger benefice. They were probably left alone to run their churches and could develop links with local people. Curates who assisted a rector or vicar, or who deputised for an absent one, were in a more precarious state. They might be dismissed when their employer ceased to require their services, or if he died or left the parish, since there was no obligation on his successor to employ them. The curate of

Marhamchurch claimed in about 1540 that he was offered his post for four years at a salary of £6, with notice of three months before termination, but was later dismissed without warning. A salary of £6 was relatively high. The maximum rate for a curate at that time was about £6 13s. 4d. but this could fall to as little as £3, or to £2 if food and clothes were provided as well. Priests employed by guilds or serving endowed chantries generally earned between £4 and £6.[173]

The activities of parish churches in the early 16th century seem to have broadly followed the pattern established during the later Middle Ages. Rebuilding continued in many places and money was spent on renewing screens and seating. In about 1520 the parishioners of Probus began a major reconstruction of their church and tower (see Figure 81), and in 1534 the vicar of Altarnun commissioned a 'carver' to fit a new roof and two new windows in his chancel. Work on Kilkhampton church was still in progress in the early years of Elizabeth I; the south porch bears the date 1567 (see Figure 82). Churchwardens went on producing their accounts, although it is not certain if all churches were well organised in this respect. The accounts, as before, refer to fund-raising and donations, including those provided by guilds and companies, and to the existence of stores in honour of saints, which suggests that people carried on venerating images.[174]

Chapels, too, continued to be popular. Bishop Vivian dedicated one at Stowe in Kilkhampton to St Christina in 1519, and another, in honour of St Katherine, was being planned at Treviddo in Menheniot as late as 1532. Pilgrimage continued to St Michael's Mount, where the receipts at the shrine were still at a high level in the 1510s. Some people continued to seek indulgences and Bishop Veysey went on granting them until 1536. There were also a few links between the Cornish and new dynamic institutions of Catholicism elsewhere. Sir John Arundell of Lanherne and Peter Bevill of St Allen both knew about and supported the reformed branch of the Franciscan friars known as 'Observants', based at Greenwich (Kent) and Richmond (Surrey).[175]

Some historians have used this kind of evidence to argue that traditional religion was flourishing on the eve of the Reformation. That is a fair argument, but it is limited by the sources on which it is based. Church buildings, wardens' accounts, and shrine receipts record the activities of people committed to religion. They tell us little of those who held aloof from religious activities, either because of their worldliness or their dissent, and it would be wise to allow for the existence of such people. There is no trace of Lollard unorthodoxy in early 16th-century Cornwall, but there would have been plenty of nonconformity of other kinds. People disobeyed the Church's moral laws, failed to attend church or

Figure 82 The south porch of Kilkhampton church, inscribed *Porta Celi* ('the gate of heaven') and the date 1567.

pay tithes, and sometimes attacked churches and clergy. Even scepticism and disbelief may have existed without being recorded, because it was not expressed or identified as heresy.

Changes were also in progress that would help to bring about the forthcoming Reformation. One was a deeper respect for the king, shown by the display in churches of royal symbols like the Tudor rose, portcullis, or coat of arms (see Figure 83). Another was the growth of seating in naves, turning the congregation into more orderly gatherings, potentially schools for instruction. In schools themselves, classical or 'humanist' Latin was replacing late-medieval Latin between 1480 and 1520, a process that must have extended to Cornwall. The new technology of printing was increasing the supply of books, some printed in England after 1476 and others imported from the Continent, so that by the 1520s the leaders of Church and state were beginning to realise the need to control what was printed and read. All these factors – royal prestige, order, education, and reading – would help change the Catholic Church of the later Middle Ages into a new and somewhat different Church of England.

Figure 83 The royal coat of arms, from St Kew church. Royal emblems began to appear in churches well before the Reformation.

THE EARLY REFORMATION, 1529–38

The English Reformation is conventionally said to begin in 1529 when a new parliament met which, for the next seven years, enacted a series of statutes that remodelled the English Church. At first these statutes centred on the clergy. In 1529 their rights and powers were restricted with regard to mortuaries (the gifts they claimed from dead parishioners), fees for administering wills, pluralities (the holding of more than one benefice at once), and involvement in business activities. In 1530 they agreed to pay a huge fine to the king for having allegedly infringed his laws, and in 1532 they promised not to make new religious laws without his authority. In 1534 Parliament passed the Act of Supremacy, making Henry the earthly head of the Church of England instead of the pope, and the clergy were required to assent to this individually. Most of the signatures by which they did so still survive in the National Archives (see Figure 84).[176]

Once the king had secured the headship of the Church, he and his chief minister, Thomas Cromwell, made it effective in two respects. The first and more immediate was financial. In 1534 a parliamentary Act of First Fruits and Tenths gave the king power to impose taxation on the Church at a heavier rate than had been previously levied by either the king or the pope. All religious houses and beneficed clergy were in future to pay the Crown one tenth of their income each year. Anyone who in future obtained a new benefice, be it as a bishop, canon, rector, or vicar, was to forfeit the whole of the first year's income to the king – ten tenths, as it were, for that year – and all candidates for benefices had to provide guarantors to ensure that the sum would be paid. The new valuation of Church incomes, the *Valor Ecclesiasticus* of 1535, tried to make sure that the incomes were properly calculated. It probably fell somewhat short of the truth, but it also produced more tax for the king from the clergy than had ever been so before.[177]

Figure 84 (opposite)
This document reads: 'The bishop of Rome has no greater jurisdiction conferred on him by God in this kingdom of England than that of any other foreign bishop.' All the Cornish clergy were obliged to sign their assent; here are some of the signatures from East and West Cornwall, beginning (top left) with the vicars of Landrake and Quethiock.

The other new application of royal policy towards the Church was spiritual and aimed at reform. This was broader in its effects than the financial one and affected the religion of lay people more directly. The first casualty of this policy was indulgences. They were so closely associated with the power of the pope that people instinctively abandoned them during the mid-1530s, and an act of Parliament in 1536 made it illegal to teach or maintain any aspect of the pope's authority. In the autumn of the same year Thomas Cromwell issued orders or 'injunctions' to the clergy in the king's name. These ordered them to preach regularly against the power of the pope and in favour of that of the king. They were warned not to promote the undue worship of saints, images, or pilgrimages, but to

Romanus episcopus non habet aliquam maiorem jurisdictionem a deo sibi collatam in hoc regno Anglie quam quivis alius externus episcopus

dns Willelmus Spaio vic' de Lanybok

mr Laurentius Travers vic' de quedyoke.

mr Laurentius Travers Rect de Donyske.

dns Nycoll bytert

dns Nycholaus pype fide Sacerdos

dns Ricardus Ryxsey de Agnethenyt

dns Johes Cad de Lanzals

dns Johes Opton de Sato Germano

dns Johes Aggett curat ibidem

decanatus de Westr

dns Robertus Hossbdo rector de Pennock

dns Stephanus Chapytell curat

dns Robertus Chamlott stip de Lyfford

dns Thomas Doneroll stip de

dns Thomas Adamps stip de

dns Thomas Douy curat de Lanstghor

dns Thomas Kynch vicar de Menwall

dns Edmundus Pyrrd stip de Sci Neclani

Dominus Wylliam Kedo curat de plynt

dominus Brasyng Wappe curatus de Lansalnis

Lantoglos

dns Rogerus Low dnt

dns Richardus Rychard Chapellanus Lantoglos

dns Radulphus Polk Capellanus Lantoglos

dns Alan Coyme stip

dns Thos Doget procur de Fardynghm

dns Johannes Kattge

dns Michaelus Walloys curatus de Atoye

dns Robtus Tubbo vic' de sci Nobti

dns Ricardus Voby Rector de Worlegan

encourage the laity to please God through their work and by giving charity to the poor.[178]

The injunctions ordered a drastic reduction in the number of holy days. Feasts commemorating the days when churches had been dedicated were to be held only on 1 October. Feasts in honour of the patron saint of the church were not to be kept as holidays unless the saint was a major figure whose day was generally observed – a threat to Cornwall where so many saints were uniquely local. Finally the clergy were told to teach the laity to say their basic prayers in English not Latin – a major change of habit. In May 1538 Veysey issued injunctions of his own for his diocese, reinforcing those of the king. In them he made the concession that the basic prayers might be taught and learnt 'in the Cornish [language] where the English tongue is not used'.[179]

In October 1538 Cromwell sent out a second and more radical set of injunctions. These had a wider impact on lay people, contradicting the view, sometimes stated, that Henry VIII's Reformation was limited to the clergy. Positively the movement in favour of the English language continued. Bible translation now received approval, and each church was ordered to acquire a Bible in English, a new translation being published for this purpose in 1539. Parishioners coming for confession in Lent were to be tested on their ability to say the Lord's Prayer and Creed in English, and warned that they might be denied communion at Easter if they did not learn them.[180]

In another innovation the injunctions of 1538 required the clergy to record every baptism, marriage, and burial in a register. This measure was claimed as helping to authenticate births for legal purposes, but it probably also aimed at ensuring that everyone was baptised, married, and buried according to law. The 1520s and '30s had seen the emergence of Anabaptists in Germany who practised adult baptism, and registration made certain that parents in England would have their children baptised as infants. Equally important in the second set of injunctions were the prohibitions. No images or relics were to be venerated by worship, lighting of candles, or by pilgrimage. Any that had been venerated were to be removed. Soon afterwards a royal proclamation of November 1538 forbade the cult of Thomas Becket altogether, because he had championed the clergy against an earlier King Henry (see Figure 85). His images were to be removed, his festivals abolished, and his very name expunged from service books.[181]

The attack on images had an immense and permanent impact on popular religion in England. It was not confined to words. During the year 1538 some images were publicly destroyed by the authorities in London and elsewhere, including the Welsh image

Figure 85 Thomas Becket, shown being martyred on a 14th-century boss in Exeter Cathedral. He was particularly detested by the leaders of the Reformation, because he had died for the privileges of the clergy against the power of the king. All possible traces of his cult were destroyed.

of Darfell Gadern and the Rood or crucifix of Boxley (Kent), the latter of which had wires to move its eyes. We do not know what happened to the two main pilgrim shrines in Cornwall, St Michael's Mount and St Day, but their activities must have been greatly curtailed. John Leland, who visited the county in 1542, implied that public pilgrimage had ceased by that time. Writing about St Elide's chapel on the Isles of Scilly, he used the past tense, 'in times past at her sepulchre was great superstition', and similarly with regard to the chapel of Our Lady in the Park near Liskeard, 'where was wont to be great pilgrimage'.[182]

The attacks on images, pilgrimages, and indulgences struck at the chapels, whose functions and resources were often bound up with such things. There was no formal abolition of chapels, but most of them ceased to be used and were demolished or converted to other purposes. Leland mentioned St Katherine's chapel in Launceston as already 'prophaned', meaning turned to secular use. Even chapels of ease eventually disappeared in some small towns, and the only chapels to survive in the long term were those that were virtually parish churches like Advent, Germoe, and Helston; a very few chapels of ease such as Marazion in St Hilary, St Enodoc and Porthilly in St Minver, St Nectan in St Winnow, and Penzance in Madron; and some of those in private houses.[183]

The religious changes of the 1530s caused some discontent in Cornwall, especially the prohibition of local saints' days in 1536.

Figure 86 The Cornish Reformer, John Tregonwell (d. 1565). A doctor of civil law, he became a royal servant and carried out the dissolution of the monasteries in Cornwall. Knighted and rewarded with monastic property, he established a magnificent household at Milton Abbey (Dorset) and is buried in its church.

In September 1536 John Tregonwell (see Figure 86), a Cornish-born lawyer who was acting as a royal commissioner in his native county, told Cromwell of rumours afoot that he, Tregonwell, was about to remove crosses, chalices, and images from churches, but said that he had personally found the county loyal and quiet. By April 1537, however, Sir William Godolphin of Breage was informing Cromwell that a fisherman named Carpyssacke of St Keverne had tried to commission a banner showing a wounded Christ with an inscription petitioning that the old holy days might be kept. St Keverne's day (5 March) fell into the forbidden category. The banner was intended for display on Pardon Monday (perhaps Rogation Monday), but Carpyssacke was arrested and consideration was given to trying him for treason.[184]

Another incident of 1537 points to religious conservatism in Cornwall. On 29 May a ship named the *Maudlyn* left Truro for

Treguier in Brittany, carrying what Alexander Carvanell, a deputy searcher (or customs officer), called a company of 'riotous' pilgrims feigning to go on a 'pope-holy pilgrimage'. They included two clergy, a merchant of Truro, and more than fifty others. Carvanell and two assistants tried to enter the vessel at Truro, ostensibly to inspect the cargo, but were thrown into the sea. They managed to get on board when the ship stopped at St Mawes, but the mariners frustrated the inspection and carried Carvanell to Brittany, obliging him to return in another boat. Although pilgrimage had not yet been forbidden, it was being discouraged, and the participants were probably as aware as Carvanell that they were defying official policy by going on such a journey.[185]

THE DISSOLUTION OF THE MONASTERIES

Soon after Parliament recognised Henry VIII as head of the Church of England, Cromwell and other royal servants began to make plans for the Crown to take control of Church property. In April 1536 an act of Parliament authorised the dissolution of small monasteries. It began by asserting that houses of fewer than thirteen clergy were unsatisfactory in their religious life, unlike larger communities which kept it well. It ordered the closure of such houses, however, not on the basis of their numbers of clergy but on whether they had an income of £200 or less.[186]

Only one Cornish monastery was dissolved under the act of 1536. This was Tywardreath whose income was reckoned at £151 in the *Valor*, although it was worth more in practice. The prior, Nicholas Guest, who had been imported from St Germans only recently, chose to withdraw from monastic life and was granted a pension of £16. The other houses did not last much longer. The compulsory dissolutions were followed by a 'voluntary' process in which they were persuaded to surrender themselves and their property into the king's hands. This was done by the two Cornish friaries in September 1538 and by the monasteries in the spring of 1539. There was no resistance. Launceston capitulated on 24 February, Bodmin on 27 February, and St Germans on 2 March. The small cells at St Anthony and St Carroc, and Tavistock's last monk on the Isles of Scilly, must have ceased to operate at about the same time. Last of all fell the Order of St John in 1540, bringing to an end whatever activities still went on at Trebeigh.[187]

Monks and canons who surrendered in 1539 were granted pensions. In contrast friars got nothing, since they were regarded as having chosen to live in poverty. The priors of the three largest Cornish monasteries were handsomely treated. Robert Swymmer of St Germans and Thomas Wandsworth of Bodmin received pensions of £66 13s. 4d. per annum, while John Shere of Launceston obtained £100, allowing them a comfortable retirement. Ordinary canons were allocated anything from £10 down to £2 and they were allowed to work as parish clergy, as were the friars. Their subsequent careers appear to have varied. Some acquired rectories or vicarages in due course and one, Stephen Gourge, became grammar schoolmaster of Launceston. Others are not recorded holding parish benefices and must have joined the crowd of ill-paid chaplains and chantry priests.

The dissolution of the monasteries had a considerable impact on Cornwall. Monastic property passed into secular hands. The Crown itself kept the temporal lands of Launceston Priory and the Isles of Scilly, some of which still belong to the duchy of Cornwall. Other lands were sold or leased by the Crown, either to courtiers or to wealthy bidders from outside the court. Thomas Sternhold, groom of the robes in the royal household, gained a lease of Bodmin Priory, and Gawen Carew, courtier and soldier, was granted the premises of Launceston. Two towns, Bodmin and Fowey, escaped from the control of the priories that had hitherto run their affairs, and became self-governing. The gentry did particularly well out of the Dissolution. They took over monastic buildings as residences at St Anthony, Bodmin, St Carroc, Trebeigh, and most notably St Michael's Mount where the church became the chapel of the house (see Figure 17). They leased or bought monastic lands. At Bodmin the prior, Thomas Wandsworth, anticipated the royal seizure of the monastery and its lands by leasing as many of the priory's lands as possible to his family and friends. The Prideaux family of Padstow was one of the beneficiaries (see Figure 87).[188]

Figure 87 Prideaux Place, Padstow, symbolises the gains that the gentry made at the Reformation at the expense of the clergy. The manor of Padstow originally belonged to Bodmin Priory, but the last prior leased it to the Prideaux family and arranged a marriage between his family and theirs. They have lived there ever since.

Not only did lands and houses change hands, but churches and tithes. In the early 1530s the patrons of the 160 rectories and vicarages in Cornwall were still predominantly churchmen. The bishop, the cathedral, and various monasteries appointed clergy to about 94 (59 per cent), and the Crown and laity to about 66 (41 per cent). After the dissolution of the monasteries their advowsons were either taken over by the Crown or sold to lay purchasers. About 66 advowsons changed hands in this way, so that by the 1560s the clergy of about 121 parishes (75 per cent) were appointed by the Crown or lay people, while the share of the churchmen fell to 25 per cent. By the 12th century church tithes had belonged to the clergy alone, and lay lords had not been allowed to receive them. Now the Crown sold off the tithes that had once belonged to the monasteries, and a new situation arose by which the great tithes of grain in many of the former vicarages had to be paid to the lay people who purchased the right to receive them, 'impropriators' as they were subsequently known.

During 1539–40, when the Crown was rich with the property of the monasteries, it considered using some of their buildings and endowments to create new dioceses and cathedrals. One of these was proposed for Cornwall, financed from the priories of Bodmin, St Germans, and Launceston; it is not clear which of the sites was intended for use. Plans were drawn up for a bishop and a cathedral foundation, but in the end the Crown founded only six new cathedrals, omitting the scheme for Cornwall. It was a sign that change was slowing down. In 1540 the Crown caused Parliament to pass the 'Act of Six Articles', which defended the traditional doctrines about the mass, the celibacy of the clergy, and confession, and threatened draconian penalties against anyone who dissented. The veneration of images remained forbidden, but most of the images in parish churches survived and so did many of the stores and guilds devoted to maintaining them.[189]

The final years of Henry's reign, from 1540 until 1547, did not produce dramatic alterations to the Church like those of the 1530s but the Reformation continued to edge forward in small steps. In 1541 a royal proclamation abolished the custom of choosing a boy-bishop to lead the church services on St Nicholas's Day and Holy Innocents Day (6 and 28 December), and tried (less successfully) to suppress the folk customs associated with these and some other saints' days. In 1544 Archbishop Cranmer produced an English version of the litany – the prayers said or sung during processions – for use in churches on Wednesdays and Fridays. This introduced worship in English on a large scale for the first time, and markedly reduced the mention of saints. Finally in 1545 the Crown turned its attention to the chantries, another group of religious institutions with property, albeit modest amounts. A Chantry Act was passed by Parliament allowing the king to take control of them for his lifetime, but Henry's death on 28 January 1547 caused the act to lapse, and the chantries gained a brief respite.[190]

THE REFORMATION UNDER EDWARD VI, 1547–49

Henry was succeeded in name by his nine year-old son Edward VI and in practice by a government led by the young king's uncle, the duke of Somerset. This government soon made plain its intention of continuing the Reformation to establish a fully Protestant Church. In the autumn of 1547 teams of royal visitors toured England, with fresh injunctions. These restated most of those of 1538 with some further requirements. The epistle and gospel at mass were to be read in English, and English lessons from the Bible were introduced at matins and evensong. As in 1538, the parish clergy were to recommend the good new practices in church once every three months, and to discourage people from the old superstitious ones. They were also to read, each Sunday, one of the new *Homilies* published by Cranmer in 1547: English sermons expounding the official doctrines of salvation, obedience, almsgiving, and so on.[191]

Figure 88 Reformation change. The late medieval chapel of St Michael, Roche. It was built of granite and hard to destroy, but its ruin remains as an eloquent statement that the Reformation abolished the Catholicism in which it had been created.

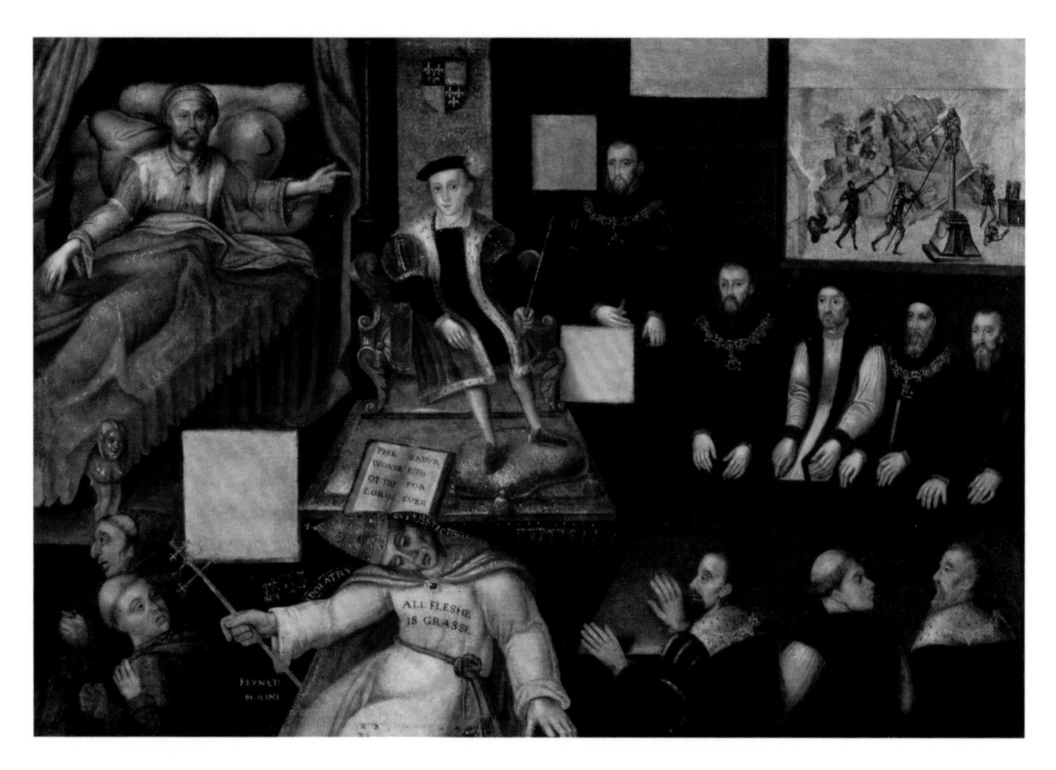

Figure 89 This painting of the English Reformation by an unknown artist (*c.*1570) depicts some of the main actors of the period. Henry VIII, on his deathbed, hands authority to his young son Edward VI. Beside the young king are his uncle, the duke of Somerset, and Archbishop Cranmer. The pope is overthrown, and monks and friars depart in despair.

Other changes of detail were made to worship, anticipating the larger alterations that were to be introduced in the next two years. Most of the processions, which had been such a large part of religious life, were forbidden. The priest was no longer allowed to lead the bodies of the dead to the church from their homes, but only to receive the dead at the churchyard. The warnings against shrines and images were repeated, and any images likely to be venerated were ordered to be removed, even from window glass. Instead the regime strove to turn people's devotion to Bible reading, Sunday observance, and works of charity. Each church was told to acquire a chest to receive donations for the needy, and the resources of the church guilds and stores were ordered to be put into the chest for that purpose.

More radical reforms came with the enactment of the second Chantry Act by Parliament in December 1547. Unlike the previous act, which had been non-committal about the future of the chantries, this one began with a robust Protestant attack on prayers for the dead. It sanctioned the dissolution of a wide range of institutions and endowments and the seizure of their property by the Crown. They included the remaining collegiate churches, the chantries, religious (but not craft) guilds, obits (masses on the anniversaries of people's deaths), and lights in front of church images. Collegiate churches and chantries were to cease their activities on Easter Day, 1 April 1548. The act promised, however, that chantry property would be applied 'to good and godly uses' such as founding grammar schools, augmenting the universities, and giving relief to the poor.[192]

The second Chantry Act had a considerable impact on Cornwall. Glasney College, the largest remaining religious house in the county, was closed, as was the ancient minster of Crantock. St Buryan, St Endellion, Probus, and St Teath lost their prebendaries, and all the chantries were dissolved. Several chapels were shorn of their endowments, notably the chapels of ease at Boscastle and Camelford, the chapel of Our Lady in the Park, and the chapel and priest of Lammana that had replaced the priory there. St Michael's Mount was spared to the extent of keeping the church and two priests to serve it, chiefly to minister to a royal garrison stationed on the island. St Buryan, too, kept some of its distinction. The chantry commissioners intended to abolish the dean as well as the prebendaries, but this turned out to be impractical and the church continued as a royal peculiar down to the 19th century, staffed by the dean (a wealthy absentee) and three poorly-paid parish chaplains.[193]

All the clergy of the colleges and the priests of the chantries and guilds were granted pensions. Some became parish chaplains and others rectors and vicars, like the ex-monks and canons. But, despite the promises of the Chantry Act, no chantry property in Cornwall was applied to educational or charitable purposes. All that the Crown did was to take over the responsibility of paying the masters of four Cornish grammar schools, one of which had been maintained by Glasney for Penryn and the others by chantries at Bodmin, Launceston, and Saltash. A fifth grammar school, Thomasine Percival's foundation at Week St Mary, was less fortunate (see Figure 90). Although its chantry priest was a good teacher and the school attracted the sons of local gentry, the government considered that it was hampered by its remote location and the authorities at Launceston appear to have suggested that it should be moved to their town. The money due to Week was therefore added to that of Launceston school, and Thomasine's foundation came to an end.[194]

The first three years of Edward VI's reign saw a succession of further reforms to the Church. In 1547 Parliament abolished Henry's 'Act of Six Articles' and the medieval heresy laws, opening the way for Protestant doctrines to become lawful. Rumours spread that the government was planning to seize church silver and jewels, and when William Body, in effect the archdeacon, visited the deanery of Penwith in December 1547, a riot broke out because of fear that he was coming with that intention. A series of royal orders in 1548 forbade the customs of lighting candles at Candlemas,

Figure 90 The remains of Thomasine Percival's grammar school at Week St Mary. Founded in 1506–8 to provide free education in Latin, this was the first endowed free school in Cornwall and an undeserved casualty of the Reformation.

receiving ashes on Ash Wednesday, carrying palms on Palm Sunday, and creeping to the cross on Good Friday. In February all images were ordered to be removed from churches. On 1 April, Easter Day, a new *Order of Communion* was introduced, bringing some English prayers into the Latin mass alongside the English epistle and gospel, and requiring communion to be given 'in both kinds': the bread and the consecrated wine. In the spring of 1549 the issue of church silver arose again. Royal commissioners told parishes to declare what they had, and lists were made of the objects, a procedure only too likely to confirm the fear that the government wanted to seize them.[195]

THE PRAYER-BOOK REBELLION AND AFTERWARDS, 1549–53

The culmination of these changes was a new prayer book, Archbishop Cranmer's *Book of Common Prayer*, which was ordered to be used in all churches from Pentecost (9 June) 1549. The Prayer Book contained three types of services, all in English. The nine daily services hitherto said by the clergy were reduced to two, morning prayer and evening prayer (approximating to the old matins and evensong). The clergy remained obliged to say both every day. The mass became the service of holy communion. Finally, the book contained the pastoral services of baptism, confirmation, marriage, churching of women, visiting the sick, and funerals. Like the communion they retained a traditional

The Prayer-Book Rebellion

The 'Prayer-Book' or 'Western' rebellion, as it is now known, was the most important attempt in England to oppose the Protestant Reformation of the reign of Edward VI (1547-53). Its leaders produced demands in writing which they sent to the royal government, led by the king's protector or regent, the duke of Somerset. These can be read in Frances Rose-Troup's book, *The Western Rebellion of 1549* (1913).

Unlike the petitions produced by some other rebellions, in which protesters asked the king to grant what they wanted, the demands of the men of Cornwall and Devon were each introduced by the robust words 'We will have…'. Most of the demands involved undoing the Church reforms that had been made under Edward VI. Doctrinally the protesters wanted the re-establishment of Henry VIII's Act of Six Articles which upheld belief in transubstantiation, confessions to priests, and the celibacy of the clergy. The death penalty should be reintroduced for heresy.

In worship the protesters wanted the restoration of the old Latin services: the mass, matins and evensong, and processions. They described the new services of Archbishop Cranmer's 'Book of Common Prayer' as 'but like a Christmas game', probably meaning a play in English such as might be staged at Christmastide. This particular demand may have come from Cornwall since it goes on to say, 'And so we the Cornish men (whereof certain of us understand no English) utterly refuse this new English'.

The protesters called for other traditions to be restored: the hanging of the pyx above the high altar, the distribution of holy bread and water after services, and the giving of communion only in the form of bread and only at Easter. Images were to be venerated again, and the dead to be prayed for. Two further demands are interesting, because they hint at undoing the religious changes of Henry VIII's reign as well. One asked for the recall of Cardinal Pole, the leading Catholic exile, and for his recruitment to the king's government. This implies a wish for the reunion of England with the Catholic Church under the pope. The other called for half of the monastic lands and chantry properties in anyone's possession to be surrendered, and used to finance two religious houses in each county. This looks like an attempt to bring back the monasteries or something similar to them.

It is never easy to be sure who took part in Tudor rebellions, who drew up their requests or demands, and whether the demands really reflected the views of those who took part. It is also worth considering that many, perhaps most, Cornish men did not take part in the rising, and might not have subscribed to all these demands either.

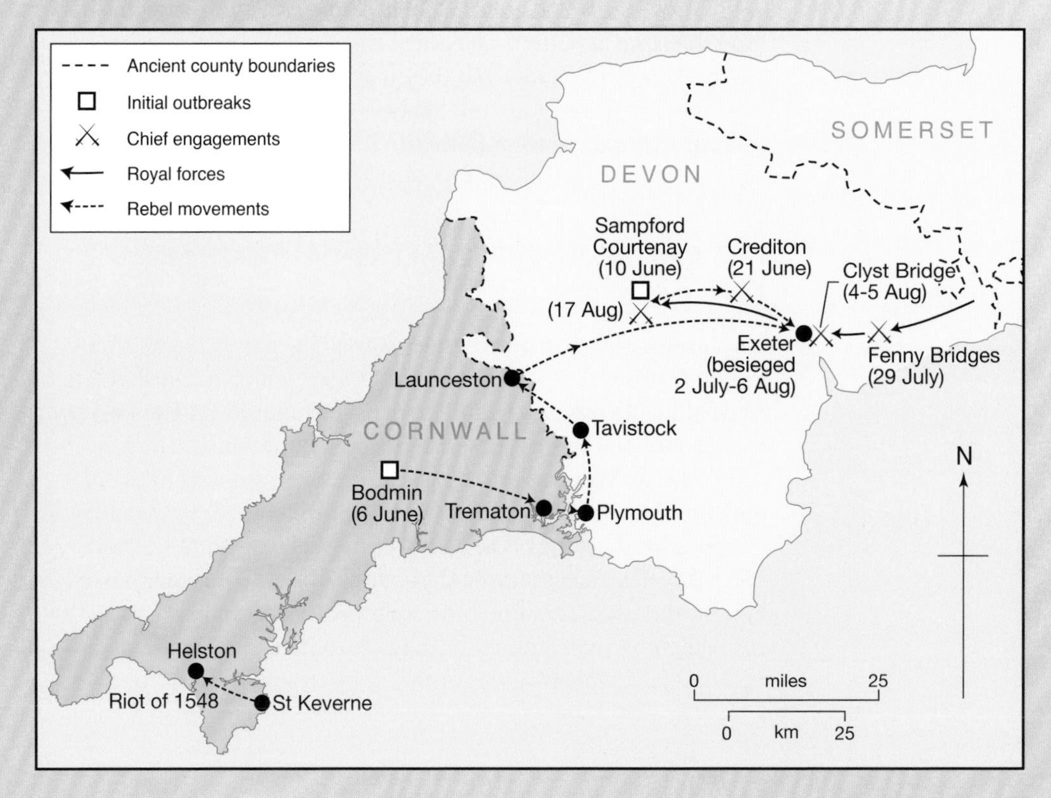

shape and continued to involve substances that were regarded as holy – water, oil, bread, and wine – but their ceremonies were simplified and their material was made more instructive. Baptism and marriage both began with explanations of what they involved, and funerals became occasions to teach the living as well as to send off the dead.[196]

Cranmer's decision to introduce the new Prayer Book at Pentecost, the day that commemorates the foundation of the Church by the Holy Spirit, was admirable in principle but maladroit in practice. Pentecost fell in the holiday period, when people had time to spare from work and when the roads allowed easy passage. This was an ancient season of unrest. The Peasants' Revolt of 1381 had taken place in May and June, and so had the Cornish rising of 1497. For all Cranmer's skill and moderation in producing the Prayer Book, the use of English would have jarred with congregations used to Latin. The new book followed a long series of unpopular changes affecting parish life, including the abolition of saints' days, guilds, and images.

While Henry VIII was king his personality was enough to keep people silent, but a government ruling for a child king was weaker and people were less inclined to obey it. Body's presence in Penwith had caused a riot as early as 1547. When he visited Kerrier deanery early in 1548 and tried to enforce the removal of images, matters grew worse. Men from St Keverne and the neighbouring parishes attacked his lodgings in Helston and murdered him on 5 April. Their leaders announced demands in the market-place that no more religious changes should be made until the king was 24 years old. Gentry loyal to the government restored order and the ringleaders were executed, but the events showed how easily religious changes could now provoke violent reactions.[197]

The Prayer Book had the same effect, but on a larger scale. In Devon the people of Sampford Courtenay revolted on Monday 10 June, the day after Pentecost, having heard the new service once. In Cornwall rebellion started at Bodmin on Thursday 6 June before the introduction of the Prayer Book, perhaps when copies of the volume arrived. The Cornish protesters gained two leaders from the gentry, Humphrey Arundell and John Winslade, and supporters from across the county. Some of the clergy of Cornwall were later accused of involvement as well. The Cornish joined up with their fellow dissenters in Devon and besieged Exeter (2 July to 6 August), but were unable to capture it (see Panel 5). The government gained time to bring up forces to restore order, and although the protesters resisted in three hard-fought battles, they were eventually crushed at Sampford Courtenay on 29 August. This put an end to the rebellion as an organised movement.[198]

Figure 91 The walls of Exeter city played a major part in defeating the Prayer-Book rebellion. They withstood a siege of six weeks by the protesters, tying them down and stopping them from taking their protest further into England.

The suppression of the rebellion left the Crown free not only to maintain the reforms it had made but to extend them further. The marriage of the clergy had already been permitted in 1548. In 1550 all altars in churches were ordered to be removed and replaced by a single wooden table in the chancel for the purpose of communion. In 1552 the Prayer Book was revised and reissued in a more radical form. Many details in the services were changed, with the broad effect that the medieval ceremonies retained in the 1549 book were mostly omitted, and services became static occasions centred on the reading of Bible lessons and prayers. The communion service of 1549 had still been said by a priest wearing vestments, facing the high altar at the east end of the church. He had put a piece of wafer bread directly into the mouth of each person as was traditional, and had said 'The body of our Lord Jesus Christ … preserve thy body and soul unto everlasting life'. The chalice was then given with comparable words.[199]

Figure 92 Teaching the new generation. An engraving from Archbishop Cranmer's *Catechism* of 1548, aimed at children. It shows Christ telling his parable of the poor man who prays humbly and the Pharisee who prays with pride. The Pharisee is dressed as a monk.

These phrases enabled people to have different views about the sense in which the bread became Christ's body, not excluding the traditional doctrine that it became so in a total and physical sense. The prayer book of 1552 took a deliberately different line. The priest was told to wear only a surplice and to stand on the north side of the new table. This was placed in the middle of the chancel on an east-west axis rather than the north-south axis of the old high altar. From there he came and put a piece of white loaf bread into the worshipper's hands, with the words 'Take and eat this in remembrance that Christ died for thee', and said a similar formula when offering the chalice. This meant that the service was not like the old Latin mass. It was not a sacrifice and it did not create Christ's body in the form of bread, thereby giving you healing. Instead it commemorated Christ's Last Supper, reminding you of his sacrifice for you and teaching you to feed on him in a spiritual sense through faith.

Now that services were simpler, the Crown considered that churches no longer needed the vestments or ornaments that they had used hitherto. In the same year, 1552, commissioners were appointed to make inventories of all such things and to take charge of them. Churches were to be left with only a surplice for the clergyman, tablecloths for the communion table, a cup for the communion, and a bell. One aspect of these further changes attracted a little support. At least seven Cornish rectors and vicars appear to have married during Edward's reign, including the incumbents of Antony, Calstock, St Kew, St Michael Penkevil, North Hill, Pelynt, and Tywardreath. Their boldness was to bring them into trouble.[200]

Throughout the religious changes from 1529 until the Prayer-Book rebellion, Bishop Veysey continued to rule the diocese (see Figure 94). Courtly and careful, he followed the policy of limiting damage by co-operating with the Crown. He did not manage to prevent any of the major changes that the Crown wished to make, however, and in 1550 he was made to surrender two of his Cornish properties to Sir Andrew Dudley, a gentleman of the royal household. He lost other property in Devon at the same time, and the wealth and power of the bishops declined in consequence. Eventually, in 1551, the government decided that it needed a more active Protestant bishop, and Veysey (now in his eighties) was told to resign. He was given a pension and retired to Sutton Coldfield. In his place the Crown appointed Miles Coverdale, the translator of the Bible and a distinguished Reformer. During his two years in office Coverdale did what he could to forward the Reformation. He even made an ill-starred visit to Cornwall, where he fell seriously ill after drinking something at Bodmin that was contaminated or, it was rumoured, poisoned.[201]

Figure 93 The 'Sunday Christ' in St Just-in-Penwith church, showing Christ wounded by the tools of those who worked on Sunday. The Protestant Reformers disliked such pictures and had them obliterated, but they agreed with their message and tried hard to ensure that people kept Sunday as a day for worship.

THE REIGN OF MARY I, 1553–8

With the death of Edward VI in July 1553, and the succession of his elder sister Mary I, there was a return to Catholicism, although it lasted for little more than five years. In the autumn of 1553 Parliament repealed the statutes of Edward that dealt with religion. This meant that the English prayer book lapsed in favour of the old Latin ones and it became lawful again to venerate saints and to pray for the dead. In 1554 the heresy laws were revived, the statutes of Henry VIII against the pope were repealed, and the English Church acknowledged the pope as its head. A clause of one of the new statutes calmed the fears of those who had acquired religious property by recognising their rights to what they held. This concession, needed to gain support for the restoration of Catholicism, made it difficult to revive the monasteries, and although a few were reinstated in England none reappeared in Cornwall.[202]

The sole institutions to be re-established in the county during Mary's reign were the prebendal church of St Endellion and the preceptory of the Order of St John at Trebeigh, or rather its property. The Crown had seized the prebends of St Endellion in 1548, leaving only the rector, but the endowments of the prebends were not sold or granted during Edward's reign, probably because their lands and tithes were mixed up with those of the rector in a complicated manner. This allowed Mary's bishop of Exeter to institute new prebendaries, and by the 1560s the church once more supported a rector and three (normally non-resident) colleagues. The Crown restored Trebeigh to the Order of St John in 1558, but the order held it for just a year before the next monarch, Elizabeth I, withdrew it again.[203]

Meanwhile in September 1553 Coverdale was removed as bishop and the aged Veysey was restored to power. He lived only until October 1554, but his second period of office saw the eviction of seven Cornish rectors and vicars from their benefices, probably for the offence of having married, and the number may have been a little higher since the records are not complete. Clergy willing to renounce their wives were allowed to occupy new parishes, if they could find a patron to present them, and one or two abandoned their wives to do so. Nicholas Nicolls, the former vicar of St Kew, moved to Marhamchurch, while William Lamb, expelled from Pelynt, started afresh at St Keyne.[204]

When Veysey died it was not easy for the crown to replace him, given that so many senior clergy had connived at the Reformation. The choice eventually fell on James Turberville, who was consecrated as bishop in September 1555. He was a doctor of divinity from a family of gentry in Dorset, who had been a cathedral canon in recent times and not prominent in Church life. His younger contemporary, the Exeter historian John Hooker who was a Protestant, characterised him as 'very gentle and courteous', 'most zealous in the Romish religion', but not personally 'cruel or bloody', although Hooker blamed him for his part in the persecution of Agnes Prest, to which we shall come. Little is known of Turberville's reign as bishop. He was in power for only four years, and his register records hardly more than the names of the clergy whom he ordained and instituted to benefices.[205]

Figure 94 Bishop John Veysey, bishop of Exeter from 1519 to 1551 and again from 1553 until his death in 1554. Here he rests from his labours on his tomb in Sutton Coldfield church (Warws.), his birthplace.

It was harder to re-establish Catholic worship. Much of the equipment of the old religion had disappeared from the parish churches, such as church silver, service books, and images, and all this had to be procured again. The Crown helped a little, since most of the church plate seized in 1552 was still being stored, and this was returned to the parishes. Churchwardens' accounts from Mary's reign list payments relating to the restoration of church interiors and worship, but there may have been much variation in the speed at which this was done. At Camborne payments were made in 1554 for altar linen, holy oil, a holy cross, a holy candle, and a holy-water bucket, while the pyx to hold the sacrament above the altar is mentioned in the following year. At Menheniot, on the other hand, although money was spent on the altar in 1554, it was not until 1557 that the pyx and the 'crucifix', presumably the rood, were set up again, or until 1558 that processional books were acquired, while a box for holy bread and rails for altar curtains were not paid for until 1559.[206]

Some people gladly returned to Catholic practices. During the 1550s Ralph Thomvy of Perranzabuloe left money for a priest to sing five masses of the five wounds of Christ for his soul. Richard Hore of St Ervan asked to be buried before the picture of St Erasmus in the parish church and to have his name put on the bead roll, while James Speryer of Mabe bequeathed a ewe to a guild in the parish named after the Holy Ghost. One Cornish cleric tried to provide preaching material for the Catholic revival. In 1555 Edmund Bonner, bishop of London, and others published a set of 12 homilies in English for reading in church, to replace those of Cranmer which had been in use up to 1553. Towards the end of the 1550s, John Tregear, vicar of St Allen, translated Bonner's homilies into Cornish, although his version now exists in a single manuscript and we do not know how far or even whether it was used in churches. There was a wider revival of the parish processions. Nicholas Roscarrock, born in St Endellion parish in the late 1540s, remembered in later life that the relics of St Piran of Perranzabuloe

Figure 95 The well house at Dupath in Callington. Smaller religious sites like wells and crosses survived the Reformation better than monasteries, shrines, and images, because they were less obtrusive or thought to be less dangerous.

'were carried about the countryside' in Mary's reign, and his description of the processions to the chapel of St Nectan in Newlyn East also relates to this time.[207]

It would be too much to expect that everyone liked the Catholic restoration. There was a notable reluctance by young men to be ordained as clergy. In 1557 and 1558, for which complete figures survive, only three and five men respectively were ordained as priests in the whole of Devon and Cornwall. We hear of a few lay dissenters. When John Come left the Christmas Eve service at Linkinhorne in 1553, he expressed his pleasure at hearing mass again and receiving holy bread and water. But Sampson Jackman allegedly replied to him, 'I would all priests were hanged', after which (according to Come) Jackman and a visitor from Stoke Climsland, John Cowlyn, slandered the queen and said that, if a woman were to reign, it ought to be her sister the Princess Elizabeth. In the parish of Boyton, Agnes Prest of Northcote voiced anti-Catholic views to such an extent that she got into trouble with the Church authorities.[208]

This woman, a wife in her fifties, had learnt Protestant ideas from sermons during the reign of Edward VI. During the 1550s she announced her disbelief in transubstantiation and the veneration of images, falling out with her husband and children and eventually leaving them. In due course she was summoned to Exeter to be examined by the bishop and his chancellor, and was put into the bishop's prison there, but was transferred to the gaoler's private house on the grounds that she was naive rather than heretical. Only when she persisted in maintaining her beliefs and declaring them to other people was she eventually found guilty of heresy and handed over to the lay power for execution. She was burnt at Exeter in August 1558 – the only person from Cornwall ever to have suffered this punishment, as far as we know, and the only one in the diocese during Mary's reign.[209]

THE ELIZABETHAN CHURCH SETTLEMENT, 1558–60

Mary died and Elizabeth succeeded her on 17 November 1558. A new parliament assembled in January 1559 and, in a session lasting until May, enacted statutes restoring the Protestant Church of England. The Church was again made subject to the English Crown, with the more tactful use of the phrase 'supreme governor' to describe the monarch instead of 'supreme head'. The English Prayer Book was re-established in a form based on the second, more radical, version of 1552, with a few conservative alterations. Most of the bishops currently in office refused to cooperate with the new regime, and voted against the new legislation in Parliament. The government hoped to win them over and, although they were suspended from power in the summer of 1559 and imprisoned in the Tower of London, it was not until March 1560 that a new bishop of Exeter was nominated in the person of William Alley. He was consecrated on 14 July.[210]

Meanwhile in September 1559 a fresh royal visitation of the Church took place throughout England. New teams of commissioners addressed articles of enquiry to the local clergy, issued injunctions to them, and required the clergy to swear an oath of allegiance to the queen as supreme governor. Bishop Jewel of Salisbury, who took part in the visitation of Exeter diocese and was a Devon man himself, said after it was finished that he and his companions found people everywhere 'well disposed towards religion', in other words to its reformed variety, 'even in those quarters where we expected most difficulty'. He complained, on the other hand, of the wilderness of superstition that had sprung up in Mary's reign. 'We found in all places votive relics of saints, nails with which the infatuated people dreamed that Christ had been pierced, and I know not what small fragments of the sacred cross.' Even in 1559 people's attitudes were not always as progressive as Jewel assumed. Many older people still clung mentally to the religion of their childhood. A few, like the Arundells of Lanherne and some of the Roscarrocks of St Endellion, remained true to Catholicism throughout Elizabeth's reign, despite disapproval and eventual persecution (see Figure 96).[211]

The injunctions of 1559 embodied a return to the policies of Henry VIII and Edward VI in many respects. The Crown once more claimed sole authority over the Church. Orders were given that worship should take place in English, English Bibles be placed in churches, parish registers and poor boxes be restored, and shrines and images abolished. The clergy were again allowed to marry. At the same time the authorities did not reinstate the Church of England to the high point of Protestantism that it had reached in the final year of Edward VI's reign. True, the new edition of the Prayer Book issued in the spring of 1559 was mainly based on the 1552 book, and Sunday worship resumed a form like that of the end of Edward's reign. Communion came to be held only about four times a year: at Christmas, Easter, Pentecost, and Michaelmas (29 September) or All Saints tide (1 November). On normal Sundays the priest read morning prayer, the litany, and the first half of the communion service in the morning, and evening prayer in the afternoon.[212]

However, the Elizabethan government ordered the communion table, when it was not in use, to be put back where the high altar

Figure 96 The Langdale Rosary, a pre-Reformation rosary with beads bearing pictures of saints. It was used by Lord William Howard, a Catholic nobleman in Cumberland in the early 17th century, who added two beads: one of St William (his name saint) and one of St Endelient, the patron saint of his friend and companion Nicholas Roscarrock.

had formerly been. When communion took place, the bread and wine given to the congregation were again considered to be consecrated objects, not merely symbols of the Last Supper. A London clergyman got into trouble in 1573 when he ran out of communion wine and dispensed more without praying over it. The communion bread returned to the traditional form of wafers, rather than the fine loaf bread stipulated under Edward VI, and the priest in giving out the wafers said the words of both 1549 and 1552: 'the body of our Lord Jesus Christ' and 'take and eat this in remembrance', and similarly with the wine.[213]

The injunctions also declared that music in parish churches was lawful. Choirs of men and boys could be organised again, and a hymn sung at the end of a service provided that it was in English. In practice, however, music in Elizabethan churches tended to centre on the singing of the psalms by the congregation in metrical versions like 'All people that on earth do dwell', rather than returning to the chanted psalms of the later Middle Ages. People were once again directed to bow at the name of Jesus, and although processions in general remained forbidden, an exception was made for Rogationtide, reflecting its great popularity. It became lawful again for clergy and people to make their customary tours around their parishes on one of the Rogation days, saying Psalm 103 and other prayers, and such processions continued to be accompanied by eating and drinking, as they had been until the 1540s.[214]

Figure 97 Coats of arms of the Pentire and Carminow families in the church of St Kew. The gentry were one of the unchanging strands of the Church during the Reformation. Powerful before it started, they maintained or increased their power as it progressed.

CHANGES AND CONTINUITIES

How far did the Church in Cornwall change during the Reformation, and how far did it continue as before? This question can be answered in three respects: landscape, worship, and people. By Elizabeth's reign the Cornish landscape was not quite the same. In four of the towns – Bodmin, Launceston, Penryn, and Truro – large churches that had dominated the skyline had been pulled down or converted to other uses. In the countryside Tywardreath Priory disappeared, St Anthony-in-Roseland and St Germans lost their chancels, and hundreds of chapels closed. Former religious structures were adapted to new uses. Bodmin Friary became a civic building, and some chapels were turned into sheds or dwellings. The gentry who bought monastic sites often converted the residential parts of the properties into houses for themselves, a transformation visible at Bodmin, St Carroc, St Germans, and Trebeigh, as well as at Rialton, the country residence of the priors of Bodmin.

As a result the Cornish landscape became somewhat less religious in appearance, although not drastically so. Holy wells and wayside crosses remained, thanks to their smaller size, their popular support, and the lesser concern of the authorities to remove them (see Figure 95). Parish churches, too, continued along with their clergy houses and glebes. In one respect they grew in strength, both institutionally and visually. The religious houses and chapels that had competed with them disappeared, and there were now no other places at which to worship or to be buried. As landscape elements, however, they stopped growing altogether (see Figure 99). Rebuilding petered out during the middle of the 16th century. The outsides of church buildings were frozen in time. For the next three hundred years the characteristic church in the Cornish (and indeed in the English) landscape was one of the 15th or early 16th century, usually with a tower and aisles. What the builders of that period achieved became what people understood churches to be, an understanding that is still with us.

Churchscapes, the internal appearances of churches, did not freeze in this way. Their walls and pillars remained the same, and so did two important parts of their furnishings. Chancels continued to be divided from naves by the screens that had been introduced in about 1300. Naves remained full of the seating that had appeared or had been upgraded during the 15th and early 16th centuries. Yet much else changed between the 1530s and the 1560s. Holy objects were removed: altars, lights, and nearly every image, whether sculpted or painted. Such images as survived did so chiefly in stained-glass windows or as carvings in lofty places. The people of St Neot were notable in defending the grand set of windows that they had recently installed. Other windows with images of saints remained in churches such as Cardinham, Feock, St Kew, and St Winnow.[215]

Nevertheless, such images were no longer focuses of devotion, and churches lacked anything to venerate apart from whatever respect people might pay to the communion table or font. Visual aids still had a place in church, but they now consisted of texts: the Lord's Prayer, the Creed, the Ten Commandments, inscriptions on tombs, or boards describing charitable benefactions. Texts, as we have seen, originated long before the Reformation, so

Figure 98 The chapel of SS Mary and George, Cotehele wood. This little chapel was later believed to have been founded by Sir Richard Edgcumbe of Cotehele House in thanksgiving for his escape from his enemies in 1483. It has survived as a building through standing on the Cotehele estate.

their proliferation after it was not something wholly new. From at least Elizabeth's reign onwards the royal coat of arms began to be displayed as well, expressing the fact that the monarch was the ruler of both Church and state. Even this had earlier origins in the popularity of royal emblems during the early 16th century.

The parish church also changed inside by expressing unity rather than variety. Before the Reformation it had consisted of two or more rooms containing several areas of devotion and activity: the chancel, the side chapels and altars, images, the font, and the porch. Now there was a single focus on most Sundays: the nave, especially the area in front of the chancel screen. In most churches the clergyman and clerk moved from the chancel to the nave side of the screen, where reading desks and a pulpit were provided for them. Nearly every service was centred here except for baptisms, which were still done at the font. The chancel came to be used only on the rare occasions of holy communion, and even then only for the prayers immediately before the communion and for the distribution of the bread and wine. Other parts of the church ceased to have religious functions. The porch was reduced to a shelter, and the side chapels were filled with seating or tombs.

A church was now a unitary space in which people gathered for almost identical services each Sunday. Most of the material at the services was repeated on every occasion. Only the psalms, the lessons, and the homily ran through a sequence, although later, as preaching developed, the sermon became something fresh and individual. Every church did the same, so that those who ignored the requirement to attend their own church had nothing to gain by attending another, unless a sermon was preached. Whereas the medieval mass had been something to watch and adore rather than to understand, the services of the Church of England were times of instruction. The churchscape came to resemble a schoolroom. The clergyman read the service from a special seat, like that of a schoolmaster. The parishioners sat on benches as if they were pupils, amid texts that could be learnt. They were taught about the nature of God, the history of his relationship with the world, the promises that he had made to his people, and the duties that he required of them.

The clergyman's duties did not change in other respects. He continued to lead the service and his clerk to lead the responses. The congregation was allocated some prayers to say, but its role remained comparatively small. In Elizabeth's reign, you still addressed the clergyman as 'Sir' John or whatever his forename was, and he was still the chief spiritual person in the parish. Economically he retained his tithes and glebe, although he was more heavily taxed than before the 1530s. His status even improved in certain respects. The Tudor monarchs turned the parish into a unit of civil government. During the mid- and late 16th century it was given responsibility for poor relief, roads and bridges, and military matters. The clergyman grew to be the leader of what became the 'vestry' or parish administration for these purposes. In this way he gained powers over his parishioners that his predecessors had not held before the Reformation. He was also free of competition from monks, friars, guild priests, and chantry priests. There were now fewer clergy than before, and they were less of an 'estate', a widely assorted group like the gentry and the labourers, than they had been before the Reformation. In future they would come closer to being a profession with a uniform way of life and public roles.

Figure 99 Reformation survival. The parish church of Altarnun, still retaining much of its pre-Reformation furnishings, and still presiding over the landscape of its village.

Lay people had a parallel experience of change and continuity. Much stayed the same for them. They still entered the Church, like it or not, by baptism, now usually done on the Sunday after the birth rather than on the birthday itself. They remained subject to the Church's laws, laws supported as before by the power of the Crown. They were still expected to learn the basic prayers, to be confirmed (although that remained hard to achieve), to attend church on Sundays, to keep the Church's times and seasons including the Lenten fast, and to be buried in the parish church or churchyard. They had to pay tithes as before. Inside church social distinctions continued to matter. The gentry had their own space, and the disappearance of chapels and images gave them more scope to erect private seating and tombs. Senior parishioners continued to act as churchwardens and, these officers, like the clergyman, acquired new parochial responsibilities. There were still Church courts to police tithe-paying and moral behaviour, especially slander and sexual immorality.

Outside church it was possible for some old religious customs to continue. Richard Carew pointed out in his *Survey of Cornwall* (1602) that the Cornish still held church ales to raise money, organised by young men of the parish. People still commemorated the days of the patron saints of their churches: no longer in church, but by entertaining friends from other parishes. Carew might have mentioned that other folk customs survived in association with these days, like those of the tinners of Perranzabuloe on 5 March (St Piran's day) and Helston's 'furry day' on 8 May (a feast of St Michael, the town's patron saint). But, as a Protestant writer he wished to play down the appeal of the religious past, just as he avoided discussing the popularity of the old holy wells. These, too, went on attracting people for purposes of healing or of divining the future.[216]

Historians have long argued over whether the Reformation should be seen as a process of destruction, or of development and renewal. In truth it was both. Much that had been lovingly created during the Middle Ages was destroyed. Equally much of what happened during the Reformation grew out of that creation. The Church of England of Elizabeth's reign embodied new ideas and laws of the 16th century. But it was also rooted in the institutions, buildings, revenues, education, and social relationships that had taken shape in the previous thousand years.

Chapter 6 Cornwall: Heir of the Ages

CELTIC OR CATHOLIC?

Many people in Cornwall today have a strong sense that their land is different from the rest of England. As we have seen, they use the word 'Celtic' to express this sense and extend it to include religion. We hear about 'Celtic Christianity' in Cornwall, Ireland, and Wales, which is often believed to have differed in its ideas and practices from the Church in other areas. Are such beliefs supported by the history that has just been described?[217]

Cornwall was Christian for at least three hundred years before it became part of England. Many of its Christian religious sites originated in that early period, including many (perhaps a majority) of the sites of the present-day parish churches, although the

Figure 100 Tremaine church, typical of Cornwall in its lonely situation, its dedication to an ancient Brittonic saint (Winwaloe), and its importance as a spiritual element in the surrounding landscape.

church buildings are later. The Cornish, like the Welsh, were distinctive in naming most of these church sites after Brittonic people, many of whom they came to regard as saints. This custom was different from England, where fewer churches were dedicated to local Anglo-Saxon saints. There most were named in honour of Mary, the apostles of Jesus, or the great saints of continental Europe. Many Cornish and Welsh church sites lie in lonely places with only a farm or a few cottages beside them. This may reflect links with earlier graveyards or rounds, but its outcome – churches that were isolated, yet centres of local life – was not a specifically 'Celtic' or Brittonic one. There were plenty of similar churches in the uplands of England, for the good reason that, where the population is scattered in farms and hamlets, no villages exist in which to put churches.

How far Christianity differed in Cornwall up to about the time of the Norman Conquest in terms of faith, worship, or people's behaviour is harder to say. The famous points of difference between the Britons and the English were the way that the clergy cut their hair and how they calculated the date of Easter. The Easter calculation was not a Celtic invention, however. It was a Roman one that had been reformed in the rest of Europe, and the peoples of western Britain and Ireland lagged behind in making the change. It may not have survived much later in Cornwall than the time of Aldhelm. We encountered a Canterbury writer of the 900s who talked of the Cornish as holding to errors and resisting the truth, and it is possible that the Cornish had varieties of behaviour and doing things that differed from the practice of the English.

In most respects, however, the early Church in Cornwall was like the Church everywhere. It was a mixture of kings, nobility, bishops, clergy, and lesser lay people, about whom we know too little to judge how differently they acted from Christians elsewhere. Its clergy read the same Bible, and they and their congregations probably prayed and worshipped in much the same way, as Catholics all over Europe. The interest in the natural world that is often thought to be special to Celtic Christianity can be found in large measure in the Old Testament of the Bible; it is not original to the British Isles.

The similarities between Cornwall and England, and beyond England with Catholic Europe, grew even stronger after 1050. Cornwall was now part of a diocese that also covered Devon. The way that this diocese functioned was uniform with the rest of England. It had English kinds of bishops, archdeacons, rural deans, and peculiars, and they worked under the supervision of the archbishop of Canterbury and the pope. When monasticism returned to Cornwall after 1100, it came in the form of international religious

Figure 101 The Norman south porch of St Anthony-in-Roseland church. The church was originally named Entenin, apparently after a local person regarded as a saint, but contact with the outside world led to the saint becoming identified with the better-known Antoninus of Alexandria.

orders: Augustinians, Benedictines, and friars. The layout and furnishing of parish churches came to resemble those of England, and so did parish organisations like churchwardens and guilds. By 1500 most of the images in any Cornish church were those of the famous saints of Christendom, not the local Brittonic saints.

True, these exterior ideas and institutions underwent some modifications in Cornwall, even after 1050. The monastic presence was not as strong as it was in some other English counties, so that few Cornish took vows as monks or even as Augustinian canons.

Cornish churches were distinctive in their building materials, and there were more freestanding chapels (and perhaps more holy wells) than in some other counties. We have noticed that, long after Cornwall was part of England, medieval Cornish people imagined their saints as coming to Cornwall not from England, or even from France or Italy, but from other 'Celtic' lands: Petroc from Wales, and Buryan, Gwinear, Ia, and Piran from Ireland. To this extent many Cornish continued to identify themselves with the peoples and Christianity of these lands.

Yet Catholic Europe was not itself uniform; nor was England. Beliefs and practices were broadly similar, but the emphasis placed on them varied from one country, region, and period to another. There were also differences in the distribution of foundations such as monasteries, and in the day-to-day functioning of institutions. Arguably, what was different in Cornwall was one subset of such variations. Lovers of the county's history must be careful about claiming for it a status that is unique.

THE MEDIEVAL ACHIEVEMENT

The Middle Ages seem a long way back. About 500 years have passed since even their latter end. Popular opinion thinks of them at best as a primitive era; people use the word 'medieval' to disparage what they think of as out of date or barbaric. The story of this book refutes such views. Christianity in medieval Cornwall turns out to have inspired achievements of wide scope and sophistication. These include worship, education, writings, architecture, art, music, hospitals, charity to the poor, travel on pilgrimages, institutions like monasteries and parishes, and social groupings such as church congregations and guilds. No one can say that the Church in Cornwall, or the human race there, slept through the Middle Ages and woke up only in the 16th century.

Some of these achievements are still around us in tangible forms that we can study and experience, not just to learn about the past but to widen our knowledge of humanity. There are church buildings, screens, seating, stained-glass windows, wall paintings, tombs, churchyards, crosses, and wells. Given the absence of much surviving art and architecture from before 1500 that is secular, the Cornish record of human achievement in these areas is preserved almost wholly in what is religious. Moving outside church buildings we can still see the impact of religion on the county's landscape. Religious objects help to form the landscape: churches, chapel ruins, crosses, and wells. Fields may, in some cases, inherit something of their shape and usage from the ecclesiastical landlords – monasteries and parish clergy – who owned them. The best historical maps that we have of these fields, the tithe maps of about 1840, were drawn for religious purposes. Roads, bridges, and quays have benefited from religious charity and indulgences.

Large numbers of documents survive from medieval Cornwall, especially after 1200. Many of them were generated by the Church and its activities, such as bishops' registers, licences for pilgrim ships, indulgences, wills, and churchwardens' accounts. These help us to trace not only religious history but also the history of towns, villages, and people, the better to understand their successors today. Books survive that the Cornish made, commissioned, or used. The most famous of these are the manuscripts containing the five plays and the few other pieces of literature in the Cornish language, most of which are religious. These manuscripts contain a very large part of that language and literature before its revival in the 19th and 20th centuries. Without this legacy from the Church in the later Middle Ages, we would have far fewer records of Cornish than we do.

Tangible objects are easy to understand because they are visible or catalogued. Less tangible, but also important, is what Christianity inspired the Cornish to create outside their own land. This has been a neglected topic, partly because most historians of medieval Cornwall have concentrated on what happened inside its borders. In fact the involvement of the Cornish with the Church beyond their coasts and the Tamar was a substantial one. They exported their religion to other areas as early as the period from 500 to 1000, as well as importing it. We know that the cult of St Petroc spread from Padstow and Bodmin to Brittany, England, and Wales, and those of St Neot and St Rumon to England.

After about 1100 the Cornish impact on the wider Church can be more clearly traced and established from documents. At least

Figure 102 Donors, perhaps guildsfolk, of the Passion window in St Kew, led by a gentleman and lady in red. At the end of this book, they may stand as emblems of all the generations of lay people who maintained the Church in Cornwall from AD 500 to 1560.

three men from the county became bishops during the 12th and early 13th centuries: Algar of Bodmin at Coutances, Walter of Coutances at Lincoln and Rouen, and Hugh le Rous at Ossory. The canons of Bodmin who went to Ireland in 1193 founded two priories that lasted until the Reformation. In the 14th and 15th centuries Cornish mariners carried English pilgrims to Compostella and back, and five or six other Cornishmen rose to be bishops in England or Ireland after 1400. We can identify Cornish deans and canons of Exeter Cathedral, Cornish parish clergy in England, and even poor Cornish chaplains – men of little account in their day, but men whose labours underpinned the Church and to whom historians, at least, can do justice.

This emigration made an important contribution to scholarship and literature outside Cornwall. Cornish students made their way to Paris in the 12th and 13th centuries, and to Oxford from its first beginnings. John of Cornwall is one of Oxford's earliest known scholars. More than 200 men who studied at Oxford can be traced from his time until the early 16th century – not a total, merely those whose names have chanced to survive. Three medieval chancellors of the university were from Cornwall. There were Cornish writers of Latin. These people are particularly hard to explain to the general reader, because their work is not usually available in English and it was often written on subjects and in ways that are unfamiliar to us. Yet John of Cornwall's *Prophecies of Merlin*, Peter of Cornwall's *Book of Revelations*, Michael of Cornwall's poems, and Richard Rufus's theological works are all highly rated by scholars. When English increased in written and scholarly use in the second half of the 14th century, it did so partly thanks to the work of John Cornwall and John Trevisa. These men's careers show that Cornwall was not isolated or introverted, but linked with the culture of western Europe.

'No man is an island', wrote John Donne, and Cornwall is not itself alone but 'a piece of the continent, a part of the main'. Its Christian history is a double story. The story is partly that of Cornwall itself, shaped by its special character. But the story also takes us beyond the Tamar, showing us that the Cornish were part of a wider Church: shaped by that Church and helping to shape it in turn. As with all local history, we can fully understand the history of the Church in Cornwall only when we consider it as part of wider history. And we can fully understand that wider history only when we make Cornwall part of it.

Guide to Technical Terms

advowson – the right to choose and present the clergyman of a parish church to the diocesan bishop for **institution**, or to be involved in choosing the head of a religious house. The owner of the right was known as the **patron**.
aisle – a subdivision of a church, usually alongside and parallel with the **nave**, **chancel**, or **choir**.
alien priory – a priory owned and ruled by a foreign abbey.
altar – a stone table at which **mass** was celebrated. The high altar was the principal altar of a church, placed at the east end of the **chancel** or **choir**.
altarage – the offerings made to the high altar of a parish church, the perquisite of the rector or vicar; sometimes the altarage was considered to include the small **tithes**.
anchorite – a man or woman who took vows to live celibately and permanently in an enclosed room or house, as opposed to having some freedom of movement like a **hermit**.
anniversary – *see* **obit**.
annuellar – an alternative name for a **chantry priest**.
antiphon – a piece of music sung in church before and after a psalm, or as an anthem in its own right.
appropriation – the practice by which a religious house was allowed to make itself rector of a parish and to take **tithes** from the parish.
arcade – a row of arches, usually separating a **nave** from an **aisle**.
archdeacon – the clergyman in charge of an archdeaconry, a subdivision of a diocese.
archpriest – a title sometimes given to the cleric in charge of a small **college** of priests.
benefice – a Church post with an income, held by a cleric such as a **rector**, **vicar**, or secular **canon**.
bishop – the Church leader in overall charge of a **diocese**. See also **suffragan**.
breviary – a book containing the daily offices or services said by the clergy.
canon, regular – a cleric, similar to a **monk**, who belonged to an abbey or priory that followed the Rule of St Augustine or comparable rules.
canon, secular – a senior cleric serving a **cathedral** or **college**, similar to a **rector** or **vicar** rather than a **monk**, but having no parish duties.
canon law – the law of the Church.
cathedral – the chief church of the bishop of the diocese. Exeter Cathedral was staffed by secular **canons**.
cell – a small religious house owned and ruled by an abbey or priory elsewhere.
chancel – the eastern part of a parish church where services were said by the clergy, and sometimes accommodating important laity. In the case of cathedrals, monasteries, and colleges the term **choir** is generally used instead.

chantry – the saying of a daily mass by a priest for the well-being of a living person, or the soul of a dead one, either for a limited period or perpetually. The term is also used for the endowment that paid the priest, and for the place where the masses were said, such as a chapel inside a church.

chantry priest – the priest of a chantry, also known in Devon and Cornwall as an **annuellar**.

chapel – an area within a church containing an **altar**, or a separate building with an altar that did not have the status of a parish church. A chapel of ease served a community a long way from a parish church.

chaplain – a term used in the Middle Ages for a priest who worked in a parish as an assistant or deputy to a **rector** or **vicar**, or in a private household.

choir – the eastern part of a cathedral, monastery, or college where services were said: the equivalent of the **chancel** of a parish church. Also the collective term for the clergy who performed the service in that part of the church.

chorister – a boy singer in a church.

chrism – a mixture of oil and balm used in baptism and in other rites.

church ale – ale brewed to help make profit for a church and sold at social functions or to individual people.

church house – a house built by parishioners close to a parish church and used for social functions.

churching – a ceremony by which a mother gave thanks after a birth, and was led back into the parish church by its **rector**, **vicar**, or **chaplain**.

clerestory – the upper part of a church, usually above an **arcade**, carrying a row of windows to light the church.

civil law – Roman law (as distinct from **canon law** and **common law**).

clerk – a term generally meaning a cleric who was not a priest, but of lower status.

collation – *see* **institution**.

college, collegiate church – a church staffed by a resident group of **secular clergy** who governed it together. In the Middle Ages the word meant a collection of clergy and did not imply any academic functions.

commendation, '*in commendam*' – the grant of a benefice to somebody as a temporary measure, pending the appointment of a permanent occupant.

common law – the law of the courts of the king of England.

communion – *see* **mass**.

confession – the process of confessing one's sins to the rector or vicar of the parish at least once a year during Lent.

consistory – the court of the bishop of the diocese.

corrody – a pension charged on a monastery, which had to provide the pensioner with board and lodging for life.

crossing – the part of a church at the east end of the nave, between the transepts.

curate – originally the **rector** or **vicar** of a parish who exercised the **cure of souls**. After the Reformation the term came to mean a priest who assisted or deputised for a rector or vicar, but until the middle of the 16th century such men were usually known as **chaplains**.

cure of souls – the right and duty to care for the souls of the inhabitants of a parish.
dean – the title given to the chief clergyman of a **cathedral** and of some **colleges**, as well as the presiding cleric of a **rural deanery**.
diocese – the territory ruled by a bishop. The diocese of Exeter covered Cornwall and Devon.
excommunication – a punishment imposed by a cleric, usually a bishop, which forbade a sinner to attend church, receive the sacraments, or mix with other people until the sinner submitted to the Church.
friar – a cleric who lived from voluntary donations, unlike monks and parish clergy who received their support from lands and other endowments.
glebe – land belonging to the **rector** or **vicar** of a parish, often known in Cornwall as **sanctuary**.
hermit – a person, usually male, who took a vow of celibacy and lived alone, but was able to travel about unlike an **anchorite**.
high altar – *see* **altar**.
holywater clerk – *see* **parish clerk**.
hospital – in the Middle Ages a religious or semi-religious institution offering long-term care for lepers or the infirm, or short-term accommodation for the sick, rather than medical treatment.
incumbent – the occupant of a **benefice** such as a **rector** or **vicar**.
indulgence (or **pardon**) – the forgiving of **penance** by a pope or a bishop in return for doing a good deed such as a crusade, pilgrimage, prayer, or contribution to a church or a hospital.
institution (or **admission**) – the act by which a bishop approved the appointment to a **benefice** of a clergyman presented to him by a **patron**. When the bishop was himself the patron of the benefice, and therefore both presented and appointed, the act was known as a **collation**.
ledger stone – a flat stone laid over a grave in a church.
Lent – the 40 weekdays (plus Sundays) from Ash Wednesday until the day before Easter, a time of fasting and penitence for sins; also an **indulgence** of 40 days of penance.
manual – a book containing the pastoral services done by clergy, such as baptisms, marriages, and funerals, so called because they took it around in their hands for these purposes.
mass – the service of the eucharist or holy communion.
mendicant – a **friar**; the term means a beggar.
minster – in modern use, a church (especially in the 10th, 11th, and 12th centuries) staffed by a group of secular **canons**, **priests**, or **clerks**, rather than **monks**. In later centuries such churches are known as **colleges** or collegiate churches.
missal – a book containing the service of the mass.
monastery – a church served by a group of **monks** or **canons regular**.
monk – a cleric who lived in a monastery that observed the Rule of St Benedict, or another similar rule.
mortuary – a due paid to a **rector** or **vicar** after someone's death.
nave – the western part of a church, also called the 'body', open to lay people.
nun – the female equivalent of a monk, living in a nunnery.

obit – a mass celebrated on the anniversary of someone's death, also known as an anniversary.

official – the deputy of a bishop or archdeacon who managed their legal affairs.

ordain, ordination – the rite by which a bishop confers religious status on a person. There were several grades of ordination, the highest of which was **priest**.

pardon, pardoner – an **indulgence** and the person who advertised it.

parish – the area belonging to a parish church, whose inhabitants had the right and duty to support that church and its clergyman and to receive care in return.

parish clerk – the assistant of a rector or vicar at the services in a parish church, usually a young man until the 15th century.

patron – the person who held the right to appoint or be involved with the appointment of the **rector** or **vicar** of a parish church, or the head of a religious house. This right was known as an **advowson** and could be held by clergy or lay people.

peculiar, peculiar jurisdiction – a territory consisting of one or more parishes which had its own system of administration for Church purposes, separate from the normal administration of the diocese.

penance – the punishment due to a sin, which had to be carried out before the sin would be obliterated.

piscina – a drain in a church wall for disposing of holy water.

polyphony, polyphonic – music sung in harmony by voices following different parts.

prebend – a share of the income of a church, equivalent to a **stipend** or salary.

prebendal church – a church staffed by two or more prebendaries, differing from a **college** in that they did not generally live together as a community.

prebendary – the holder of a **prebend**, a member of the **secular clergy** similar to a secular **canon**, differing from a **rector** or **vicar** in not usually having parish duties.

presbytery – the eastern part of a choir of a church, near the high altar, where the clergy celebrated mass.

priest – a cleric with the power to say mass, baptise, and administer the other **sacraments. Rectors, vicars**, and **chaplains** were normally priests, and by the later Middle Ages so were **monks** and **friars**.

prior – the head of a **priory**, sometimes of a **hospital.**

priory – a monastery, generally less large and wealthy than an abbey. There were no abbeys in medieval Cornwall.

proctor – a legal representative or agent.

provision, papal provision – an appointment of a bishop, abbot, prior, cathedral canon, rector, or vicar by the pope instead of by the **patron** normally responsible for making the appointment. Such appointments were common in 14th-century England, but only replaced the rights of other clergy, never challenging those of lay patrons.

provost – the title given to some heads of colleges, including Glasney in Cornwall.

rector – the clergyman of a parish who received all its revenues; his **benefice** and house were known as a rectory.

regency – a period after graduation at university in which the graduate was expected to lecture and hold disputations.

regular clergy – **monks**, regular **canons**, and **friars**, so called because they all followed written codes of rules.

religious house – any church served by a group of clergy, such as a **cathedral**, **monastery**, or **friary**.

reliquary – a wooden or metal container holding bones or other relics of Christ or the saints.

requiem – a **mass** including prayers for the soul of a dead person.

retrochoir – the area behind the high altar of a large church, similar to a choir **aisle**.

rood – a large image of Christ on the cross, placed on the rood screen – a screen (normally of wood) between the chancel and the nave.

rural deanery – a group of parishes administered by a rural **dean**.

sacraments – one of seven solemn rites of the medieval Church: baptism, confirmation, marriage, confession, communion, ordination, and the anointing of the sick.

sanctuary – the part of the church around the high altar at the east end of the chancel or choir; also a privilege by which people accused of a crime could take refuge in a church or on certain pieces of Church property; also an alternative name for **glebe**.

Sarum, **Use of** – **breviaries**, **manuals**, **missals**, and other service books following the usages of Salisbury Cathedral, commonly used in southern England in the 14th, 15th, and early 16th centuries.

secular clergy – clergy who did not follow the monastic life, such as parish clergy and the **canons** of **cathedrals** and **colleges**.

sexton – a sacristan who helped look after a church, eventually coming to mean someone who did physical tasks like ringing bells and digging graves.

Sir – a title given to all priests, as well as to knights; it did not necessarily signify possession of a university degree.

stipend – the income of a **benefice** received by the cleric who held it.

suffragan – an assistant bishop.

tithe – the obligation of all householders to pay the rector of their parish one tenth of the produce of their land, including all crops and young animals. Fish, dairy products, and the milling of grain were also tithed. Tithes of grain were known as 'great tithes' or 'garb tithes'; other tithes as 'small tithes'.

transept – transverse space at right angles to the nave and often projecting to form arms, as in cross plan. Often applied to those arms alone.

tympanum – a panel within an archway above a church door or between the chancel and the nave.

vicar – the clergyman of an **appropriated** parish, who received part not all of its revenues; his **benefice** and house were known as a vicarage.

vicar choral – a clergyman in a **cathedral** or **college** who deputised for a **canon** in saying the daily services.

vicar general – the deputy of a bishop, with general responsibility for administering his affairs in his absence other than confirmations and ordinations which were done by a **suffragan**.

Endnotes

References to books and articles in the Bibliography adopt the 'Harvard' form. The author's surname is followed by the date of publication (if the author is represented by more than one work), a letter of the alphabet after the date (if the author published more than one work in the same year), and the page number(s). Other references are spelt out in full. The following abbreviations are used:

BL	British Library, London
Bodleian	Bodleian Library, Oxford
Cal. Inq. Misc.	*Calendar of Inquisitions Miscellaneous*
CRO	Cornwall Record Office, Truro
DCNQ	*Devon and Cornwall Notes and Queries*
DCRS	Devon and Cornwall Record Society
DNB	*The Oxford Dictionary of National Biography*
DRO	Devon Record Office, Sowton, Exeter
ECA, D&C	Exeter Cathedral Archives, Dean and Chapter
ed.	edited
edn.	edition
L. & P. Hen VIII	*Letters and Papers, Foreign and Domestic, Henry VIII*
TDA	*Transactions of the Devonshire Association*
TNA	The National Archives, Kew, London
VCH	*Victoria County History*

CHAPTER 1 The Early Middle Ages (500–1100), pp. 1–25

1 The Romans applied the word *Celticus* to the people of ancient Gaul (modern France). The earliest English uses, recorded from 1656, had a similar application (*Oxford English Dictionary*, s.n. 'Celtic').
2 On the Dumnonii, see A. Fox, and Todd, and on Wessex, Yorke.
3 For the campaigns and battles, see *Anglo-Saxon Chronicle*, 16, 21, 26, 30, 39-41, and for Dungarth, D. N. Dumville (ed.), *Annales Cambriae, A.D. 682-954* (Cambridge, 2002), 12-13.
4 For Alfred, see Keynes and Lapidge, 89, 175.
5 On Christianity in Roman Britain, see Thomas, 1981, and Blair, 10-15.
6 On the stones, see Okasha, 1993, 1998-9; Thomas, 1994; and Sims-Williams.
7 Gildas, 29-30, 99-100.
8 Orme, 2000a, 11-14; *VCH Cornwall*, II, chapter 1.
9 The best edition of the First Life is now Flobert, esp. 212-23 (Latin text with French translation). An English translation of an older edition, T. Taylor, *The Life of St. Samson of Dol* (London, 1925), is now out-of-date.
10 On Aldhelm, see *DNB*; for his letter, Aldhelm, *The Prose Works*, trans. M. Lapidge and M. Herren (Cambridge, 1979), 155-60; and for his journey, Aldhelm, *The Poetic Works*, trans. M. Lapidge and J. L. Rosier (Woodbridge, 1985), 177-9.
11 For Gerontius's grant, see M. A. O'Donovan (ed.), *Charters of Sherborne*, British Academy, Anglo-Saxon Charters 3 (London, 1988), 81; on Sherborne, see also K. Barker, 'The Early History of Sherborne', in Pearce, 77-116.
12 On Kenstec, see Olson, 51-6, and for Asser, Keynes and Lapidge, 97.
13 For the Canterbury letter, see Whitelock, 893.
14 Ibid., and on the Church in the South West after 909, Barlow, 1979, 211-15.
15 Olson, 78-84 (royal charters); *Anglo-Saxon Chronicle*, 80 (Viking attack).
16 *Domesday Book*, sections 1/4, 5/7/6, 5/24/14 (St Kew), 4/21 (Bodmin); Orme,

2000a, 201-2, 226-7 (relics).

17 Orme, 2000a, 214-19.

18 Barlow, 1979, 211-24.

19 Ibid., 212-15; on Leofric, see *DNB*, and F. Barlow and others, *Leofric of Exeter* (Exeter, 1972).

20 The records of slave freeing are printed in Förster, 83-99 (Latin and Old English), with extracts in modern English in Whitelock, 608-10. On education in this period, see Gwara, and Orme, 2006a, chapter 1.

21 On minsters generally, see Blair.

22 On minsters in Cornwall, see Olson, 51-97, and *VCH Cornwall*, II, sub 'Religious Houses before 1066'.

23 For the endowments of these churches, see *Domesday Book*, section 4/1-24; on tax immunity, Olson, 87n, 92-4; and on sanctuaries, ibid., 72-3, 79, 107. It is possible that St Keverne was a fourth early sanctuary.

24 On the list of saints, see Olson and Padel; Olson, 56-60; and Roscarrock, 42-51.

25 On early Cornish churchyards, see the good survey by Preston-Jones in Edwards and Lane, especially 82-4, and in *Cornish Archaeology* especially 114-15 (on Merther Uny and rounds).

26 On holy wells, see above, pp. 111-12.

27 On this, and the next three paragraphs, see Orme, 2000a, especially 20-7.

28 Translations of texts of medieval saints' Lives are printed in Doble, 1960-97, and Wade-Evans.

29 On the Petroc bell, see Förster, 88, and on Perranzabuloe and Veryan, Orme, 2000a, 221, 240.

30 On the Bodmin Gospels, see Jenner, 1922-5, 113-45, 235-60; for the Pontifical, G. H. Doble (ed.), *Pontificale Lanaletense*, Henry Bradshaw Soc. 74 (1937); and on the *Codex*, F. Madan and H. H. E. Craster (ed.), *A Summary Catalogue of Western Manuscripts in the Bodleian Library at Oxford* (Oxford, 1922-53), II(i), 170-4.

31 On early estates in Cornwall that may have helped shape parishes, see Hooke. Parishes are also discussed above, pp. 30-3. For glebes, see Potts.

32 There is no convenient history of tithes. Most has been written on the tithe surveys and maps in the 19th century: Kain and Oliver, Kain and Prince, 1985, 2000. On tithes in medieval Cornwall, see also *VCH Cornwall*, II, and for the duties of the clergy in England generally, Tinti, especially 17-26.

33 Förster, 83, 88, 96; Okasha, 1993, 213-17, 291-5.

34 On Osbern, see Barlow, 1996a, pp. xxxii-xxxiii, and *DNB*, and on Robert of Mortain, Golding and *DNB*.

35 *Domesday Book*, especially sections 4/1-24.

36 For the Bodmin estate, see ibid., section 4/21, and on Robert's alleged seizures of property, ibid., sections 3/7, 4/1, 4/2, 4/7-15, 4/20, 4/23-4.

37 On Robert's relations with St Stephen-by-Launceston, see Hull, 1987, pp. xi-xiii, and *VCH Cornwall*, II, chapter 1 and sub 'Religious Houses before 1066: Launceston'.

CHAPTER 2 The High Middle Ages (1100-1300), pp. 27-61

38 Bishops of Exeter to 1300 are listed in Le Neve, 2005, 1-7, and their biographies in Barlow, 1996a, pp. xxxii-liv, and *DNB*. The 1123 charter is in *Regesta Regum Anglo-Normannorum*, II, 185, and cf. 72.

39 For Cargoll, see Rowe, I, 118-19.

40 Archdeacons of Cornwall to 1300 are listed in Le Neve, 2005, 32-5. On archdeacons in general, see B. R. Kemp (ed.), *Twelfth-Century English Archidiaconal and Vice-Archidiaconal Acta*, Canterbury & York Soc. 92 (2001), especially pp. xlii-lv, 27-30, and on rural deaneries in general, Thompson, 1943, 153-94, and idem, 1947, 63-9. By the 19th century rural deans in Exeter diocese were considered to be elected by their fellow clergy, but earlier evidence for this is elusive.

41 The list of 1291 is in *Reg. Bronescombe*, ed. Hingeston-Randolph, 465-72.

42 On peculiars, see ibid., 465-7, and Fig.18. The St Buryan case is discussed in *VCH Cornwall*, II.

43 The earliest maps of Cornish parish boundaries are reproduced in Orme, 2006c, 34-8 (Fig. 21 in this book), Gascoyne, and the tithe maps of *c.*1840 housed (for Cornwall) in TNA and CRO. Tithe maps are discussed in Kain and Oliver, and Kain and Prince 1985, 2000.
44 On monasticism in general in the 12th and 13th centuries, see D. Knowles, *The Monastic Order in England 943-1216* (2nd edn, Cambridge, 1963), idem, *The Religious Orders in England* (Cambridge, 1948-59), vol I; J. C. Dickinson, *The Origins of the Austin Canons and their Introduction into England* (London, 1950); and J. E. Burton, *Monastic and Religious Orders in Britain, 1000-1300* (Cambridge, 1994).
45 On histories of these and the houses that follow, see *VCH Cornwall*, II.
46 On friars in general, see Knowles, *Religious Orders*, I, 114-252, and on the Cornish friaries, *VCH Cornwall*, II, sub 'Bodmin Friary' and 'Truro Friary'.
47 Examples of Cornish men and women who became monks and nuns outside Cornwall are listed in *VCH Cornwall*, II, chapter 2.
48 This is discussed above, pp. 69-71.
49 Hale and Ellacombe, 28-9; Orme and Webster, 170-7.
50 On Guy, Algar, and the four Bodmin canons of 1193, see *VCH Cornwall*, II, sub 'Bodmin Priory'; and on Peter of Cornwall, Hull and Sharpe; Sharpe, 425-6; and *DNB*.
51 On Peter, see Sharpe, 426, and on Rufus, ibid., 503-5; P. G. J. M. Raedts, *Richard Rufus of Cornwall and the Tradition of Oxford Theology* (Oxford, 1987); R. Wood, 'Richard Rufus of Cornwall and Aristotle's Physics', *Franciscan Studies* 52 (1996), 247-81; and *DNB*.
52 Hull and Sharpe, 16-27.
53 Grosjean, 1956, 470-96; Doble, 1939, 403-15; Jankulak, 1-39, 153-201.
54 The earliest register is *Reg. Bronescombe*, ed. Hingeston-Randolph, and ed. Robinson; on Bodmin and Launceston, see *VCH Cornwall*, II.
55 On Richard, see *Reg Bronescombe*, ed. Hingeston-Randolph, 31-2, 315; ed. Robinson, II, 66-7, 111, and on Plympton, *Register of Bishop Godfrey Giffard*, ed. J. W. Willis Bund, III, Worcs. Hist. Soc. (1900), 293.
56 On parish clergy in England between 1100 and 1200, pending forthcoming work by Dr Julia Barrow, see M. Brett, *The English Church under Henry I* (1975), 216-33; Dr Barrow's articles in *Historical Research* 60 (1987), 1-8, *Anglo-Norman Studies* 26 (2004), 37-53, and in Tinti, 17-26; and C. Harper-Bill in *Anglo-Norman Studies* 11 (1989), 113-32. On parish clergy between 1200 and 1300, see J. R. H. Moorman, *Church Life in England in the 13th Century* (Cambridge, 1945). Schooling throughout the period is covered by Orme, 2006a.
57 For Quinil's order, see Powicke and Cheney, II, 1026-7. On parish clerks, see Orme, 2006a, 205-7, and above, pp. 81, 90.
58 The 'Vocabulary' is BL, Cotton Vespasian A.xiv, ff. 7-10, edited by Graves. For Quinil, see Powicke and Cheney, II, 1017, and for the handbook, ibid. 1059-77. The latter was an abridgement of Quinil's synodal statutes mentioned above, p. 56.
59 On universities from 1100 to 1300, see J. I. Catto (ed.), *The Early Oxford Schools*, History of the University of Oxford, I (Oxford, 1984), and A. B. Cobban, *The Medieval English Universities: Oxford and Cambridge to c.1500* (Aldershot, 1988).
60 On Cornwall, see *DNB*, and on his *Prophecies of Merlin*, Curley.
61 On Walter of Coutances, see *DNB*; on the two Richards of Cornwall, Emden, 1957-9I, 490-1; on John of St Goran, Barlow, 1996b, 312, 320; on Philip of St Austell, J. Le Neve, *Fasti Ecclesiae Anglicanae 1300-1541*, IV: *Monastic Cathedrals*, ed. B. Jones (London, 1963), 50; and on Michael of Cornwall, Sharpe, 376-7, and *DNB*.
62 On this subject, see also Page; his method of counting differs slightly from that used here.
63 For (much undervalued) incomes in 1291, see *Reg. Bronescombe*, ed. Hingeston-Randolph, 465-72.
64 Taxations (financial ordinances) of vicarages are listed in *Reg. Bronescombe*, ed. Robinson, III, 125. For stipends, see Powicke and Cheney, II, 1025, and for hospitality, ibid, I, 232.
65 For chaplains' wages, see ibid., I, 236; II, 1025.

66 Buildings in this period are discussed in more detail in *VCH Cornwall*, II, chapter 2.
67 On Norman churches in Cornwall, see Sedding.
68 Powicke and Cheney, I, 227-37 (Brewer); II, 982-1077 (Quinil).
69 The report of 1281 is ECA, D&C 2672A, ff. 7v-8, 9-11. The churches were Altarnun, St Breward, St Erth, Gwennap, St Issey, Perranzabuloe, Veryan, and St Winnow, and the chapel St Nectan in St Winnow parish.
70 The report of 1331 is ECA, D&C 2851, printed in *Reg. Grandisson*, II, 605-11. The churches were Altarnun, Boconnoc, Bradoc, St Breward, Constantine, St Erth, Gwennap, Gwinear, St Issey, Mullion, Perranzabuloe, Sancreed, Veryan, and St Winnow, and the chapels St Agnes (in Perranzabuloe), and St Nectan and Respryn (in St Winnow).
71 Powicke and Cheney, II, 1007 (Quinil on seating).
72 For the obligations of lay people to the Church, see Powicke and Cheney, I, 228, 233-5; II, 987-99.
73 On children and the Church, see Orme, 2001, 200-36.
74 Powicke and Cheney, I, 228 (Brewer on clergy teaching children).
75 Lepine and Orme, 259-61 (early guilds near Exeter); *Cat. Ancient Deeds*, IV, 449 (Truro); H. R. Moulton, *Palaeography, Genealogy and Topography: selections from the collection of H. R. Moulton* (Richmond, 1930), 179 (Nancecuke).
76 For the St Michael's Mount miracles, see G. H. Doble, 'Miracles at St. Michael's Mount in Cornwall in 1262', *Truro Diocesan Gazette* (October, 1934), 130-1, and Fletcher and Stéphan, 67-9; for St Buryan, Barlow, 1996b, 259-61; and on the crusade of 1188, Orme and Padel, 2005, 71-7.

CHAPTER 3 The Later Middle Ages (1300-1500): The Clergy, pp. 63–93

77 On the Black Death in England, see M. Prestwich, *Plantagenet England 1225-1360* (Oxford, 2005), 538-50, and for Bodmin especially, Worcester, 94-5, and *Reg. Grandisson*, II, 1076-7.
78 *Reg. Grandisson*, III, 1338-1425.
79 A. Hinde, *England's Population* (London, 2003), especially 38-52, 68-73; J. Hatcher, *Rural Economy and Society in the Duchy of Cornwall, 1300-1500* (Cambridge, 1970), 102-21.
80 For Bodmin in 1381, see *Cal. Inq. Misc.* IV, 102; on Lollardy, A. Hudson, *The Premature Reformation* (Oxford, 1988); and on Stephen, Emden, 1957-9, III, 1772, and *DNB*.
81 Further details of these changes are given in *VCH Cornwall*, II, chapter 3.
82 *Regg. Stapeldon, Grandisson, Brantyngham, Stafford*, and *Lacy*, vol. I, ed. Hingeston-Randolph, and *Reg. Lacy*, ed. Dunstan, vols I-V. For their biographies, see Emden, 1957-9, passim, and *DNB*; and for their itineraries, *Reg. Stapeldon*, 547-60; *Reg. Grandisson*, III, 1524-32; *Reg. Brantyngham*, II, 890-6; *Reg. Stafford*, 476-9; and *Reg. Lacy*, ed. Hingeston-Randolph and Dunstan, passim.
83 *Reg. Bronescombe*, ed. Hingeston-Randolph, 202; ed. Robinson, II, 74; *Reg. Stapeldon*, 384. For a provisional list of suffragan bishops, see Fryde et al., 284-7.
84 For the list of archdeacons, 1300-1540, see Le Neve, 1964, 15-17; many of their biographies are in Emden, 1957-9 and 1974.
85 Matthew, 72-142.
86 Detailed histories of all the houses that follow will be found in *VCH Cornwall*, II.
87 On the Launceston elections of 1430 and 1534, see ibid., sub 'Launceston Priory'.
88 For Launceston, see *Reg. Grandisson*, I, 564-5; II, 837, 955-6, 989-2, 1003-8, and for Bodmin, ibid., II, 979-83, 1009-14.
89 For Bodmin, see *Reg. Bronescombe*, ed. Hingeston-Randolph, 31; ed. Robinson, II, 66-7; for St Germans, *Reg. Grandisson*, III, 1226, and *Lettres communes des papes du XIVe siècle: Urbain V, letters communes*, 3 (Paris, 1974-6), 542; and for Tywardreath, CRO, RS/60, pp. 2-67.
90 BL, Harley 2399, ff. 47-64v (John Bowyer's manuscript); Worcester, 88-91.

91 For libraries, see R. H. and M. A. Rouse (ed.), *Registrum Anglie de Libris Doctorum et Auctorum Veterum*, Corpus of British Medieval Library Catalogues, vol 2 (London, 1991), 281-2, and for university study, Emden, 1957-9, II, 711, 1035; III, 1691, and *Reg. Lacy*, ed. Dunstan, III, 196, 324.

92 On friars' education in general, see Orme, 2006a, 258-66, and on Bodmin and Truro in particular, *VCH Cornwall*, II, sub 'Bodmin Friary' and 'Truro Friary'.

93 *Reg. Grandisson*, II, 632, 1146.

94 Worcester, 84-7, 92-3, 98-9 (calendars); *Reg. Lacy*, ed. Hingeston-Randolph, I, 32-3 (Clerk); TNA, C 85/81/25 (friars as parish chaplains).

95 Orme, 2007, 70; Orme, 1976, 167-8.

96 On hospitals in medieval England, see N. Orme and M. Webster, *The English Hospital, 1070-1570* (New Haven and London, 1995). The articles on Cornwall in that book have been revised in *VCH Cornwall*, II.

97 Ibid., under the foundations concerned.

98 On hermits and anchorites in general, see R. M. Clay, *The Hermits and Anchorites of England* (London, 1914) and A. K. Warren, *Anchorites and their Patrons in Medieval England* (Berkeley, Cal., 1985). Those recorded in Cornwall are listed in *VCH Cornwall*, II, sub 'Anchorites and Hermits'.

99 *Reg. Stapeldon*, 448-50, 452-5.

100 On school education in England, 1300-1500, see Orme, 2006a; on parish clerks, Orme, 2001, 231; and on education in Cornwall, also above, pp. 46-7, 121-2.

101 Medieval Oxford students are listed in Emden, 1957-9, and 1974. On students from Camborne, see Orme, 2006d.

102 On St Edmund Hall, see A. B. Emden, *An Oxford Hall in Medieval Times* (Oxford, 1968), 105-10, and on Hart Hall, N. Saul, 'The Pre-History of an Oxford College: Hart Hall and its Neighbours in the Middle Ages', *Oxoniensia* 54 (1991), 327-43.

103 On the history of the college, with lists of fellows, see Boase.

104 *Reg. Grandisson*, II, 621-2, 627, 660, 1147-9, 1179-81; III, 1305.

105 The dignitaries and canons of Exeter Cathedral, 1300-1540, are listed in Le Neve, 1964, and discussed by D. Lepine, *A Brotherhood of Canons Serving God: English Secular Cathedrals in the Later Middle Ages* (Woodbridge, 1995), especially 47. On Cobbethorn, see R. and O. B. Peter, 13, 116. 149.

106 For biographies of Oxford scholars from Cornwall, see Emden, 1957-9, and *DNB*.

107 *Reg. Grandisson*, II, 957-8, 1193-5; III, 1231-4; *Reg. Brantyngham*, I, 148, 156, 354-5, 434, 438, 466, 490; *Reg. Stafford*, 42.

108 *Reg. Stapeldon*, 342, *Reg. Grandisson*, II, 606 (clergy houses); Orme, 2007, passim (clergy wills).

109 Greke's breviary is Aberystwyth, National Library of Wales, NLW 22253A, described in Orme, 1999 and 2000b; on Waryn, see Orme, 2007, 60-2, 251.

110 For chaplains' stipends, see *Statutes of the Realm*, I, 373-4; II, 188, and W. Lyndwood, *Provinciale seu Constitutiones Angliae* (Oxford, 1679), 240-1. On Cornish chaplains at Exeter Cathedral, see Orme, 1979, passim.

111 For the poll-tax of 1381, see TNA, E 179/25/5, and for compulsions, *Reg. Lacy*, ed. Dunstan, II, 114, and cf. II, 400; III, 16, 47-8, 49, 92.

112 Perpetual chantries and chantry priests in 1546-8 are listed in Snell, *c.*1953; on teaching by such priests, see Orme, 1976; and 2006a, especially 228-9, 237-8, 298-9, 312-24.

113 TNA, E 179/25/5 (poll tax); Orme, 2007, 62, 251 (John Walle).

114 On elderly clergy, see Orme, 1991b, 62-73.

115 On Clyst Gabriel, see Orme, 1994, 107-121, especially 114-21.

116 Leland, 1907-10, I, 175, 180.

117 On medieval Cornish brasses, see Dunkin, 1882, especially 9-11; M. Stephenson, *A List of Monumental Brasses in the British Isles* (2nd edn, London, 1964), 70-7, 731; and, most thoroughly, W. Lack et al. Waryn's brass is in Bodleian, Gough Cornwall 22 (printed book: R. Carew, *The Survey of Cornwall* [1602]), drawing opp. f. 135; Lack et al., 85.

CHAPTER 4 The Later Middle Ages: The People, pp. 95–125

118 A. Clifton-Taylor, 'Building Materials', in N. Pevsner, *Cornwall*, The Buildings of England, rev. edn (1970), 29-34.
119 For Lady chapels, see ECA, D&C 1145, printed in Oliver, 1846, 413 (Launceston), and *Reg. Grandisson*, II, 982 (Bodmin, reference to an altar of St Mary, implying a Lady chapel).
120 ECA, D&C 1403 (St Merryn); Orme, 2007, 103-4, 140, 164, 168, 177 (will references); J. Mattingly et al., 96-100 (tin miner).
121 *Reg. Brantyngham*, I, 379-80; II, 891, and *Reg. Stafford*, 74 (all Crantock); Mattingly, 2000, 2001, 2003, and 2005 (St Neot); Wilkinson, 1-49 (Bodmin).
122 On the origin of roods, see C. D. Cragoe, 'Belief and Patronage in the English Parish before 1300: some evidence from roods', *Architectural History* 48 (2005), 21-48. For Quinil, see Powicke and Cheney, II, 1005-8, and for the visitations, ECA, D&C 2851, printed in *Reg. Grandisson*, II, 605-11.
123 Goulding, 91-4.
124 Maclean, 1873-9, I, 15; on bench-ends, see Mattingly, 1991, 58-72.
125 On Cornish wall painting, see Enys et al., and Coomber; on the Sunday Christ, Reiss; and on St Neot, Mattingly, 2000, 2001, and 2003.
126 For the earliest Latin text of the Sarum mass, see J. Wickham Legg (ed.), *The Sarum Missal* (Oxford, 1916), 205-29, and, for a text based on later printed editions, F. H. Dickinson (ed.), *Missale ad Usum Insignis et Praeclarae Ecclesiae Sarum* (Oxford, 1861-83).
127 Orme, 2006d (bead-rolls).
128 On statues of patron saints and Mary, see Orme, 1996, 6-7; other saint cults in churches are listed by Orme, 2000a.
129 Orme, 2000a, 63-4, 141-2, 150-1, 225, 241-2; an earlier store of St Anne is mentioned at St Ive in 1387 (Orme, 2007, 41).
130 On the St Cleer stores, see Orme, 2007, 42-3. Stores in general are listed by Mattingly, 1989.
131 Cornish guilds are analysed and listed by Mattingly, 1989 and 2005. On those of Bodmin, see also Wilkinson, 5-6.
132 On medieval chapels, see Orme, 1996b, and (with more emphasis on Cornwall), Orme, 2006b.
133 On chapels in Cornwall, see Henderson, 1953-6, 1957-60, and Adams, and on those in Devon, James. Canon Adams's detailed notes on Cornish chapels are held at the Institute of Cornish Studies, Tremough.
134 For Bodmin, see Wilkinson, 5-7, and for Padstow, Henderson, 1957-60, 376-9. The Padstow chapels of St Saviour and Trinity were probably identical.
135 *Reg. Stafford*, 276 (Chapel Amble); CRO, PD/322/1, ff. 1-14 (Camborne); and CRO, P/19/5/1, ff. 4, 6 (Burlawn Eglos).
136 On holy wells, see Quiller-Couch, Lane-Davies, and Meyrick, and for Samson's well, Flobert, 220.
137 Orme, 2000a, 89, 90, 92, 95, 120, 137, 148, 150-1, 169-71, 180, 187, 203, 216, 228.
138 Ibid., 80-2, 120, 170, 180, 206, 228.
139 On Cornish crosses, see A. G. Langdon and the more recent thorough surveys by A. [i.e. Andrew] Langdon, listed in the bibliography; and on chairs, Orme 2000a, 129, 182, 194.
140 On trees, see Orme, 2000a, 137, and Roscarrock, 61, 79; and on other features, Orme, 2000a, 60, 72, 107, 189, 215, 228.
141 For Quinil, see Powicke and Cheney, II, 1008.
142 On churchwardens' accounts, see Cox, especially 15-52; for those of Launceston, CRO, B/LAUS/148-172, extracted in R. and O. B. Peter, 140-88; and for Bodmin, Wilkinson, pp. iii-vii, 1-49. Later Bodmin accounts are preserved in CRO, B/BOD/314/4-6, and the borough accounts (B/BOD/314/3) also include some parish church items. The other early Cornish accounts are BL, Add. MSS 32,243-4 (Stratton); CRO, P/7/5/1 (Antony); P/19/5/1 (St Breock); P/102/5/1 (Kilkhampton); P/144/5/2 (Menheniot); P/167/5/1 (North Petherwin); P/192/5/1 (Poughill); and PD/322/1-3 (Camborne).

143 In the west of England such choirs are recorded at Ashburton, Cirencester, and Lyme Regis (Orme, 1976, 111, 130, 150); for the Bodmin evidence, see CRO, B/BOD/314/3/22d, and Wallis, 41.
144 On the calendar, see Wright; R. Hutton, *The Rise and Fall of Merry England: The Ritual Year 1400-1700* (Oxford, 1994); and idem, *The Stations of the Sun: A History of the Ritual Year in Britain* (Oxford, 1996).
145 On confession, see Orme, 2002, 57-68.
146 Parishioners at Lanteglos-by-Fowey are mentioned receiving communion on the evening before Easter in 1504×1515 (TNA, C 1/363/39).
147 On processions at Perranzabuloe, see Orme, 2000a, 221-2, and on St Buryan and St Michael's Mount, *VCH Cornwall*, II.
148 Roscarrock, 94.
149 Orme, 2007, passim.
150 On the Fowey prayer book, see Orme, 1999, 69.
151 On money raising in Cornwall for crusading between 1300 and 1536, see *VCH Cornwall*, II, sub 'Trebeigh'; on indulgences in general, R. N. Swanson, *Indulgences in Medieval England* (forthcoming); and on indulgences in Cornwall, Orme, 1992a, 149-69.
152 For cathedral indulgences, see A. M. Erskine (ed.), *The Accounts of the Fabric of Exeter Cathedral, 1279-1353*, 2 parts, DCRS new ser. 24, 26 (1981-3), I, 162, 172; II, 218, 228, 237, 247, 253, and on those of Lacy, Orme, 1992a, 162-9.
153 Significations of excommunication relating to Cornwall, from 1264 to 1558, are preserved in TNA, C 85/71-84. For the pretended priest, see C 85/77/16, and for the pollution of North Tamerton church, C 85/81/6.
154 Surveys of medieval pilgrimage include J. Sumption, *Pilgrimage: an image of medieval religion* (London, 1975); R. Finucane, *Miracles and Pilgrims: popular beliefs in medieval England* (London, 1977); and D. Webb, *Medieval European Pilgrimage, c.700-c.1500* (Basingstoke, 2002). These centre on major pilgrim shrines, however, and have little to say about Cornwall.
155 Orme, 2000a, 69, 72, 86, 111, 113-14, 119, 124, 128-9, 137, 144, 147, 155, 173, 190, 196, 202, 207, 215-16, 221, 236, 255.
156 Orme, 1992b, 107-18.
157 On St Day, see Orme, 2000a, 103-4, 246, and on the Mount, ibid., 193-4, and *VCH Cornwall*, II.
158 Licences to carry pilgrims are listed in Storrs, 173-82. Those of 1434 are in TNA, C 76/116, mm. 9-14, printed in T. Rymer, *Foedera* (London, 1704-35), X, 567-82; for Dabernon, see Orme, 2007, 32.
159 On education in England from 1300 to 1500, see Orme, 2006a, and on Cornwall in particular, Orme, 1976, 100-1, 111-14, 148-50, 167-8, and 173-82, and (on Camborne), Orme, 1993, 1-13, while on Bodmin should be added Wilkinson, 47, and CRO, B/BOD314/3/42d (a schoolmaster in 1524-5).
160 Other tombs with inscriptions in French survive at Bodmin, St Breock, and Little Petherick.
161 On works by Cornish scholars, see above, pp. 47-9, 88; on saints' lives, Orme, 2000a, 72, 112, 137, 144-5, 211, 214-15, 220-1; and for Grandisson, *Reg. Grandisson*, I, 585.
162 For the Arundell documents, see CRO, O. J. Padel and L. McCann, 'Catalogue of Arundell Deeds', passim, and for Blanchminster's books, Orme, 2007, 27-8.
163 Ranulf Higden, *Polychronicon*, ed. C. Babington (London, Rolls Series, 1865-86), II, 158-61. On the languages of teaching, see Orme, 2006a, 105-6, and on Cornwall, Emden, 1957-9, I, 490, *DNB*, and Orme, 2007, 30-1, 218.
164 On Trevisa, see Emden, 1957-9, III, 1903-4, Fowler, and *DNB*.
165 I am grateful to Dr O. J. Padel for advice on the linguistic boundary. Published maps of the Cornish-speaking area in the Middle Ages should be used with caution. For a good survey of medieval Cornish, see Padel, 2005a; for evidence on the speaking of Cornish, Spriggs; for *Pascon agan Arluth*, Stokes, 1861; and for the 'Charter Endorsement', Toorians. The life of St Columb is mentioned in Roscarrock, 67-8.
166 For an edition of the trilogy manuscript (Bodleian, Bodley 791), see Norris, and for a modern study, Bakere. For *Bewnans Meriasek* (Aberystwyth, Nat. Lib. of

Wales, Peniarth 105), see Stokes, 1872, and Combellack, and for *Bewnans Ke* (Aberystwyth, Nat. Lib. of Wales, 23,849D) the edition of that name (2007).

167 On Tremur, see above, pp. 83-4, and *Reg. Grandisson*, II, 1180.

CHAPTER 5 The Reformation (1500-1559), pp. 127–60

168 For the bishops' biographies, see *DNB*; for Oldham's visits to Cornwall (1506, 1509), DRO, Chanter XIII, ff. 87v, 98; and for a possible visit by Veysey (1541), Chanter XV f. 110v-111r, printed in Oliver, 1846, 53.

169 *Valor Ecclesiasticus*, II, 296. On Winter, Body, and Pollard, see Rowse, 149-51, and for the lease of 1543, DRO, Chanter 1073.

170 There are several lists of clergy in early 16th-century Cornwall. They include Stoate 1987 (parish clergy, 1522, parts of Cornwall only), TNA, E 25 (clergy of some religious houses, 1534), TNA, E 36/64, pp. 35-46 (parish clergy, 1534), ECA, D&C 3688 (parish clergy, *c.*1535-6), and Snell, *c.*1953 (perpetual chantry priests, 1546-8).

171 *Valor Ecclesiasticus*, II, 392-408.

172 Ibid.

173 For chaplains' and chantry priests' salaries, see Stoate, 1987, and on Marhamchurch, TNA, C 1/1055/34, /35.

174 TNA, STAC 2/17/209 (Probus); ECA, D&C 606 (Altarnun).

175 Orme, 2000a, 87 (Stowe); Orme, 2007, 188 (Treviddo); *VCH Cornwall*, II (St Michael's Mount); Orme, 2007, 140, 153 (Greenwich and Richmond). Stowe was not necessarily a new chapel; one is recorded there in 1386 (*Reg. Brantyngham*, II, 621).

176 *Statutes of the Realm*, III, 285-8, 288-9, 292-6, 334-8, 460-1, 492. The signed documents are TNA, E 25 (some religious houses) and E 36/64, pp. 35-46 (parish clergy).

177 *Statutes of the Realm*, III, 493-9; *Valor Eccl.* II, 392-408.

178 *Statutes of the Realm*, III, 663-6 (act of 1536); Frere and Kennedy, 1908-10, II, 1-11 (injunctions).

179 D. Wilkins (ed.), *Concilia Magnae Britanniae et Hiberniae* (London, 1737), III, 823-4 (holy days); Frere and Kennedy, II, 61-4 (Veysey's injunctions).

180 Frere and Kennedy, II, 34-43.

181 Ibid. (injunctions); P. L. Hughes and J. F. Larkin (ed.), *Tudor Royal Proclamations* (New Haven and London, 1964-9), I, 275-6 (Thomas Becket).

182 On image-destruction in general, see M. Aston, *England's Iconoclasts* (Oxford, 1988); E. Duffy, *The Stripping of the Altars* (New Haven and London, 1992), 402-10; and Leland, 1907-10, I, 190, 208.

183 Leland, 1907-10, I, 175 (St Katherine's).

184 On Tregonwell, see *DNB* and *L. & P. Hen VIII*, XI, 166, and on St Keverne, *L. & P. Hen VIII*, XII(1), 450-1, 522; XII(2), 220.

185 *L. & P. Hen VIII*, XII(2), 124, 476.

186 *Statutes of the Realm*, III, 575-8.

187 The dissolutions are described in more detail in *VCH Cornwall*, II.

188 On the dissolutions and disposal of property, see *VCH Cornwall*, II.

189 For the cathedral scheme, see H. Cole (ed.), *King Henry VIII's Scheme of Bishopricks* (London, 1838), 68-9, 74 and *L&P Hen. VIII*, XIV(2), 152, and Addenda, I (2), 498; and for the Act of Six Articles, *Statutes of the Realm*, III, 739-43.

190 Hughes and Larkin, *Proclamations*, I, 302 (proclamation); *Statutes of the Realm*, III, 988-93 (Chantry Act). The surveys of Cornish chantries generated by the act are in Snell, *c.*1953 (certificate 15).

191 Frere and Kennedy, II, 103-30.

192 *Statutes of the Realm*, IV(1), 24-33.

193 The surveys of Cornish chantries generated by the act are in Snell, *c.*1953 (certificate 9) and grants of pensions (certificate 10).

194 Orme, 1976, 113-14, 148-50, 168-9, 172-3, 180-2.

195 *Statutes of the Realm*, IV(1), 18-22 (repeal of heresy laws); Rowse, 253-4 (William

Body); Duffy, *Stripping of the Altars*, 547-8 (royal orders of 1548); and TNA, E 117, printed in Snell, *c.*1955, 1-25 (church goods).

196 *Statutes of the Realm*, IV(1), 37-9. The best edition of the 1549 prayer book is F. E. Brightman (ed.), *The English Rite* (2nd edn, London, 1970).

197 Rose-Troup, and Rowse, 253-4, 257-9.

198 Rose-Troup; Rowse, 253-90; and I. Arthurson, 'Fear and Loathing in West Cornwall: seven new letters on the 1548 rising', *JRIC* new ser. II, 3/3-4 (2000), 68-96.

199 *Statutes of the Realm*, IV(1), 67, 146-7 (clergy marriage); Frere and Kennedy, II, 242-4 (altar removal); *Statutes of the Realm*, IV(1), 130-1 (act imposing prayer book of 1552); and Brightman (ed.), *English Rite* (text of prayer book).

200 Duffy, *Stripping of the Altars*, 476-7 (church ornaments); DRO, Chanter XVI, ff. 21-31v, and Rowse, 307-10 (married clergy).

201 *Cal. Pat.* 1549-51, 7, 333 (bishop's loss of properties); DRO, Exeter City Archives, Book 51, f. 350 (Coverdale at Bodmin). The bishop kept his other Cornish estates at Burniere, Cargoll, Lawhitton, Penryn, and Tregaire.

202 *Statutes of the Realm*, IV(1), 202 (repeal of 1553); ibid., 246-54 (repeal of 1554).

203 On St Endellion and Trebeigh, see *VCH Cornwall*, II.

204 DRO, Chanter XVI, ff. 14-31v; Rowse, 307-10. Not all institutions of clergy in this period state what had happened to the previous incumbent, and the records after October 1554 are less informative.

205 On Turberville, see Emden, 1974, 579; *DNB*; and J. Hooker, *A Catalog of the Bishops of Excester* (London, 1584), sig. Iiiv. His bishop's register is in DRO, Chanter XVIII-XIX.

206 Snell, *c.*1955, 35-51 (church plate); CRO, PD/322/1, ff. 35v-40 (Camborne); and CRO, P/144/5/2, ff. 6-10v (Menheniot).

207 Truro, Royal Institution of Cornwall, Henderson MS 66, p. 159 (Thomvy); ibid., p. 149 (Hore); ibid., p. 150 (Speryer); BL, Add. 46397 (Tregear's homilies); Frost (discussion of the homilies); and Roscarrock, 94, 159-60 (processions).

208 DRO, Chanter XVIII (ordinations); TNA, SP 11/2, f. 2 (Linkinhorne).

209 J. Foxe, *Acts and Monuments*, ed. J. Pratt (London, 1877), VIII, 737-8, and DRO, Exeter City Archives, Book 51, f. 352.

210 *Statutes of the Realm*, IV(1), 350-8, 359-64, 397-400 (Reformation statutes). On Alley, see *DNB*; Turberville died in the Tower of London in about 1570.

211 Frere and Kennedy, III, 1-29 (visitation); J. Jewel, *Works*, ed. J. Ayre, Parker Soc. (1847-50), IV, 1216-18 (Jewel's assessment); *DNB* s.n. 'Arundell Family', and Roscarrock, 1-14 (Roscarrock family).

212 Modern editions of the 1559 prayer book are W. K. Clay (ed.), *Liturgies and Occasional Forms of Prayer set forth in the reign of Queen Elizabeth*, Parker Soc. (1847), 23-245, 272-98, and E. Benham (ed.), *The Prayer-Book of Queen Elizabeth 1559* (Edinburgh, 1890)

213 *DNB*, s.n. Robert Johnson (died 1574) (case of 1573).

214 Frere and Kennedy, III, 15 (processions), 22-3 (singing), 25 (bowing). On post-Reformation Rogation processions, see Cox, 264-5.

215 Mattingly, 2000), 9-55 (St Neot windows).

216 Carew, ff. 68-71 (church ales and holy days); Wright, II, 162, 247-51 (calendar customs outside church); and Carew, ff. 123, 126v-127, 129v-130, 144-v (holy wells).

CHAPTER 6 Cornwall: Heir of the Ages, pp. 161–6

217 Recent discussions of 'Celtic Christianity' in general include I. Bradley, *Celtic Christianity: making myths and chasing dreams* (1999) and (in relation to early medieval England), Blair, 5.

Bibliography

This is a list of the printed works that are cited several times in the foot-notes of this book, together with others that are useful for further reading or research. The unprinted sources that have been used are listed at the end of the *Victoria County History of Cornwall*, volume II. For abbreviations, see above, p. 181.

Adams, J. H. 'The Mediaeval Chapels of Cornwall,' *JRIC* new series 3 (1957–60), 48-65

The Anglo-Saxon Chronicle, trans. D. Whitelock (London, 1965)

Bakere, J. *The Cornish Ordinalia: a critical study* (Cardiff, 1980)

Barlow, F. *The English Church 1000–1066* (2nd edn, London, 1979)

Barlow, F. (ed.) *English Episcopal Acta,* vol. XI: *Exeter 1046–1184* (London and Oxford, 1996a)

Barlow, F. (ed.) *English Episcopal Acta,* vol. XII: *Exeter 1186–1257* (London and Oxford, 1996b)

Bewnans Ke, ed. C. G. Thomas and N. J. A. Williams (Exeter, 2007)

Black Prince, Register of Edward the, 4 parts (London, Public Record Office, 1930–3)

Blair, J. *The Church in Anglo-Saxon Society* (Oxford, 2005)

Boase, C. W. *Registrum Collegii Exoniensis*, Oxford Historical Society 27 (1894)

Calendar of Charter Rolls, 6 vols (London, Public Record Office, 1903–27)

Calendar of Close Rolls, 47 vols (London, Public Record Office, 1892–1963)

Calendar of Fine Rolls, 22 vols (London, Public Record Office, 1911–63)

Calendar of Inquisitions Miscellaneous, 8 vols (London, Public Record Office, 1916–2003)

Calendar of Inquisitions Post Mortem (London, Public Record Office, 1904–, in progress)

Calendar of Papal Petitions, vol. I (London, Public Record Office, 1897)

Calendar of Papal Registers (London, Public Record Office, and Dublin, Irish Historical Manuscripts Commission, 1894–, in progress)

Calendar of Patent Rolls (London, Public Record Office, 1891–, in progress)

Carew, R. *The Survey of Cornwall* (London, 1602; 1603 modern style); reprinted with introduction and index, ed. J. Chynoweth, N. Orme, and A. Walsham, DCRS new series 47 (2004)

Catalogue of Ancient Deeds, 6 vols (London, Public Record Office, 1890–1915)

Chambers, D. S. *Faculty Office Registers 1534–1549* (Oxford, 1966)

Close Rolls: Henry III, 14 vols (London, Public Record Office, 1902–38).

Cockerham, P. D. *Continuity and Change: Memorialisation and the Cornish Funeral Monument Industry, 1497–1660* (Oxford, 2006)

Cokayne, G. E. *The Complete Peerage*, ed. V. Gibbs and H. A. Doubleday, 13 vols in 14 (London, 1910–59)

Cole, D., et al. *Glasney College, Penryn, Cornwall* (Truro, Cornwall County Council, Historic Environment Service, Report No. 2005R061, 2005)

Combellack, M. (ed.) *The Camborne Play: a translation of Beunans Meriasek* (Truro, 1988)

Coomber, J. E. 'Medieval Painting in Cornwall', University of Exeter, unpublished MA thesis (1980)

Cornwall, John of – *see* Curley

Cox, J. C. *Churchwardens' Accounts* (London, 1913)

Curley, M. J. 'A New Edition of John of Cornwall's *Prophetia Merlini*', *Speculum* 57 (1982), 217-49

Doble, G. H. 'The Relics of St Petroc', *Antiquity* 13 (1939), 403-15

Doble, G. H. *The Saints of Cornwall*, 6 vols (Truro and Felinfach, 1960–97)

Domesday Book, vol. X: *Cornwall*, ed. C. and F. Thorn (Chichester, 1979)

Dunkin, E. H. W. *The Church Bells of Cornwall* (London and Derby, 1878)

Dunkin, E. H. W. *The Monumental Brasses of Cornwall* (London, 1882)

Emden, A. B. *A Biographical Register of the University of Oxford to A.D. 1500*, 3 vols (Oxford, 1957–9)

Emden, A. B. *A Biographical Register of the University of Cambridge to 1500* (Cambridge, 1963)

Emden, A. B. *A Survey of Dominicans in England*, Institutum Historicum FF. Praedicatorum, Dissertationes Historicae 18 (Rome, 1967)

Emden, A. B. *A Biographical Register of the University of Oxford A.D. 1501 to 1540* (Oxford, 1974)

Enys, J. D., et al. 'Mural Painting in Cornish Churches', *JRIC* 15 (1901–2), 136-60

Fletcher, J. R. and Stéphan, J. *Short History of St. Michael's Mount Cornwall* (St Michael's Mount, 1951)

Flobert, P. (ed.) *La Vie ancienne de Saint Samson de Dol* (Paris, 1997)

Förster, M. 'Die Freilassungsurkunden des Bodmin-Evangeliars', in N. Bøgholm, A. Brusendorff, and C. Bodelsen (ed.), *A Grammatical Miscellany offered to Otto Jespersen* (Copenhagen and London, 1930), 77-99

Fowler, D. C. *The Life and Times of John Trevisa, Medieval Scholar* (Seattle and London, 1995)

Fox, Aileen. *South-West England, 3500BC–AD600* (2nd edn, Newton Abbot, 1973)

Fox, H. S. A. and Padel, O. J. (ed.) *The Cornish Lands of the Arundells of Lanherne*, DCRS new series 41 (2000)

Frere, W. H. and Kennedy, W. M. (ed.) *Visitation Articles and Injunctions of the Period of the Reformation*, 3 vols, Alcuin Club 14-16 (1908–10)

Frost, D. H. '*Sacrament an Alter*: a Tudor Cornish Patristic Catena', *Cornish Studies* new series 11 (2003), 291-307

Fryde, E. B., Greenway, D. E. Porter, S., and Roy, I. (ed.) *Handbook of British Chronology* (3rd edn, London, Royal Historical Society, 1986)

Gascoyne, J. *A Map of the County of Cornwall*, ed. W. L. D. Ravenhill and O. J. Padel, DCRS new series 34 (1991)

Gilbert, C. S. *Historical and Topographical Survey of the County of Cornwall*, 2 vols (Plymouth and London, 1817–20)

Gilbert, D. *The Parochial History of Cornwall*, 4 vols (London, 1838)

Gildas. *The Ruin of Britain and Other Works*, ed. M. Winterbottom (London, 1978)

Golding, B. 'Robert of Mortain', *Anglo-Norman Studies* 13 (1990), 19-44

Goulding, R. W. *Records of the Charity known as Blanchminster's Charity* (Louth, Stratton, and Bude, 1898)

Graves, E. van T. (ed.) 'The Old Cornish Vocabulary' (Columbia University, New York, PhD thesis, 1962)
Grosjean, P. 'Vie et Miracles de. S. Petroc', *Analecta Bollandiana* 74 (1956), 131-88, 470-96
Gwara, S. *Education in Wales and Cornwall in the Ninth and Tenth Centuries: Understanding* De raris fabulis (Cambridge, Kathleen Hughes Memorial Lectures, 4, 2004)
Hale, W. H. and Ellacombe, H. T. (ed.) *Accounts of the Executors of Richard Bishop of London 1303, and of the Executors of Thomas Bishop of Exeter 1310*, Camden Society new series 10 (1874)
Henderson, C. G. *The Cornish Church Guide* (Truro, 1927)
Henderson, C. G. *Records of the Church and Priory of St Germans* (Long Compton, 1929)
Henderson, C. G. *St. Columb Major Church and Parish, Cornwall* (Shipston-on-Stour, 1929; Long Compton, [1930])
Henderson, C. G. *Essays in Cornish History* (Oxford, 1935)
Henderson, C. G. *A History of the Parish of Constantine in Cornwall*, ed. G. H. Doble (Long Compton, 1937)
Henderson, C. G. 'The Ecclesiastical History of the 109 Parishes of West Cornwall', *JRIC* new series 2 (1953–6), 1-210; 3 (1957–60), 211-382, 383-497. Pagination is independent of the rest of these volumes
Henderson, C. G. and Coates, H. *Old Cornish Bridges and Streams* (Exeter, 1928, reprinted Truro, 1972)
Hooke, D. *Pre-Conquest Charter-Bounds of Devon and Cornwall* (Woodbridge, 1994)
Hull, P. L. (ed.) *The Cartulary of St Michael's Mount*, DCRS new series 5 (1962)
Hull, P. L. 'The Foundation of St.-Michael's Mount in Cornwall: a Priory of the Abbey of Mont St.-Michel', in *Millénaire monastique du Mont Saint-Michel: mélanges commemoratifs: I. Histoire et vie monastique* (Paris, 1967), 703-24
Hull, P. L. (ed.) *The Caption of Seisin of the Duchy of Cornwall (1337)*, DCRS new series 17 (1971)
Hull, P. L. (ed.) *The Cartulary of Launceston Priory*, DCRS new series 30 (1987)
Hull, P. L. and Sharpe, Richard. 'Peter of Cornwall and Launceston', *Cornish Studies* 13 (1985), 5-53
Iago, W. 'The Ecclesiastical Seals of Cornwall', *JRIC* 8 (1883–5), 28-79
James, J. 'The Medieval Chapels of Devon', University of Exeter, unpublished MPhil thesis, 1997
Jankulak, K. *The Medieval Cult of St Petroc* (Woodbridge, 2000)
Jenner, H. 'The Bodmin Gospels', *JRIC* 21 (1922–5), 113-45
Jenner, H. 'The Manumissions in the Bodmin Gospels', *JRIC* 21 (1922–5), 235-60
Jenner, H. and Taylor, T. 'The Legend of the Church of the Holy Cross in Cornwall', *JRIC* 20 (1915–21), 295-309
Kain, R. J. P. and Oliver, R. R. *The Tithe Maps of England and Wales: a cartographic analysis and county-by-county catalogue* (Cambridge, 1995)
Kain, R. J. P. and Prince, H. C. *The Tithe Surveys of England and Wales* (Cambridge, 1985)
Kain, R. J. P. and Prince, H. C. *Tithe Surveys for Historians* (Chichester, 2000)

Kain, R. J. P. and Ravenhill, W. L. D. (ed.) *Historical Atlas of South-West England* (Exeter, 1999)
Ker, N. R. *Medieval Libraries of Great Britain* (2nd edn, London, 1964); *Supplement to the Second Edition*, ed. A. G. Watson (London, 1987)
Keynes, S. and Lapidge, M. (ed.) *Alfred the Great: Asser's life of King Alfred and other contemporary sources* (London, 1983)
Lack, W., Stuckfield, H. M., and Whittemore, P. *The Monumental Brasses of Cornwall* (London, 1997)
Lane-Davies, A. *Holy Wells of Cornwall* (No place, 1970)
Langdon, A. *Stone Crosses in North Cornwall* (2nd edn, [St Austell,] 1996)
Langdon, A. *Stone Crosses in West Penwith* ([St Austell,] 1997)
Langdon, A. *Stone Crosses in West Cornwall* ([St Austell,] 1999)
Langdon, A. *Stone Crosses in Mid Cornwall* (2nd edn, [St Austell,] 2002)
Langdon, A. *Stone Crosses in East Cornwall* (2nd edn, [St Austell,] 2002)
Langdon, A. G. *Old Cornish Crosses* (Truro, 1896)
Leland, J. *The Itinerary of John Leland*, ed. L. Toulmin Smith, 5 vols (London, 1907–10)
Le Neve, J. *Fasti Ecclesiae Anglicanae 1066–1300*, vol. X: *Exeter*, ed. D. E. Greenway (London, 2005)
Le Neve, J. *Fasti Ecclesiae Anglicanae 1300–1541*, vol. IX: *Exeter Diocese*, ed. J. M. Horn (London, 1964)
Lepine, D. and Orme, N. *Death and Memory in Medieval Exeter*, DCRS new series 46 (2003)
Letters and Papers, Foreign and Domestic, Henry VIII, ed. S. J. Brewer, J. Gairdner and R. H. Brodie, 21 vols in 33 parts (London, 1864–1932)
Lysons, D. and S. *Magna Britannia*, vol. III: *Cornwall* (London, 1814)
Maclean, Sir J. *The Parochial and Family History of the Deanery of Trigg Minor*, 3 vols. (London and Bodmin, 1873–9)
Matthew, D. J. A. *The Norman Monasteries and their English Possessions* (London, 1962)
Mattingly, J. 'The Medieval Parish Guilds of Cornwall', *JRIC* new series 10/3 (1989), 290-329
Mattingly, J. 'The Dating of Bench-ends in Cornish Churches', *JRIC* new series II, 1/1 (1991), 58-72
Mattingly, J. 'Stories in the Glass: reconstructing the St Neot pre-Reformation glazing scheme', *JRIC* new series II, 3/3–4 (2000), 9-55
Mattingly, J. et al. 'A Tin Miner and a Bal Maiden: further research on the St Neot windows', *JRIC* (2001), 96-100
Mattingly, J. 'Pre-Reformation Saints' Cults in Cornwall, with particular reference to the St Neot windows', in J. Cartwright (ed.), *Celtic Hagiography and Saints' Cults* (Cardiff, 2003), 249-70
Mattingly, J. 'Going A-Riding: Cornwall's late-medieval guilds revisited', *JRIC* (2005), 78-103
Meyrick, J. *A Pilgrims Guide to the Holy Wells of Cornwall* (Falmouth, 1982)
Norden, John. *Speculi Britanniae Pars: Cornwall* (London, 1728)
Norden, John. *John Norden's Manuscript Maps of Cornwall and its Nine Hundreds*, ed. W. L. D. Ravenhill (Exeter, 1972)
Norris, E. (ed.) *The Ancient Cornish Drama*, 2 vols (Oxford, 1859)
Okasha, E. *Corpus of Early Christian Inscribed Stones of South-West Britain* (London, 1993)
Okasha, E. 'A Supplement to Corpus of Early Christian Inscribed Stones of South-West Britain', *Cornish Archaeology* 37-8 (1998–9), 137-52

Oliver, G. *Monasticon Diocesis Exoniensis*, with supplement (Exeter and London, 1846)
Oliver, G. *Additional Supplement to the Monasticon Dioecesis Exoniensis* (Exeter, 1854)
Olson, L. *Early Monasteries in Cornwall* (Woodbridge, 1989)
Olson, L. and Padel, O. J. 'A Tenth-Century List of Cornish Parochial Saints', *Cambridge Medieval Celtic Studies* 12 (1986), 33-71
Orme, N. *Education in the West of England, 1066–1548* (Exeter, 1976)
Orme, N. *The Minor Clergy of Exeter Cathedral* (Exeter, 1979)
Orme, N. 'St Michael and his Mount', *JRIC* new series 10/1 (1986–7), 32-43
Orme, N. 'Indulgences in the Diocese of Exeter', *TDA*, 120 (1988), 15-32
Orme, N. 'Music and Teaching at Tywardreath Priory, 1522–1536', *DCNQ* 36/8 (1990), 277-80
Orme, N. (ed.) *Unity and Variety: a history of the Church in Devon and Cornwall* (Exeter, 1991a)
Orme, N. 'Sufferings of the Clergy': illness and old age in Exeter diocese, 1300–1540', in M. Pelling and R. M. Smith (ed.), *Life, Death, and the Elderly: historical perspectives* (London, 1991b), 62-73
Orme, N. 'Indulgences in Medieval Cornwall', *JRIC* new series II, 1/2 (1992a), 149-70
Orme, N. 'Bishop Grandisson and Popular Religion', *TDA* 124 (1992b), 107-18
Orme, N. 'Education in the Cornish Play *Beunans Meriasek*', *Cambridge Medieval Celtic Studies* 25 (1993), 1-13
Orme, N. 'The Clergy of Clyst Gabriel, 1312–1508', *TDA* 126 (1994), 107-21
Orme, N. *English Church Dedications* (Exeter, 1996a)
Orme, N. 'Church and Chapel in Medieval England', *Transactions of the Royal Historical Society* 6th series 6 (1996b), 75-102
Orme, N. 'A Fifteenth-century Prayer-Book from Cornwall: MS NLW 22253A', *JRIC* new series II, 3/2 (1999), 69-73
Orme, N. *The Saints of Cornwall* (Oxford, 2000a)
Orme, N. 'The Lanteglos Prayer-Book: a further note', *JRIC* new series II, 3/3-4 (2000b), 67
Orme, N. *Medieval Children* (New Haven and London, 2001)
Orme, N. 'Confession in a Fifteenth-Century Devon Parish', *TDA* 134 (2002), 57-68
Orme, N. 'Popular Religion and the Reformation in England: a View from Cornwall', in J. A. Tracy and M. Ragnow (ed.), *Official Religion and Lived Religion* (Cambridge, 2004), 351-75
Orme, N. *Medieval Schools* (New Haven and London, 2006a)
Orme, N. 'The Other Parish Churches: Chapels in Late Medieval England', in C. Burgess and E. Duffy (ed.), *Parish Churches in Late Medieval England* (Donington, 2006b), 78-94
Orme, N. 'The Church and Clergy of St Buryan, *c.*1200–*c.*1574', *JRIC* (2006c), 32-44
Orme, N. 'Prayer and Education in Fifteenth-Century Camborne', *JRIC* (2006d), 95-104
Orme, N. *Cornish Wills 1342–1540*, DCRS new series 50 (2007)
Orme, N. – *see also Victoria County History of Cornwall*
Orme, N. and Padel, O. J. 'The Medieval Lepers of *Lamford*, Cornwall', *Historical Research* 69 (1995), 102-7

Orme, N. and Padel, O. J. 'Cornwall and the Third Crusade', *JRIC* (2005), 71-7

Orme, N. and Webster, M. *The English Hospital, 1070–1570* (New Haven and London, 1995)

The Oxford Dictionary of National Biography, ed. C. Matthew and B. Harrison, 60 vols (Oxford, 2004); updated electronic edition: http://www.oxforddnb.com

The Oxford English Dictionary, ed. J. Simpson and E. S. C. Weiner, 40 vols (2nd edn, Oxford, 1989)

Padel, O. J. 'Cornish Language Notes: 5. Cornish Names of Parish Churches', *Cornish Studies* 4-5 (1976–7), 15-27

Padel, O. J. 'Two New Pre-Conquest Charters for Cornwall', *Cornish Studies* 6 (1978), 20-7

Padel, O. J. *Cornish Place-Name Elements*, English Place-Name Society 56-57 (1985)

Padel, O. J. *A Popular Dictionary of Cornish Place-Names* (Penzance, 1988)

Padel, O. J. 'Glastonbury's Cornish Connections', in L. Abrams and J. P. Carley (ed.), The *Archaeology and History of Glastonbury Abbey* (Woodbridge, 1991), 245-56

Padel, O. J. 'Notes on the New Edition of the Middle Cornish "Charter Endorsement"', *Cambrian Medieval Celtic Studies* 30 (1995), 123-7

Padel, O. J. 'Local Saints and Place-Names in Cornwall', in A. Thacker and R. Sharpe (ed.), *Local Saints and Local Churches in the Early Medieval Period* (Oxford, 2002), 303-60

Padel, O. J. 'Oral and Literary Culture in Medieval Cornwall', in H. Fulton (ed.), *Medieval Celtic Literature and Society* (Dublin, 2005a), 95-116

Padel, O. J. 'The Charter of Lanlawren (Cornwall)', in K. O'Brien O'Keeffe and A. Orchard (ed.), *Latin Learning and English Lore*, 2 vols (Toronto and London, 2005b), II, 74-85

Page, M. 'The Ownership of Advowsons in Thirteenth-Century Cornwall', *DCNQ*, 37/10 (1996), 336-41

Pearce, S. M. (ed.) *The Early Church in Western Britain and Ireland*, British Archaeological Reports, British Series 102 (Oxford, 1982)

Peter, R. and O. B. *The Histories of Launceston and Dunheved* (Plymouth, 1885)

Peter, T. C. *The History of Glasney Collegiate Church, Cornwall* (Camborne, 1903)

Picken, W. M. M. *A Medieval Cornish Miscellany*, ed. O. J. Padel (Chichester, 2000)

[Polsue, J.] *A Complete Parochial History of the County of Cornwall*, 4 vols (Truro and London, 1867–72)

Pool, P. A. S. 'The Ancient and Present State of St. Michael's Mount, 1762', *Cornish Studies* 3 (1976), 29-47

Potts, R. (ed.) *A Calendar of Cornish Glebe terriers 1673–1735*, DCRS new series 19 (1974)

Powicke, F. M. and Cheney, C. R. (ed.) *Councils and Synods II: A.D. 1205–1313*, 2 vols (Oxford, 1964)

Preston-Jones, A. 'Decoding Cornish Churchyards', in N. Edwards and A. Lane (ed.), *The Early Church in Wales and the West* (Oxford, 1992), 104-24, reprinted in *Cornish Archaeology* 33 (1994), 71-95

Preston-Jones, A. and Rose, P. 'Medieval Cornwall', *Cornish Archaeology* 25 (1986), 155-85

Quiller-Couch, M. and L. *Ancient and Holy Wells of Cornwall* (London, 1894, reprinted Liskeard, 1994)
Rashleigh, J. and Vincent, J. A. C. (ed.) *Abstract of the Glasney Cartulary* (Truro, 1879)
Ratcliffe, J. *The Archaeology of Scilly* (Truro, Cornwall Archaeology Unit, 1989)
Regesta Regum Anglo-Normannorum, ed. H. W. C. Davis et al., 4 vols. (Oxford, 1913–59); vol. I, ed. D. Bates (2nd edn, Oxford, 1998)
The Register of Thomas de Brantyngham, Bishop of Exeter, ed. F. C. Hingeston-Randolph, 2 vols (London and Exeter, 1901–6)
The Registers of Walter Bronescombe and Peter Quivil, Bishops of Exeter, ed. F. C. Hingeston-Randolph (London and Exeter, 1889)
The Register of Walter Bronescombe Bishop of Exeter 1258–1280, ed. O. F. Robinson, 3 vols, Canterbury & York Society 82, 87, 94 (1995–2003)
The Register of John de Grandisson, Bishop of Exeter, ed. F. C. Hingeston-Randolph, 3 vols (London and Exeter, 1894–9)
The Register of Edmund Lacy, Bishop of Exeter, ed. F. C. Hingeston-Randolph, 2 vols (London and Exeter, 1901–15). Vol. II is now superseded by the edition of G.R. Dunstan, next following
The Register of Edmund Lacy, Bishop of Exeter: Registrum Commune, ed. G. R. Dunstan, 5 vols, DCRS new series 7, 10, 13, 16, 18 (1963–72)
The Register of Edmund Stafford, ed. F. C. Hingeston-Randolph (London and Exeter, 1886)
The Register of Walter de Stapeldon, Bishop of Exeter, ed. F. C. Hingeston-Randolph (London and Exeter, 1892)
Reiss, A. *The Sunday Christ: Sabbatarianism in English medieval wall painting*, British Archaeological Reports, British Series 292 (Oxford, 2000)
Roscarrock, N. *Lives of the Saints: Cornwall and Devon*, ed. N. Orme, DCRS new series 35 (1992)
Rose-Troup, F. *The Western Rebellion of 1549* (London, 1913)
Rotuli Chartarum, ed. T. D. Hardy (London, Record Commission, 1837)
Rotuli Litterarum Clausarum in Turri Londinensi asservati, ed. T. D. Hardy, 2 vols (London, Record Commission, 1833–44)
Rotuli Litterarum Patentium, 1201–1216, ed. T. D. Hardy (London, Record Commission, 1835)
Rowe, J. H. (ed.) *Cornwall Feet of Fines*, 2 vols, DCRS (1914–50)
Rowse, A. L. *Tudor Cornwall* (London, 1941)
Salter, H. E. (ed.) *Chapters of the Augustinian Canons*, Canterbury & York Society 29 (1922)
Sawyer, P. H. *Anglo-Saxon Charters: an annotated list and bibliography* (London, Royal Historical Society, 1968); online updated version http://www.trin.cam.ac.uk/sdk13/chartwww/charthome.html
Sedding, E. H. *Norman Architecture in Cornwall* (London, 1909)
Sharpe, R. *A Handlist of the Latin Writers of Great Britain and Ireland before 1540* (Brussels, 1997)
Sheppard, P. *The Historic Towns of Cornwall: an archaeological survey* (Truro, 1980)
Sims-Williams, P. *The Celtic Inscriptions of Britain: phonology and chronology, c.400–1200* (Oxford, 2003)
Snell, L. S. *Documents towards a History of the Reformation in Cornwall: vol. I, The Chantry Certificates for Cornwall* (Exeter, *c.*1953)
Snell, L. S. *Documents towards a History of the Reformation in Cornwall:*

vol. II, *The Edwardian Inventories of Church Goods for Cornwall* (Exeter, *c.*1955)

Sowell, C. R. 'The Collegiate Church of St. Thomas of Glasney', *JRIC* 1/3 (1864–5), 21-34 with 4 plates

Spriggs, M. 'Where Cornish Was Spoken and When: a provisional synthesis', *Cornish Studies* new series 11 (2003), 228-69

The Statutes of the Realm, from Magna Carta to the end of the reign of Queen Anne, 10 vols (London, Record Commission, 1810–24)

Stoate, T. L. (ed.) *Cornwall Subsidies in the Reign of Henry VIII* (Almondsbury, 1985)

Stoate, T. L. (ed.) *The Cornwall Military Survey 1522* (Almondsbury, 1987)

Stoate, T. L. (ed.) *Cornwall Manorial Rentals and Surveys* (Almondsbury, 1988)

Stokes, W. (ed.) *The Passion* (London, 1861)

Stokes, W. (ed.) *Beunans Meriasek: The Life of St Meriasek* (London, 1872)

Storrs, C. M. *Jacobean Pilgrims from England to St. James of Compostella* (Compostella, 1994; reprinted London, 1998)

Thomas, C. *Christian Antiquities of Camborne* (St Austell, 1967)

Thomas, C. *Christianity in Britain to AD500* (London, 1981)

Thomas, C. *Exploration of a Drowned Landscape* (London, 1985)

Thomas, C. *And Shall These Mute Stones Speak? Post-Roman inscriptions in western Britain* (Cardiff, 1994)

Thompson, A. Hamilton. 'Diocesan Organization in the Middle Ages: archdeacons and rural deans', *Proceedings of the British Academy* 29 (1943), 153-94

Thompson, A. Hamilton. *The English Clergy and their Organization in the Later Middle Ages* (Oxford, 1947)

Tinti, F. (ed.) *Pastoral Care in Late Anglo-Saxon England* (Woodbridge, 2005)

Todd, M. *The South West to AD 1000* (London, 1987)

Toorians, L. (ed.) *The Middle Cornish Charter Endorsement: the making of a marriage in medieval Cornwall*, Innsbrucker Beiträge zur Sprachwissenschaft, 67 (Innsbruck, 1991)

Valor Ecclesiasticus tempore Henrici VIII auctoritate regia institutus, ed. J. Caley, 6 vols (London, Record Commission, 1810–24)

The Victoria County History of Cornwall, vol. II: *Religious History to 1559*, by Nicholas Orme (London and Woodbridge, 2007)

Wade-Evans, A. W. (ed.) *Vitae Sanctorum Britanniae et Genealogiae* (Cardiff, 1944)

Wallis, J. *The Bodmin Register* (Bodmin, 1827–38)

Whetter, J. *The History of Glasney College* (Padstow, 1988)

Whitelock, D. (ed.) *English Historical Documents* c.*500–1042* (2nd edn, London, 1979)

Wilkinson, J. J. 'The Receipts and Expenses in the Building of Bodmin Church', *The Camden Miscellany: Vol. VII*, Camden Society new series 14 (1875)

Worcester, W. *Itineraries*, ed. J. H. Harvey (Oxford, 1969)

Wormald, F. 'The Calendar of the Augustinian Priory of Launceston in Cornwall', *The Journal of Theological Studies* 39 (1938), 1-21

Wright, A. R. *British Calendar Customs: England*, ed. T. E. Lones, 3 vols, Folk-Lore Society 97, 102, 106 (1936–40)

Yorke, B. *Wessex in the Early Middle Ages* (London, 1995)

Index

The index follows the Cornish convention of ignoring 'St' when indexing place-names. All places are in Cornwall unless otherwise stated.

Picture Credits

The author and publisher would like to thank the following for permission to reproduce their material. Any infringement of copyright is entirely inadvertent and accidental. Every care has been taken to contact or trace all copyright owners. We would be pleased to correct any errors or omissions brought to our attention in future editions. References are to page numbers unless otherwise noted.

Anova Books Company Ltd, 121
Bodleian Library (University of Oxford), 7 (MS. Bodl 557, fol. iir), 21 (Corpus Christi Coll. MS. 285, fol. 6r), 46 Fig. 28 (MS. Douce 245, fol. 264v), 56 (MS. Douce 118, fol. 140v), 62 (MS. Gough Liturg 12, fol. 111r), 76 Rawl. Poet. 223, fol. 142r), 77 (MS. Douce 104, fol. 11v), 83 (MS. Bodl 13, fol. 12v), 92 (Gough Cornwall 22 opp. fol. 135r), 100 (MS. Douce 266, fol. 11a verso), 115 (MS. Douce 135, fol. 3r), 124 (MS. Add. A 185, fol. 65v), 125 (MS. Bodl. 791, fol. 56v)
Bridgeman Art Library (with special permission of the Musée de la Tapisserie, Bayeux), 24
The British Library Board, 22 (Add. MS. 9381 fol. 50), 40 (Lansdowne 451, fol. 127), 48 (Cotton MS. Vespasian A, xiv, fol. 8), 79 (Royal 19, E.iii, recto).
Cameracraft Photography, 118
English Heritage (Derek Kendall), x, 4, 9, 10, 12, 17, 35, 39, 46 (Fig. 27), 70, 85, 91, 97, 102, 104, 106, 108, 111, 113, 114, 126, 129, 131, 133 (Fig. 82), 140, 145, 150, 151, 152, 161, 163
English Heritage (NMR), 74
Exeter Cathedral (the Dean and Chapter), 72
Nash Ford Publishing, 19
The National Archives, 34, 135
National Portrait Gallery, London, 143
Penryn Town Council, 78
Royal Institution of Cornwall, 138
St Samson's Church, Golant (the Revd P. de Frey-Warter and Wardens), 6, 120
Dae Sasitorn/www.Lastrefuge.co.uk, 26
University of Exeter, 3, 15, 25, 49, 59, 68, 80, 87, 109, 110, 137, 157, 159
University of London (Nicholas Orme), 29, 44, 50, 55, 61, 64, 66, 86, 89, 94, 99, 105, 112, 116, 122, 123, 127, 133 (Fig. 83), 142, 148, 149, 156, 165
Victoria & Albert Museum/V&A Images, London, 155
Arthur Wills and John Lyne, 43

New maps and plans for this volume were drawn by Cath d'Alton (Figs. 2, 10, 18, 20, 23, 48 and Panel 5 map) and Alan Fagan (Panel 2 plan, Figs. 32 and 42) using Ordnance Survey 1st edition map © University of London.